THE OXFORD BOOK OF
CANADIAN
GHOST STORIES

Edited by Alberto Manguel

TORONTO OXFORD NEW YORK

OXFORD UNIVERSITY PRESS

1990

Oxford University Press, 70 Wynford Drive, Don Mills, Ontario, M3C 1J9

Toronto   Oxford   New York
Delhi   Bombay   Calcutta   Madras   Karachi   Petaling Jaya
Singapore   Hong Kong   Tokyo   Nairobi   Dar es Salaam
Cape Town   Melbourne   Auckland

and associated companies in
Berlin   Ibadan

*To Lucinda Vardey, for the ghost of a bathtub in Frankfurt,
the ghost of a certain Mr Crook, and the ghost of a
cat-scented basement.*

Selection © copyright Oxford University Press Canada 1990
Introduction and Notes © copyright Alberto Manguel 1990

Canadian Cataloguing in Publication Data
Main entry under title:

The Oxford book of Canadian ghost stories

ISBN 0-19-540761-X

1. Ghost stories, Canadian (English).* I. Manguel,
Alberto, 1948–   .

PS8323.G5093 1990   C813'.0873'08   C90-093156-6
PR9197.35.G5093 1990

Cover painting by Matt Gould

CONTENTS

INTRODUCTION

Few literary genres have a nationality. The ghost story, that venerable institution, has at least two. One is the Chinese ghost story, which flourished during the Tang dynasty (A.D. 618-907) and described a world of demonic foxes and vampire spirits, which was, we are told, as real to its readers as the vast Chinese geography. The other is the British ghost story, of which the first literary exponent is usually considered to be Daniel Defoe's 'True Relation of the Apparition of one Mrs Veal', published in 1706. Written, according to Sir Walter Scott, as an appendix to enhance the sales of a dreary Christian's Defence Against the Fears of Death, 'Mrs Veal' sought its effectiveness in the documentary style that Defoe perfected in his Journal of the Plague Year, and suffers from it. If it is one of the first, it is also one of the worst ghost stories, mild and predictable. The classic rules of the genre, as perceived in the Western world, were not established until much later, after the noble experiments in fantastic literature by the European Romantics and the Gothic novelists. The masters of literary hauntings belong to the late nineteenth century: Montague Rhodes James (1862-1936) and Joseph Sheridan Le Fanu (1814-73). James, in his classic introduction to an anthology published in 1924, observed that the 'two ingredients most valuable in the concocting of a ghost story are, to me, the atmosphere and the nicely managed crescendo.' This simple formula still defines the best stories of this genre.

The Canadian ghost story has various origins. In Quebec and Acadia, literature in general and the ghost story in particular sprang from early legends and tall tales: sometimes local stories, sometimes stories from Brittany and Normandy retold in colder settings. One of the first Québécois *raconteurs* was Philippe Aubert de Gaspé, an aristocrat who at the age of seventy began to collect anecdotes and folktales that, held together by a thin connecting plot, became the romance *Les Anciens Canadiens*, published in 1863. The work was an immediate success, and in 1890 Charles G.D. Roberts translated it into English under the title *The Canadians of Old*. Even today the folkloric source has not been forgotten: Antonine Maillet, the best-known of contemporary Acadian writers, deliberately echoes the voice and style of those early storytellers.

It is interesting to note that after those promising beginnings, French Canada has not been fruitful in ghosts. Ghosts are conjured up in several novels—including Anne Hébert's *In the Shadow of the Wind* and one of the Plateau Mont Royal volumes of Michel Tremblay—but the best-known modern Québécois writers have not imagined ghost stories. There are no *histoires de fantômes* by Marie-Claire Blais, Gabrielle Roy, Victor-Lévy Beaulieu, Jacques Poulin, Claude Jasmin, Hubert Aquin, even Anne Hébert. 'Our reality—political, physical—is perhaps too haunting in itself to allow for ghosts,' the novelist Yves Beauchemin has said.

In English Canada ghosts do appear, but not immediately. Two of Canada's earliest writers, Catharine Parr Traill and her younger sister Susanna Moodie, both regretted the absence of hauntings in the New World. 'As to ghosts or spirits,' wrote Traill in 1836, 'they appear totally banished from Canada. This is too matter-of-fact a country for such supernaturals to visit.' Sixteen years later, Moodie quoted one of her fellow-settlers: '"Ghosts! There are no ghosts in Canada!" said Mr D—. "The country is too new for ghosts. No Canadian is afeard of ghosts. It is only in old countries, like your'n, that are full of sin and wickedness, that people believe in such nonsense."' The poet Earle Birney insisted, only a few years ago: 'it's only by our lack of ghosts / we're haunted.' However, John Robert Colombo's *Mysterious Canada*, published in 1988 and listing over 400 pages of uncanny and ghostly Canadiana, seems to contradict these assertions.

And yet, by the turn of the century the ghost story, whether in local or in foreign settings, was well-recognized enough in Canada for Stephen Leacock to poke the kind of fun at it, in 'Buggam Grange', that Oscar Wilde had poked at his Gothic ancestors in 'The Canterville Ghost'. British and American ghost-story practitioners such as Charles Dickens, Henry James, and Edith Wharton found several excellent disciples in Canada, such as Duncan Campbell Scott and Mazo de la Roche. More recently, Robertson Davies' Dickensian spoof is a homage to the master.

M.R. James, more powerfully than anyone else, realized that the reader of ghost stories requires no explanations. The witness of the apparition need not be mad, need not be dreaming, need not be lying. In fact, the author need not comment on the narrator's credentials at all: the ghost and its victim are left alone with the reader, and from their unchaperoned encounter is born the horror. In Canada this distillation of the ghostly essence of a story is carried to the point of mere inference. In Brian Moore's 'The Sight', for instance, the haunting is a gift, albeit the terrible gift of second sight; there is no ghost as such—only a horror akin to the one produced by a ghost. In Timothy Findley's 'Dreams', the ghosts instead are of too, too solid flesh, husband and wife inhabiting the same dream. And in Margaret Atwood's 'Death By Landscape' the ghostly presence is an absence, as it is in her novel *Surfacing* (which Eli Mandel called the foremost Canadian ghost story).

Few Canadian writers have sought inspiration for their nightmares in native lore. There is a sad lack of native writers in Canada, whether because for a long time they were refused access to the mainstream white culture, or because they have now consciously decided not to be part of the system that exploited them for so long. Non-native writers like W.H. Blake and Farley Mowat have tried to interpret some of the native ghosts—the Wendigo and the Sasquatch have powerful ghostly qualities—but what we lack is a sighting of these apparitions from inside the particular kind of fear experienced by the people who bred them.

It is impossible to define a Canadian ghost story through its local colour. In fact, if one must define it at all, what is notable about the ghost stories written in Canada—especially in the past twenty years— is their universality. For the immigrant writers—in Canada today they are probably the majority of the literary community—the ghosts of the past, of back home, must seem strangely comforting, and it is from the new antiseptic land that they best draw their fears. These and Canadian-born writers have set their stories in Paris (Mavis Gallant), in Iowa (W.P. Kinsella), in Africa (Audrey Thomas), in New York (Brian Moore), in Bombay (Rohinton Mistry); but in a sense the ghostly experience is common to them all in the land Traill and Moodie saw as 'so new'. British and American ghosts seldom travel. The Canadian ghost story, like so much of Canadian literature today, seems to be about the rest of the world as much as it is about Canada. It demands a new reader as much as a different kind of writer, a reader aware of different codes, different languages, different fears from his or her own. The 'atmosphere' that M.R. James said he required can be found—the reader discovers—almost anywhere on earth; the 'nicely managed crescendo' has, in the Canadian ghost story, a Scottish lilt or an Eastern inflection.

'The digging up of ancestors, calling up of ghosts, exposure of skeletons in the closet which are so evident in many cultural areas,' wrote Margaret Atwood in her essay 'Canadian Monsters', 'have numerous motivations, but one of them surely is a search for reassurance.' That reassurance, however, is paradoxically unnerving. It produces in the reader a primordial shiver that, sought in Canada, is sparked by something suspected and yet unknown, lying just beyond the horizon.

ALBERTO MANGUEL

The editor wishes to thank John Robert Colombo, Geoff Hancock, Sally Livingston, Professors Neil Besner, Maurice Elliott, Carole Gerson, Reginald Hamel, John Lennox, and Robert McDougall, typist Jaye Mastalerz, and the editor of editors, Richard Teleky. — A.M.

ACKNOWLEDGEMENTS

MARGARET ATWOOD 'Death by Landscape'. Reprinted by permission of Margaret Atwood © 1989 by Margaret Atwood, originally appeared in *Saturday Night*.

PHILIPPE AUBERT DE GASPÉ 'The Canadians of Old' from *The Canadians of Old*. English translation by Charles G.D. Roberts. Used by permission of the Canadian Publishers, McClelland and Stewart, Toronto.

HONORÉ BEAUGRAND 'The Miser's Ghost'. English translation copyright © 1989 by Alberto Manguel.

VIRGIL BURNETT 'Fallowfields' from *Farewell Tour*. Used by permission of The Porcupine's Quill Inc.

ROBERTSON DAVIES 'Dickens Digested' from *High Spirits* by Robertson Davies. Copyright © 1982 by Robertson Davies. All rights reserved. Reprinted by permission of Penguin Books Canada Limited and Viking Penguin, a division of Penguin Books USA Inc.

MAZO DE LA ROCHE 'Portrait of a Wife' from *Selected Stories*. University of Ottawa Press, 1979.

TIMOTHY FINDLEY 'Dreams' from *Stones* by Timothy Findley. Copyright © Pebble Productions, Inc. 1988. Reprinted by permission of Penguin Books Canada Limited and Timothy Findley.

MAVIS GALLANT 'From the Fifteenth District' from *From the Fifteenth District*. Reprinted by permission of Georges Borchardt, Inc. and the author. Copyright © 1973, 1974, 1975, 1976, 1977, 1978, 1979 by Mavis Gallant.

W.P. KINSELLA 'Shoeless Joe Jackson Comes to Iowa' reprinted from *Shoeless Joe Jackson Comes to Iowa* by permission of Oberon Press.

A.M. KLEIN 'No Traveller Returns . . . ' from *Short Stories* edited by M.W. Steinberg. Used by permission of University of Toronto Press.

STEPHEN LEACOCK 'Buggam Grange: A Good Old Ghost Story' from *Laugh With Leacock*. Used by permission of the Canadian Publishers, McClelland and Stewart, Toronto.

ERIC MCCORMACK 'No Country for Old Men' from *Inspecting the Vaults* by

Eric McCormack. Copyright © Eric McCormack, 1987. Reprinted by permission of Penguin Books Canada Limited.

ALISTAIR MACLEOD 'As Birds Bring Forth the Sun' from *As Birds Bring Forth the Sun.* Used by permission of the Canadian Publishers, McClelland and Stewart, Toronto.

ANTONINE MAILLET 'The Ghost of Lovers' Lane' translated from 'Le Revenant du chemin des amoureux' from *Les Contes de par derrière chez mon père* © Leméac 1987. Reprinted by permission of Leméac Éditeur. English translation copyright © 1989 by Alberto Manguel.

ROHINTON MISTRY 'The Ghost of Firozsha Baag' from *Tales of Firozsha Baag* by Rohinton Mistry. Copyright © 1987 by Rohinton Mistry. Reprinted by permission of Penguin Books Canada Limited and Houghton Mifflin Co.

BRIAN MOORE 'The Sight'. Reprinted by permission of Curtis Brown, Ltd. Copyright © 1977 by Brian Moore.

FARLEY MOWAT 'The Snow Walker' from *The Snow Walker.* Reprinted by permission of Jack McClelland and Associates Inc.

JANE RULE 'If There Is No Gate'. Reprinted by permission of Jane Rule. Copyright © by Jane Rule.

DUNCAN CAMPBELL SCOTT 'Vengeance Is Mine' from *In the Village of Viger and Other Stories.* Used by permission of John G. Aylen, Ottawa.

AUDREY THOMAS 'Joseph and his Brother' from *Two in the Bush and Other Stories.* Used by permission of the Canadian Publishers, McClelland and Stewart, Toronto.

SEAN VIRGO 'Haunt' © Sean Virgo. Used by permission of Sean Virgo.

ETHEL WILSON 'Mr Sleepwalker' from *Mrs Golightly & Other Stories* © 1961. Reprinted by permission of Macmillan of Canada, A Division of Canada Publishing Corporation.

TIM WYNNE-JONES 'The Woman With the Lounge-Act Hair' © Tim Wynne-Jones. Used by permission of Lucinda Vardey Agency.

PHILIPPE AUBERT DE GASPÉ · 1786-1871

La Corriveau

As soon as our young travellers, crossing the St Lawrence opposite Quebec, have reaching Point Lévis, José makes haste to harness a splendid Norman horse into one of those low sledges which furnish the only means of transport at this season, when the roads are only covered here and there with snow and ice, and when overflowing streams intercept the way at intervals. When they come to one of these obstacles José unharnesses the horse, all three mount, and the brook is speedily forded. It is true that Jules, who clasps José around the waist, tries every now and then to throw him off, at the risk of partaking with him the luxury of a bath at a little above zero. He might as well have tried to throw Cape Tourmente into the St Lawrence. José, who, in spite of his comparatively small stature, is as strong as an elephant, laughs in his sleeve and pretends not to notice it. The brook forded, José goes back for the sledge, reharnesses the horse, climbs into the sledge with the baggage in front of him lest he should get it wet, and speedily overtakes his fellow-travellers, who have not halted a moment in their march.

Thanks to Jules, the conversation never flags during the journey. Archie does nothing but laugh over the witticisms that Jules perpetrates at his expense. He has long given up attempting any retort.

'Now,' said Archie, 'since you seem to have emptied your budget of all the absurdities that a hair-brained French head can contain, try and speak seriously, and tell me why the Isle of Orleans is called the Isle of the Sorcerers.'

'For the very simple reason', answered Jules, 'that a great many sorcerers live there.'

'There you begin again with your nonsense,' said Lochiel.

'I am in earnest,' said Jules. 'These Scotch are unbearably conceited. They can't acknowledge any excellence in other nations. Do you think, my dear fellow, that Scotland has the monopoly of witches and wizards? I would beg you to know that we too have our sorcerers;

and that two hours ago, between Point Lévis and Beaumont, I might as easily as not have introduced you to a very respectable sorceress. I would have you know, moreover, that on the estate of my illustrious father you shall see a witch of the most remarkable skill. The difference is, my dear boy, that in Scotland you burn them, while here we treat them in a manner fitting their power and social influence. Ask José if I am not telling the truth?'

José did not fail to confirm all he said. In his eyes the witches of Beaumont and St Jean Port Joli were genuine and mighty sorceresses.

'But to speak seriously,' continued Jules, 'since you would make a reasonable man of me, *nolens volens*, as my sixth-form master used to say when he gave me a dose of the strap, I believe the fable takes its rise from the fact that the *habitants* on the north and south shores of the river, seeing the islanders on dark nights go out fishing with torches, mistake their lights for will-o'-the-wisps. Then, you know that our country folk regard the will-o'-the-wisps as witches, or as evil spirits who endeavour to lure the wandering wretch to his death. They even profess to hear them laugh when the deluded traveller falls into the quagmire. The truth is, that there is an inflammable gas continually escaping from our bogs and swampy places, from which to the hobgoblins and sorcerers is but a single step.'

'Impossible,' said Archie; 'your logic is at fault, as the professor so often had to tell you. You see the inhabitants of the north and south shores themselves go fishing with torches, whence, according to your reasoning, the islanders should have called them sorcerers; which is not the case.'

While Jules was shaking his head, with no answer ready, José took up the word.

'If you would let me speak, gentlemen, I might explain your difficulty by telling you what happened to my late father who is now dead.'

'Oh, by all means, tell us that; tell us what happened to your late father who is now dead,' cried Jules, with a marked emphasis on the last four words.

'Yes, my dear José, do us the favour of telling us about it,' added Lochiel.

'I can't half tell the story,' answered José, 'for, you see, I have neither the fine accent nor the splendid voice of my lamented parent. When he used to tell us what happened to him in his vigil, our bodies would shake so, as if with ague, as would do you good to see. But I'll do my best to satisfy you:

'It happened one day that my late father, who is now dead, had left the city for home somewhat late. He had even diverted himself a little so to speak, with his acquaintances in Point Lévis. Like an honest man, he loved his drop; and on his journeys he always carried a flask of brandy in his dogfish-skin satchel. They say the liquor is the milk for old men.'

'*Lac dulce*,' interjected Archie, sententiously.

'Begging your pardon, Mr Archie,' answered José, with some warmth, 'it was neither *sweet water* (*de l'eau douce*) nor *lake-water* (*eau de lac*), but very good, unadulterated brandy which my late father, now dead, was carrying in his satchel.'

'Capital, upon my word!' cried Jules. 'It serves you right for your perpetual Latin quotations!'

'I beg your pardon, José,' said Lochiel, very seriously. 'I intended not the shadow of disrespect to your late father.'

'You are excused, sir,' said José, entirely mollified. 'It happened that it was quite dark when my father at last got under way. His friends did their best to keep him all night, telling him that he would have to pass, all by himself, the iron cage wherein *La Corriveau* did penance for having killed her husband.

'You saw it yourselves, gentlemen, when leaving Point Lévis at one o'clock. She was quiet then in her cage, the wicked creature, with her eyeless skull. But never you trust to her being blind. She is a cunning one, you had better believe! If she can't see in the daytime, she knows well enough how to find her way to torment poor folks at night. Well, as for my late father, who was as brave as his captain's sword, he told his friends that he didn't care—that he didn't owe *La Corriveau* a farthing—with a heap more reasons which I can not remember now. He put the whip to his horse, a fine brute that could travel like the wind, and was gone in a second.

'As he was passing the skeleton, he thought he heard a noise, a sort of wailing; but, as a heavy southwest wind was blowing, he made up his mind it was only the gale whistling through the bones of the corpse. It gave him a kind of a start, nevertheless, and he took a good pull at the flask to brace himself up. All things considered, however, as he said to himself, Christians should be ready to help each other; perhaps the poor creature was wanting his prayers. He took off his cap and devoutly recited a *de profundis* for her benefit, thinking that, if it didn't do her any good, it could at least do her no harm, and that he himself would be the better for it. Well, then he kept on as fast as he could; but, for all that, he heard a queer sound behind him—tic-tac, tic-tac, like a piece of iron striking on the stones. He thought it was the tire of his wheel, or some piece of the wagon, that had come unfastened. He got out to see, but found everything snug. He touched the horse to make up for lost time, but after a little he heard again that tic-tac, tic-tac, on the stones. Being brave, he didn't pay much attention.

'When he got to the high ground of St Michel, which we passed a little way back, he grew very drowsy. "After all," said my late father, "a man is not a dog! let us take a little nap; we'll both be the better for it, my horse and I." Well, he unharnessed his horse, tied his legs so he would not wander too far, and said: "There, my pet, there's good grass, and you can hear the brook yonder. Good-night."

'As my late father crawled himself into the wagon to keep out of the dew, it struck him to wonder what time it was. After studying the "Three Kings" to the south'ard and the "Wagon" to the north'ard, he made up his mind it must be midnight. "It is time", said he, "for honest men to be in bed."

'Suddenly, however, it seemed to him as if Isle d'Orlèans was on fire. He sprang over the ditch, leaned on the fence, opened his eyes wide, and stared with all his might. He saw at last that the flames were dancing up and down the shore, as if all the will-o'-the-wisps, all the damned souls of Canada, were gathered there to hold the witches' sabbath. He stared so hard that his eyes which had grown a little dim grew very clear again, and he saw a curious sight; you would have said they were a kind of men, a queer breed altogether. They had a head big as a peck measure, topped off with a pointed cap a yard long; then they had arms, legs, feet, and hands armed with long claws, but no body to speak of. Their crotch, begging your pardon, gentlemen, was split right up to their ears. They had scarcely anything in the way of flesh; they were kind of all bone, like skeletons. Every one of these pretty fellows had his upper lip split like a rabbit's, and through the split stuck out a rhinoceros tusk a foot long, like you see, Mr Archie, in your book of unnatural history. As for the nose, it was nothing more nor less, begging your pardon, than a long pig's snout, which they would rub first on one side and then on the other of their great tusk, perhaps to sharpen it. I almost forgot to say that they had a long tail, twice as long as a cow's, which they used, I suppose, to keep of the flies.

'The funniest thing of all was that there were but three eyes to every couple of imps. Those that had but one eye, in the middle of the forehead, like those Cyclopes that your uncle, who is a learned man, Mr Jules, used to read to us about out of that big book of his, all Latin, like the priest's prayer-book, which he called his Virgil—those that had but one eye held each by the claw two novices with the proper number of eyes. Out of all these eyes spurted the flames which lit up Isle d'Orléans like broad day. The novices seemed very respectful to their companions, who were, as one might say, half blind; they bowed down to them, they fawned upon them, they fluttered their arms and legs, just like good Christians dancing the minuet.

'The eyes of my late father were fairly starting out of his head. It was worse and worse when they began to jump and dance without moving from their places, and to chant in a voice as hoarse as that of a choking cow, this song:

> *Hoary Frisker, Goblin gay.*
> *Long-nosed Neighbour, come away!*
> *Come my Grumbler in the mud,*
> *Brother Frog of tainted blood!*
> *Come, and on this juicy Christian*
> *Let us feast it while we may!*

'"Ah! the accursed heathens," exclaimed my late father, "an honest man can not be sure of his property for a moment! Not satisfied with having stolen my favourite song, which I always keep to wind up with at weddings and feasts, just see how they've played the devil with it! One would hardly recognize it. It is Christians instead of good wine that they are going to treat themselves to, the scoundrels!"

'Then the imps went on with their hellish song, glaring at my late father, and curling their long snouts around their great rhinoceros tusks:

> *Come, my tricksy Traveler's Guide,*
> *Devil's Minion true and tried,*
> *Come, my Sucking-Pig, my Simple,*
> *Brother Wart and Brother Pimple;*
> *Here's a fat and juicy Frenchman*
> *To be pickled, to be fried!*

'"All that I can say to you just now, my darlings," cried my late father, "is that if you get no more fat to eat than what I'm going to bring you on my lean carcass you'll hardly need to skim your broth."

'The goblins, however, seemed to be expecting something, for they kept turning their heads every moment. My late father looked in the same direction. What was that he saw on the hill-side? A mighty devil, built like the rest, but as long as the steeple St Michel, which we passed awhile back. Instead of the pointed bonnet, he wore a three-horned hat, topped with a big thorn bush in place of a feather. He had but one eye, blackguard that he was, but that was as good as a dozen. He was doubtless the drum-major of the regiment, for he held in his hand a saucepan twice as big as our maple-sugar kettles, which hold twenty gallons, and in the other hand a bell-clapper, which no doubt the dog of a heretic had stolen from some church before its consecration. He pounded on his saucepan, and all the scoundrels began to laugh, to jump, to flutter, nodding to my late father as if inviting him to come and amuse himself with them.

'"You'll wait a long time, my lambs," thought my late father to himself, his teeth chattering in his head as if he had the shaking fever—"you will wait a long time, my gentle lambs. I'm not in any hurry to quit the good Lord's earth to live with the goblins!"

'Suddenly the tall devil began to sing a hellish round, accompanying himself on the saucepan, which he beat furiously, and all the goblins darted away like lightening—so fast, indeed, that it took them less than a minute to go all the way around the island. My poor late father was so stupefied by the hubbub that he could not remember more than three verses of the song, which ran like this:

> *Here's the spot that suits us well*
> *When it gets too hot in hell—*
> *Toura-loura;*
> *Here we go all round,*
> *Hands all round,*
> *Here we go all round.*
>
> *Come along and stir your sticks,*
> *You jolly dogs of heretics—*
> *Toura-loura;*

'Well,' said José, 'it happened that my father, brave as he was, was in such a devil of a funk that the sweat was hanging from the end of his nose like a head of oats. There he was, the dear man, with his eyes bigger than his head, never daring to budge. Presently he thought he heard behind him the "tic-tac," "tic-tac", which he had already heard several times on the journey; but he had too much to occupy his attention in front of him to pay much heed to what might pass behind. Suddenly, when he was least expecting it, he felt two great bony hands, like the claws of a bear, grip him by the shoulders. He turned around horrified, and found himself face to face with La Corriveau, who was climbing on his back. She had thrust her hands through the bars of her cage and succeeded in clutching him; but the cage was heavy, and at every leap she fell back again to the ground with a hoarse cry, without losing her hold, however, on the shoulders of my late father, who bent under the burden. If he had not held tight to the fence with both hands, he would have been crushed under the weight. My poor late father was so overwhelmed with horror that one might have heard the sweat that rolled off his forehead dropping down on the fence like grains of duck-shot.

"'My dear Francis," said La Corriveau, "do me the pleasure of taking me to dance with my friends of Isle d'Orléans?"

"'Oh, you devil's wench!" cried my late father. That was the only oath the good man ever used, and that only when very much tried.'

'The deuce!' exclaimed Jules, 'it seems to me that the occasion was a very suitable one. For my own part, I should have been swearing like a heathen.'

'And I,' said Archie, 'like an Englishman.'

'Isn't that much the same thing?' answered D'Haberville.

'You are wrong, my dear Jules. I must acknowledge that the heathen acquit themselves very well; but the English? Oh, my! Le Roux who, soon as he got out of college, made a point of reading all the bad books he could get hold of, told us, if you remember, that that blackguard of a Voltaire, as my uncle the Jesuit used to call him, had declared in a book of his, treating of what happened in France in the reign of Charles VII, when that prince was hunting the islanders out of his kingdom—Le Roux told us that Voltaire had put it on record that "every Englishman swears". Well, my boy, those events took place about the year 1445—let us say, three hundred years ago. Judge, then, what dreadful oaths that ill-tempered nation must have invented in the course of three centuries!'

'I surrender,' said Jules. 'But go on, my dear José.'

"'Devil's wench!" exclaimed my late father, "is that your gratitude for my *de profundis* and all my other prayers? You'd drag *me* into the orgy, would you? I was thinking you must have been in for at least three or four thousand years of purgatory for your pranks; and you had only killed two husbands—which was a mere nothing. So having always a tender heart for everything. I felt sorry for you, and said to myself we must give you a helping hand. And this is the way you thank me, that you want to straddle my shoulders and ride me to hell like a heretic!"

"'My dear Francis," said La Corriveau, "take me over to dance with my dear friends;" and she knocked her head against that of my late father till her skull rattled like a dry bladder filled with pebbles.

"'You may be sure," said my late father, "You hellish wench of Judas Iscariot, I'm not going to be your jackass to carry you over to dance with those pretty darlings!"

"'My dear Francis," answered the witch, "I can not cross the St Lawrence, which is a consecrated stream, except with the help of a Christian."

"'Get over as best you can, you devilish gallows bird," said my late father. "Get over as best you can; every one to his own business. Oh, yes, a likely thing that I'll carry you over to dance with your dear friends; but that will be a devil of a journey you have come, the Lord knows how, dragging that fine cage of yours, which must have torn up all the stones on the king's highway! A nice row there'll be when the inspector passes this way one of these days and finds the road in such a condition! And then, who but the poor *habitant* will have to suffer for your frolics, getting fined for not having kept the road properly!"

'The drum-major suddenly stopped beating on his great sauce-pan. All the goblins halted and gave three yells, three frightful whoops, like the Indians give when they have danced that war-dance with which they always begin their bloody expeditions. The island was shaken to its foundation, the wolves, the bears, all the other wild beasts, and the demons of the northern mountains took up the cry, and the echoes repeated it till it was lost in the forests of the far-off Saguenay.

'My poor, late father thought that the end of the world had come, and the Day of Judgement.

'The tall devil with the sauce-pan struck three blows; and a silence most profound succeeded the hellish hubbub. He stretched out his arm toward my late father, and cried with a voice of thunder: "Will you make haste, you lazy dog? will you make haste, you cur of a Christian, and ferry our friend across? We have only fourteen thousand four hundred times more to prance around the island before cock-crow. Are you going to make her lose the best of the fun?"

"'Go to the devil, where you all belong," answered my late father, losing all patience.

"'Come, my dear Francis," said La Corriveau, "be a little more obliging. You are acting like a child about a mere trifle. Moreover, see how the time is flying. Come, now, one little effort!"

"'No, no, my wench of Satan," said my late father. "Would to Heaven you still had on the fine collar which the hangman put around your neck two years ago. You wouldn't have so clear a wind-pipe."

'During this dialogue the goblins on the island resumed their chorus:

> *Here we go all round,*
> *Hands all round,*
> *Here we go all round.*

"'My dear Francis," said the witch, "if your body and bones won't carry me over, I'm going to strangle you. I will straddle your soul and ride over to the festival." With these words, she seized him by the throat and strangled him.'

'What,' exclaimed the young men, 'she strangled your poor, late father, now dead?'

'When I said strangled, it was very little better than that,' answered José, 'for the dear man lost his consciousness.

'When he came to himself he heard a little bird, which cried *Qué-tu?* (Who art thou?)

"'Oh, ho!" said my late father, "it's plain I'm not in hell, since I hear the dear Lord's birds!" He opened first one eye, then the other, and saw that it was broad daylight. The sun was shining right in his face; the little bird, perched on a neighbouring branch, kept crying *qué-tu?*

"'My dear child," said my father, "it is not very easy to answer your question, for I'm not very certain this morning just who I am. Only yesterday I believed myself to be a brave, honest, and God-fearing man; but I have had such an experience this night that I can hardly be sure that it is I, Francis Dubé, here present in body and soul. Then the dear man began to sing:

> *Here we go all round,*
> *Hands all round,*
> *Here we go all round.*

'In fact, he was half bewitched. At last, however, he perceived that he was lying full length in a ditch where, happily, there was more mud than water; but for that my poor, late father, who now sleeps with the saints, surrounded by all his relations and friends, and fortified by all the holy sacraments, would have died without absolution, like a monkey in his old tree, begging your pardon for the comparison, young gentlemen. When he had got his face clear from the mud of the ditch, in which he was stuck fast as in a vise, the first thing he saw was his flask on the bank above him. At this he plucked up his courage and stretched out his hand to take a drink. But no such luck! The flask was empty! The witch had drained every drop.'

'My dear José,' said Lochiel, 'I think I am about as brave as the next one. Nevertheless, if such an adventure had happened to me, never again would I have travelled alone at night.'

'Nor I either,' said D'Haberville.

'To tell you the truth, gentlemen,' said José, 'since you are so discriminating, I will confess that my late father, who before this adventure would not have turned a hair in the graveyard at midnight, was never afterward so bold; he dared not even go alone after sunset to do his chores in the stable.'

'And very sensible he was; but finish your story,' said Jules.

'It is finished,' said José. 'My late father harnessed his horse, who appeared, poor brute, to have noticed nothing unusual, and made his way home as fast as possible. It was not till a fortnight later that he told us his adventure.'

'What do you say to all that, my self-satisfied skeptic who would refuse to Canada the luxury of witches and wizards?' inquired D'Haberville.

'I say,' answered Archie, 'that our Highland witches are mere infants compared with those of New France, and what's more, if ever I get back to my Scottish hills, I'm going to imprison all our hobgoblins in bottles, as Le Sage did with his wooden-legged devil, Asmodeus.'

'Hum-m-m!' said José. 'It would serve them just right, accursed blackguards; but where would you get bottles big enough? There'd be the difficulty.'

Translated by Charles G.D. Roberts

JOHN CHARLES DENT · 1841-1888

The Gerrard Street Mystery

I

My name is William Francis Furlong. My occupation is that of a commission merchant, and my place of business is on St Paul Street, in the City of Montreal. I have resided in Montreal ever since shortly after my marriage in 1862, to my cousin, Alice Playter, of Toronto. My name may not be familiar to the present generation of Torontonians, though I was born in Toronto, and passed the early years of my life there. Since the days of my youth my visits to the Upper Province have been few, and—with one exception—very brief; so that I have doubtless passed out of the remembrance of many persons with whom I was once on terms of intimacy. Still, there are several residents of Toronto whom I am happy to number among my warmest personal friends at the present day. There are also a good many persons of middle age, not in Toronto only, but scattered here and there throughout various parts of Ontario, who will have no difficulty in recalling my name as that of one of their fellow-students at Upper Canada College. The name of my late uncle, Richard Yardington, is of course well known to all old residents of Toronto, where he spent the last thirty-two years of his life. He settled there in the year 1829, when the place was still known as Little York. He opened a small store on Yonge Street, and his commercial career was a reasonably prosperous one. By steady degrees the small store developed into what, in those times, was regarded as a considerable establishment. In the course of years the owner acquired a competency, and in 1854 retired from business altogether. From that time up to the day of his death he lived in his own house on Gerrard Street.

After mature deliberation, I have resolved to give to the Canadian public an account of some rather singular circumstances connected with my residence in Toronto. Though repeatedly urged to do so, I have hitherto refrained from giving any extended publicity to those circumstances, in consequence of my inability to see any good to be served thereby. The only person, however, whose reputation can be injuriously affected by the details has been dead for some years. He has left behind him no one whose feelings can be shocked by the disclosure, and the story is in itself sufficiently remarkable to be worth the telling. Told, accordingly, it shall be; and the only fictitious element introduced into the narrative shall be the name of one of the persons most immediately concerned in it.

At the time of taking up his abode in Toronto—or rather in Little York—my uncle Richard was a widower, and childless; his wife having died several months previously. His only relatives on this side of the Atlantic were two maiden sisters, a few years younger than himself. He never contracted a second matrimonial alliance, and for some time after his arrival here his sisters lived in his house, and were dependent upon him for support. After the lapse of a few years both of them married and settled down in homes of their own. The elder of them subsequently became my mother. She was left a widow when I was a mere boy, and survived my father only a few months. I was an only child, and as my parents had been in humble circumstances, the charge of my maintenance devolved upon my uncle, to whose kindness I am indebted for such educational training as I have received. After sending me to school and college for several years, he took me into his store, and gave me my first insight into commercial life. I lived with him, and both then and always received at his hands the kindness of a father, in which light I eventually almost came to regard him. His younger sister, who was married to a watchmaker called Elias Playter, lived at Quebec from the time of her marriage until her death, which took place in 1846. Her husband had been unsuccessful in business, and was moreover of dissipated habits. He was left with one child—a daughter—on his hands; and as my uncle was averse to the idea of his sister's child remaining under the control of one so unfit to provide for her welfare, he proposed to adopt the little girl as his own. To this proposition Mr Elias Playter readily assented, and little Alice was soon domiciled with her uncle and myself in Toronto.

Brought up, as we were, under the same roof, and seeing each other every day of our lives, a childish attachment sprang up between my cousin Alice and myself. As the years rolled by, this attachment ripened into a tender affection, which eventually resulted in an engagement between us. Our engagement was made with the full and cordial approval of my uncle, who did not share the prejudice entertained by many persons against marriage between cousins. He stipulated, however, that our marriage should be deferred until I had seen somewhat more of the world, and until we had both reached an age when we might reasonably be presumed to know our own minds. He was also, not unnaturally, desirous that before taking upon myself the responsibility of marriage I should give some evidence of my ability to provide for a wife, and for other contingencies usually consequent upon matrimony. He made no secret of his intention to divide his property between Alice and myself at his death; and the fact that no actual division would be necessary in the event of our marriage with each other was doubtless one reason for his ready acquiescence in our engagement. He was, however, of a vigorous constitution, strictly regular and methodical in all his habits, and likely to live to an advanced age. He could hardly be called parsimonious, but, like most men who have successfully fought their own way through life, he was rather fond of authority, and little disposed to divest himself of his wealth until he should have no further occasion for it. He expressed his willingness to establish me in business, either in Toronto or elsewhere, and to give me the benefit of his experience in all mercantile transactions.

When matters had reached this pass I had just completed my twenty-first year, my cousin being three years younger. Since my uncle's retirement I had engaged in one or two little speculations on my own account, which had turned out fairly successful, but I had not devoted myself to any regular or fixed pursuit. Before any definite arrangements had been concluded as to the course of my future life, a circumstance occurred which seemed to open a way for me to turn to good account such mercantile talent as I possessed. An old friend of my uncle's opportunely arrived in Toronto from Melbourne, Australia, where, in the course of a few years, he had risen from the position of a junior clerk to that of senior partner in a prominent commercial house. He painted the land of his adoption in glowing colours, and assured my uncle and myself that it presented an inviting field for a young man of energy and business capacity, more especially if he had a small capital at his command. The matter was carefully debated in our domestic circle. I was naturally averse to a separation from Alice, but my imagination took fire at Mr Redpath's glowing account of his own splendid success. I pictured myself returning to Canada after an absence of four or five years with a mountain of gold at my command, as the result of my own energy and acuteness. In imagination, I saw myself settled down with Alice in a palatial mansion on Jarvis Street, and living in affluence all the rest of my days. My uncle bade me consult my own judgement in the matter, but rather encouraged the idea than otherwise. He offered to advance me £500, and I had about half that sum as the result of my own speculations. Mr Redpath, who was just about returning to Melbourne, promised to aid me to the extent of his power with his local knowledge and advice. In less than a fortnight from that time he and I were on our way to the other side of the globe.

We reached our destination early in the month of September, 1857. My life in Australia has no direct bearing upon the course of events to be related, and may be passed over in a very few words. I engaged in various enterprises, and achieved a certain measure of success. If none of my ventures proved eminently prosperous, I at least met with no serious disasters. At the end of four years—that is to say, in September, 1861—I made up my account with the world, and found I was worth ten thousand dollars. I had, however, become terribly homesick, and longed for the termination of my voluntary exile. I had, of course, kept up a regular correspondence with Alice and Uncle Richard, and of late they had both pressed me to return home. 'You have enough', wrote my uncle, 'to give you a start in Toronto, and I see no reason why Alice and you should keep apart any longer. You will have no housekeeping expenses, for I intend you to live with me. I am getting old, and shall be glad of your companionship in my declining years. You will have a comfortable home while I live, and when I die you will get all I have between you. Write as soon as you receive this, and let us know how soon you can be here,—the sooner the better.'

The letter containing this pressing invitation found me in a mood very much disposed to accept it. The only enterprise I had on hand which would be likely to delay me was a transaction in wool, which, as I believed, would be closed by the end of January or the beginning of February. By the first of March I should certainly be in a condition to start on my homeward voyage, and I determined that my departure should take place about that time. I wrote both to Alice and my uncle, apprising them of my intention, and announcing my expectation to reach Toronto not later than the middle of May.

The letters so written were posted on the 19th of September, in time for the mail which left on the following day. On the 27th, to my huge surprise and gratification, the wool transaction referred to was unexpectedly concluded, and I was at liberty, if so disposed, to start for home by the next fast mail steamer, the *Southern Cross*, leaving Melbourne on the 11th of October. I *was* so disposed, and made my preparations accordingly. It was useless, I reflected, to write to my uncle or to Alice, acquainting them with the change in my plans, for I should take the shortest route home, and should probably be in Toronto as soon as a letter could get there. I resolved to telegraph from New York, upon my arrival there, so as not to take them altogether by surprise.

The morning of the 11th of October found me on board the *Southern Cross*, where I shook hands with Mr Redpath and several other friends who accompanied me on board for a last farewell. The particulars of the voyage to England are not pertinent to the story, and may be given very briefly. I took the Red Sea route, and arrived at Marseilles about two o'clock in the afternoon of the 29th of November. From Marseilles I travelled by rail to Calais, and so impatient was I to reach my journey's end without loss of time, that I did not even stay over to behold the glories of Paris. I had a commission to execute in London, which, however, delayed me there only a few hours, and I hurried down to Liverpool, in the hope of catching the Cunard Steamer for New York. I missed it by about two hours, but the *Persia* was detailed to start on a special trip to Boston the following day. I secured a berth, and at eight o'clock the next morning steamed out of the Mersey on my way homeward.

The voyage from Liverpool to Boston consumed fourteen days. All I need say about it is, that before arriving at the latter port I formed an intimate acquaintance with one of the passengers—Mr Junius H. Gridley, a Boston merchant, who was returning from a hurried business trip to Europe. He was—and is—a most agreeable companion. We were thrown together a good deal during the voyage, and we then laid the foundation of a friendship which has ever since subsisted between us. Before the dome of the State House loomed in sight he had extracted a promise from me to spend a night with him before pursuing my journey. We landed at the wharf in East Boston on the evening of the 17th of December, and I accompanied him to his house on West Newton Street, where I remained until the following morning. Upon consulting the time-table, we found that the Albany express would leave at 11:30 A.M. This left several hours at my disposal, and we sallied forth immediately after breakfast to visit some of the lions of the American Athens.

In the course of our peregrinations through the streets, we dropped into the post office, which had recently been established in the Merchants' Exchange Building, on State Street. Seeing the countless piles of mail-matter, I jestingly remarked to my friend that there seemed to be letters enough there to go around the whole human family. He replied in the same mood, whereupon I banteringly suggested the probability that among so many letters, surely there ought to be one for me.

'Nothing more reasonable,' he replied. 'We Bostonians are always bountiful to strangers. Here is the General Delivery, and here is the department where letters addressed to the Furlong family are kept in stock. Pray inquire for yourself.'

The joke I confess was not a very brilliant one; but with a grave countenance I stepped up to the wicket and asked the young lady in attendance:

'Anything for W.F. Furlong?'

She took from a pigeon-hole a handful of correspondence, and proceeded to run her eye over the addresses. When about half the pile had been exhausted she stopped, and propounded the usual inquiry in the case of strangers:

'Where do you expect letters from?'

'From Toronto,' I replied.

To my no small astonishment she immediately handed me a letter, bearing the Toronto postmark. The address was in the peculiar and well-known handwriting of my uncle Richard.

Scarcely crediting the evidence of my senses I tore open the envelope, and read as follows:—

Toronto, 9th December, 1861.

My Dear William—
I am so glad to know that you are coming home so much sooner than you expected when you wrote last, and that you will eat your Christmas dinner with us. For reasons which you will learn when you arrive, it will not be a very merry Christmas at our house, but your presence will make it much more bearable than it would be without you. I have not told Alice that you are coming. Let it be a joyful surprise for her, as some compensation for the sorrows she has had to endure lately. You needn't telegraph. I will meet you at the GWR station.

Your affectionate uncle,
Richard Yardington.

'Why, what's the matter?' asked my friend, seeing the blank look of surprise on my face. 'Of course the letter is not for you; why on earth did you open it?'

'It *is* for me,' I answered. 'See here, Gridley, old man; have you been playing me a trick? If you haven't, this is the strangest thing I ever knew in my life.'

Of course he hadn't been playing me a trick. A moment's reflection showed me that such a thing was impossible. Here was the envelope, with the Toronto postmark of the 9th of December, at which time he had been with me on board the *Persia*, on the Banks of Newfoundland. Besides, he was a gentleman, and would not have played so poor and stupid a joke upon a guest. And, to put the matter beyond all possibility of doubt, I remembered that I had never mentioned my cousin's name in his hearing.

I handed him the letter. He read it carefully through twice over, and was as much mystified at its contents as myself; for during our passage across the Atlantic I had explained to him the circumstance under which I was returning home.

By what conceivable means had my uncle been made aware of my departure from Melbourne? Had Mr Redpath written to him, as soon as I acquainted that gentleman with my intentions? But even if such were the case, the letter could not have left before I did, and could not possibly have reached Toronto by the 9th of December. Had I been seen in England by some one who knew me, and had not one written from there? Most unlikely; and even if such a thing had happened, it was impossible that the letter could have reached Toronto by the 9th. I need hardly inform the reader that there was no telegraphic communication at that time. And how could my uncle know that I would take the Boston route? And if he *had* known, how could he foresee that I would do anything so absurd as to call at the Boston post office and inquire for letters? '*I will meet you at the GWR station.*' How was he to know by what train I would reach Toronto, unless I notified him by telegraph? And that he expressly stated to be unnecessary.

We did no more sight-seeing. I obeyed the hint contained in the letter, and sent no telegram. My friend accompanied me down to the Boston and Albany station, where I waited in feverish impatience for the departure of the train. We talked over the matter until 11:30, in the vain hope of finding some clue to the mystery. Then I started on my journey. Mr Gridley's curiousity was aroused, and I promised to send him an explanation immediately upon my arrival at home.

No sooner had the train glided out of the station than I settled myself in my seat, drew the tantalizing letter from my pocket, and proceeded to read and re-read it again and again. A very few perusals sufficed to fix its contents in my memory, so that I could repeat every word with my eyes shut. Still I continued to scrutinize the paper, the penmanship, and even the tint of the ink. For what purpose, do you ask? For no purpose, except that I hoped, in some mysterious manner, to obtain more light on the subject. No light came, however. The more I scrutinized and pondered, the greater was my mystification. The paper was a simple sheet of white letter-paper, of the kind ordinarily used by my uncle in his correspondence. So far as I could see, there was nothing peculiar about the ink. Anyone familiar with my uncle's writing could have sworn that no hand but his had penned the lines. His well-known signature, a masterpiece of involved hieroglyphics, was there in all its indistinctness, written as no one but himself could ever have written it. And yet, for some unaccountable reason, I was half disposed to suspect forgery. Forgery! What nonsense. Anyone clever enough to imitate Richard Yardington's handwriting would have employed his talents more profitably than indulging in a mischievous and purposeless jest. Not a bank in Toronto but would have discounted a note with that signature affixed to it.

Desisting from all attempts to solve these problems, I then tried to fathom the meaning of other points in the letter. What misfortune had happened to mar the Christmas festivities at my uncle's house? And what could the reference to my cousin Alice's sorrows mean? She was not ill. *That*, I thought, might be taken for granted. My uncle would hardly have referred to her illness as 'one of the sorrows she had to endure lately'. Certainly, illness may be regarded in the light of a sorrow; but 'sorrow' was not precisely the word which a straightforward man like Uncle Richard would have applied to it. I could conceive of no other cause of affliction in her case. My uncle was well, as was evinced by his having written the letter, and by his avowed intention to meet me at the station. Her father had died long before I started for Australia. She had no other near relation except myself, and she had no cause for anxiety, much less for 'sorrow', on my account. I thought it singular, too, that my uncle, having in some strange manner become acquainted with my movements, had withheld the knowledge from Alice. It did not square with my preconceived ideas of him that he would derive any satisfaction from taking his niece by surprise.

All was a muddle together, and as my temples throbbed with the intensity of my thoughts, I was half disposed to believe myself in a troubled dream from which I should presently awake. Meanwhile, on glided the train.

A heavy snowstorm delayed us for several hours, and we reached Hamilton too late for the mid-day express for Toronto. We got there, however, in time for the accommodation leaving at 3:15 P.M., and we would reach Toronto at 5:05. I walked from one end of the train to the other in hopes of finding some one I knew, from whom I could make enquiries about home. Not a soul. I saw several persons whom I knew to be residents of Toronto, but none with whom I had ever been personally acquainted, and none of them would be likely to know anything about my uncle's domestic arrangements. All that remained to be done under these circumstances was to restrain my curiosity as well as I could until reaching Toronto. By the by, would my uncle really meet me at the station, according to his promise? Surely not. By what means could he possibly know that I would arrive by this train? Still, he seemed to have such accurate information respecting my proceedings that there was no saying where his knowledge began or ended. I tried not to think about the matter, but as the train approached Toronto my impatience became positively feverish in its intensity. We were not more than three minutes behind time, as we glided in font of the Union Station I passed out on to the platform of the car, and peered intently through the darkness. Suddenly my heart gave a great bound. There, sure enough, standing in front of the door of the waiting-room, was my uncle, plainly discernible by the fitful glare of the overhanging lamps. Before the train came to a stand-still, I sprang from the car and advanced towards him. He was looking out for me, but his eyes not being as young as mine, he did not recognize me until I grasped him by the hand. He greeted me warmly, seizing me by the waist, and almost raising me from the ground. I at once noticed several changes in his appearance; changes for which I was wholly unprepared. He had aged very much since I had last seen him, and the lines about his mouth had deepened considerably. The iron-grey hair which I remembered so well had disappeared; its place being supplied with a new and rather dandified-looking wig. The old-fashioned great-coat which he had worn ever since I could remember, had been supplanted by a modern frock of spruce cut, with seal-skin collar and cuffs. All this I noticed in the first hurried greetings that passed between us.

'Never mind your luggage, my boy,' he remarked. 'Leave it till tomorrow, when we will send down for it. If you are not tired we'll walk home instead of taking a cab. I have a good deal to say to you before we get there.'

I had not slept since leaving Boston, but was too much excited to be conscious of fatigue, and as will readily be believed, I was anxious enough to hear what he had to say. We passed from the station, and proceeded up York Street, arm in arm.

'And now, Uncle Richard,' I said, as soon as we were well clear of the crowd,—'keep me no longer in suspense. First and foremost, is Alice well?'

'Quite well, but for reasons you will soon understand, she is in deep grief. You must know that—'

'But,' I interrupted, 'tell me, in the name of all that's wonderful, how you knew I was coming by this train; and how did you come to write me at Boston?'

Just then we came to the corner of Front Street, where was a lamp-post. As we reached the spot where the light of the lamp was most brilliant, he turned half round, looked me full in the face, and smiled a sort of wintry smile. The expression of his countenance was almost ghastly.

'Uncle,' I quickly said, 'What's the matter? Are you not well?'

'I am not as strong as I used to be, and I have had a good deal to try me of late. Have patience and I will tell you all. Let us walk more slowly, or I shall not finish before we get home. In order that you may clearly understand how matters are, I had better begin at the beginning, and I hope you will not interrupt me with any questions till I have done. How I knew you would call at the Boston postoffice, and that you would arrive in Toronto by this train, will come last in order. By the by, have you my letter with you?'

'The one you wrote to me at Boston? Yes, here it is,' I replied, taking it from my pocket-book.

'Let me have it.'

I handed it to him, and he put it into the breast pocket of his inside coat. I wondered at this proceeding on his part, but made no remark upon it.

We moderated our pace, and he began his narration. Of course I don't pretend to remember his exact words, but they were to this effect. During the winter following my departure to Melbourne, he

had formed the acquaintance of a gentleman who had then recently
settled in Toronto. The name of this gentleman was Marcus Weatherley, who had commenced business as a wholesale provision merchant immediately upon his arrival, and had been engaged in it ever
since. For more than three years the acquaintance between him and
my uncle had been very slight, but during the last summer they had
had some real-estate transactions together, and had become intimate.
Weatherley, who was comparatively a young man and unmarried,
had been invited to the house on Gerrard Street, where he had more
recently become a pretty frequent visitor. More recently still, his visits
had become so frequent that my uncle suspected him of a desire to
be attentive to my cousin, and had thought proper to enlighten him
as to her engagement with me. From that day his visits had been
voluntarily discontinued. My uncle had not given much consideration
to the subject until a fortnight afterwards, when he had accidentally
become aware of the fact that Weatherley was in embarrassed circumstances.

Here my uncle paused in his narrative to take a breath. He then
added, in a low tone, and putting his mouth almost close to my ear:

'And, Willie, my boy, I have at last found out something else. He
has forty-two thousand dollars falling due here and in Montreal within
the next ten days, and *he has forged my signature to acceptances for
thirty-nine thousand seven hundred and sixteen dollars and twenty-
four cents.*'

Those to the best of my belief, were his exact words. We had
walked up York Street to Queen, and then had gone down Queen to
Yonge, when we turned up the east side on our way homeward. At
the moment when the last words were uttered we had got a few yards
north of Crookshank Street, immediately in front of a chemist's shop
which was, I think, the third house from the corner. The window of
this shop was well lighted, and its brightness was reflected on the
sidewalk in front. Just then, two gentlemen walking rapidly in the
opposite direction to that we were taking brushed by us; but I was
too deeply absorbed in my uncle's communication to pay much
attention to passers-by. Scarcely had they passed, however, ere one
of them stopped and exclaimed:

'Surely that is Willie Furlong!'

I turned, and recognized Johnny Gray, one of my oldest friends. I
relinquished my uncle's arm for a moment, and shook hands with
Gray, who said:

'I am surprised to see you. I heard only a few days ago, that you were not to be here till next spring.'

'I am here,' I remarked, 'somewhat in advance of my own expectations.' I then hurriedly enquired after several of our common friends, to which enquiries he briefly replied.

'All well,' he said; 'but you are in a hurry, and so am I. Don't let me detain you. Be sure and look in on me tomorrow. You will find me at the old place, in the Romain Buildings.'

We again shook hands, and he passed on down the street with the gentleman who accompanied him. I then turned to re-possess myself of my uncle's arm. The old gentleman had evidently walked on, for he was not in sight. I hurried along, making sure of overtaking him before reaching Gould Street, for my interview with Gray had occupied barely a minute. In another minute I was at the corner of Gould Street. No signs of Uncle Richard. I quickened my pace to a run, which soon brought me to Gerrard Street. Still no signs of my uncle. I had certainly not passed him on my way, and he could not have got farther on his homeward route than here. He must have called in at one of the stores; a strange thing for him to do under the circumstances. I retraced my steps all the way to the front of the chemist's shop, peering into every window and doorway as I passed along. No one in the least resembling him was to be seen.

I stood still for a moment, and reflected. Even if he had run at full speed—a thing most unseemly for him to do—he could not have reached the corner of Gerrard Street before I had done so. And what should he run for? He certainly did not wish to avoid me, for he had more to tell me before reaching home. Perhaps he had turned down Gould Street. At any rate, there was no use waiting for him. I might as well go home at once. And I did.

Upon reaching the old familiar spot, I opened the gate, passed on up the steps to the front door, and rang the bell. The door was opened by a domestic who had not formed part of the establishment in my time, and who did not know me; but Alice happened to be passing through the hall, and heard my voice as I inquired for Uncle Richard. Another moment and she was in my arms. With a strange foreboding at my heart I noticed that she was in deep mourning. We passed into the dining-room, where the table was laid for dinner.

'Has Uncle Richard come in?' I asked, as soon as we were alone. 'Why did he run away from me?'

'Who?' exclaimed Alice, with a start; 'what do you mean, Willie? Is it possible you have not heard?'

'Heard what?'

'I see you have *not* heard,' she replied. 'Sit down, Willie, and prepare yourself for painful news. But first tell me what you meant by saying what you did just now,—who was it that ran away from you?'

'Well, perhaps I should hardly call it running away, but he certainly disappeared most mysteriously, down here near the corner of Yonge and Crookshank Streets.'

'Of whom are you speaking?'

'Of Uncle Richard, of course.'

'Uncle Richard! The corner of Yonge and Crookshank Streets! When did you see him there?'

'When? A quarter of an hour ago. He met me at the station and we walked up together till I met Johnny Gray. I turned to speak to Johnny for a moment, when—'

'Willie, what on earth are you talking about? You are labouring under some strange delusion. *Uncle Richard died of apoplexy more than six weeks ago, and lies buried in St James's Cemetery.*'

II

I don't know how long I sat there, trying to think, with my face buried in my hands. My mind had been kept on a strain during the last thirty hours, and the succession of surprises to which I had been subjected had temporarily paralyzed my faculties. For a few moments after Alice's announcement I must have been in a sort of stupor. My imagination, I remember, ran riot about everything in general, and nothing in particular. My cousin's momentary impression was that I had met with an accident of some kind, which had unhinged my brain. The first distinct remembrance I have after this is, that I suddenly awoke from my stupor to find Alice kneeling at my feet, and holding me by the hand. Then my mental powers came back to me, and I recalled all the incidents of the evening.

'When did uncle's death take place?' I asked.

'On the 3rd of November, about four o'clock in the afternoon. It was quite unexpected, though he had not enjoyed his usual health for some weeks before. He fell down in the hall, just as he was returning from a walk, and died within two hours. He never spoke or recognized anyone after his seizure.'

'What has become of his old overcoat?' I asked.

'His old overcoat, Willie—what a question?' replied Alice, evidently thinking that I was again drifting back into insensibility.

'Did he continue to wear it up to the day of his death?' I asked.

'No. Cold weather set in very early this last fall, and he was compelled to don his winter clothing earlier than usual. He had a new overcoat made within a fortnight before he died. He had it on at the time of his seizure. But why do you ask?'

'Was the new coat cut by a fashionable tailor, and had it a fur collar and cuffs?'

'It was cut at Stovel's, I think. It had a fur collar and cuffs.'

'When did he begin to wear a wig?'

'About the same time that he began to wear his new overcoat. I wrote you a letter at the time, making merry over his youthful appearance and hinting—of course only in jest—that he was looking out for a young wife. But you surely did not receive my letter. You must have been on your way home before it was written.'

'I left Melbourne on the 11th of October. The wig, I suppose, was buried with him?'

'Yes.'

'And where is the overcoat?'

'In the wardrobe upstairs, in uncle's room.'

'Come and show it to me.'

'I led the way upstairs, my cousin following. In the hall of the first floor we encountered my old friend Mrs Daly, the housekeeper. She threw up her hands in surprise at seeing me. Our greeting was very brief; I was too intent on solving the problem which had exercised my mind ever since receiving the letter at Boston, to pay much attention to anything else. Two words, however, explained to her where we were going, and at our request she accompanied us. We passed into my uncle's room. My cousin drew the key of the wardrobe from a drawer where it was kept, and unlocked the door. There hung the overcoat. A single glance was sufficient. It was the same.

The dazed sensation in my head began to make itself felt again. The atmosphere of the room seemed to oppress me, and closing the door of the wardrobe, I led the way downstairs again to the dining-room, followed by my cousin. Mrs Daly had sense enough to perceive that we were discussing family matters, and retired to her own room.

I took my cousin's hand in mine, and asked:

'Will you tell me what you know of Mr Marcus Weatherley?'

This was evidently another surprise for her. How could I have heard of Marcus Weatherley? She answered, however, without hesitation:

'I know very little of him. Uncle Richard and he had some dealings a few months since, and in that way he became a visitor here. After a while he began to call pretty often, but his visits suddenly ceased a short time before uncle's death. I need not affect any reserve with you. Uncle Richard thought he came after me, and gave him a hint that you had a prior claim. He never called afterwards. I am rather glad that he didn't, for there is something about him that I don't quite like. I am at a loss to say what the something is; but his manner always impressed me with the idea that he was not exactly what he seemed to be on the surface. Perhaps I misjudged him. Indeed, I think I must have done so, for he stands well with everybody, and is highly respected.'

I looked at the clock on the mantelpiece. It was ten minutes to seven. I rose from my seat.

'I will ask you to excuse me for an hour or two, Alice. I must find Johnny Gray.'

'But you will not leave me, Willie, until you have given me some clue to your unexpected arrival, and to the strange questions you have been asking? Dinner is ready, and can be served at once. Pray don't go out again till you have dined.'

She clung to my arm. It was evident that she considered me mad, and thought it probable that I might make away with myself. This I could not bear. As for eating any dinner, that was simply impossible in my then frame of mind, although I had not tasted food since leaving Rochester. I resolved to tell her all. I resumed my seat. She placed herself on a stool at my feet, and listened while I told her all that I have set down as happening to me subsequently to my last letter to her from Melbourne.

'And now, Alice, you know why I wish to see Johnny Gray.'

She would have accompanied me, but I thought it better to prosecute my inquiries alone. I promised to return sometime during the night, and tell her the result of my interview with Gray. That gentleman had married and become a householder on his own account during my absence in Australia. Alice knew his address, and gave me the number of his house, which was on Church Street. A few minutes' rapid walking brought me to his door. I had no great expectation of finding him at home, as I deemed it probable he had not returned from wherever he had been going when I met him; but I should be able to find out when he was expected, and would either wait or go in search of him. Fortune favoured me for once, however; he had returned more than an hour before. I was ushered into the drawing-room, where I found him playing cribbage with his wife.

'Why, Willie,' he exclaimed, advancing to welcome me, 'this is kinder than I expected. I hardly looked for you before tomorrow. All the better; we have just been speaking of you. Ellen, this is my old friend, Willie Furlong, the returned convict, whose banishment you have so often heard me deplore.'

After exchanging brief courtesies with Mrs Gray, I turned to her husband.

'Johnny, did you notice anything remarkable about the old gentleman who was with me when we met on Yonge Street this evening?'

'Old gentleman! who? There was no one with you when I met you.'

'Think again. He and I were walking arm in arm, and you had passed us before you recognized me, and mentioned my name.'

He looked hard in my face for a moment, and then said positively:

'You are wrong, Willie. You were certainly alone when we met. You were walking slowly, and I must have noticed if anyone had been with you.'

'It is you who are wrong,' I retorted, almost sternly. 'I was accompanied by an elderly gentleman, who wore a great coat with fur collar and cuffs, and we were conversing earnestly together when you passed us.'

He hesitated an instant, and seemed to consider, but there was no shade of doubt on his face.

'Have it your own way, old boy,' he said. 'All I can say is, that I saw no one but yourself, and neither did Charley Leitch, who was with me. After parting from you we commented upon your evident abstraction, and the sombre expression of your countenance, which we attributed to your having only recently heard of the sudden death of your Uncle Richard. If any old gentleman had been with you we could not possibly have failed to notice him.'

Without a single word by way of explanation or apology, I jumped from my seat, passed out into the hall, seized my hat, and left the house.

III

Out into the street I rushed like a madman, banging the door after me. I knew that Johnny would follow me for an explanation, so I ran like lightning round the next corner, and thence down to Yonge Street. Then I dropped into a walk, regained my breath, and asked myself what I should do next.

Suddenly I bethought me of Dr Marsden, an old friend of my uncle's. I hailed a passing cab, and drove to his house. The doctor was in his consultation-room, and alone.

Of course he was surprised to see me, and gave expression to some appropriate words of sympathy at my bereavement. 'But how is it that I see you so soon?' he asked—'I understood that you were not expected for some months to come.'

Then I began my story, which I related with great circumstantiality of detail, bringing it down to the moment of my arrival at his house. He listened with the closest attention, never interrupting me by a single exclamation until I had finished. Then he began to ask questions, some of which I thought strangely irrelevant.

'Have you enjoyed your usual good health during your residence abroad?'

'Never better in my life. I have not had a moment's illness since you last saw me.'

'And how have you prospered in your business enterprises?'

'Reasonably well; but pray doctor, let us confine ourselves to the matter in hand. I have come for friendly, not professional, advice.'

'All in good time, my boy,' he calmly remarked. This was tantalizing. My strange narrative did not seem to have disturbed his serenity in the least degree.

'Did you have a pleasant passage?' he asked, after a brief pause. 'The ocean, I believe, is generally rough at this time of year.'

'I felt a little squeamish for a day or two after leaving Melbourne,' I replied, 'but I soon got over it, and it was not very bad even while it lasted. I am a tolerably good sailor.'

'And you have had no special ground of anxiety of late? At least not until you received this wonderful letter'—he added, with a perceptible contraction of his lips, as though trying to repress a smile.

Then I saw what he was driving at.

'Doctor,' I exclaimed, with some exasperation in my tone—'pray dismiss from your mind the idea that what I have told you is the result of diseased imagination. I am as sane as you are. The letter itself affords sufficient evidence that I am not quite such a fool as you take me for.'

'My dear boy, I don't take you for a fool at all, although you are a little excited just at present. But I thought you said you returned the letter to—ahem—your uncle.'

For a moment I had forgotten that important fact. But I was not altogether without evidence that I had not been the victim of a disordered brain. My friend Gridley could corroborate the receipt of the letter and its contents. My cousin could bear witness that I had displayed an acquaintance with facts which I would not have been likely to learn from anyone but my uncle. I had referred to his wig and overcoat, and had mentioned to her the name of Mr Marcus Weatherley—a name which I had never heard before in my life. I called Dr Marsden's attention to these matters, and asked him to explain them if he could.

'I admit', said the doctor, 'that I don't quite see my way to a satisfactory explanation just at present. But let us look the matter squarely in the face. During an acquaintance of nearly thirty years, I always found your uncle a truthful man, who was cautious enough to make no statements about his neighbours that he was not able to prove. Your informant, on the other hand, does not seem to have confined himself to facts. He made a charge of forgery against a gentleman whose moral and commercial integrity are unquestioned by all who know him. I know Marcus Weatherley pretty well, and am not disposed to pronounce him a forger and a scoundrel upon the unsupported evidence of a shadowy old gentleman who appears and disappears in the most mysterious manner, and who cannot be laid hold of and held responsible for his slanders in a court of law. And it is not true, as far as I know and believe, that Marcus Weatherley is embarrassed in his circumstances. Such confidence have I in his solvency and integrity that I would not be afraid to take up all his outstanding paper without asking a question. If you will make inquiry, you will find that my opinion is shared by all the bankers in the city. And I have no hesitation in saying that you will find no acceptances with your uncle's name to them, either in this market or elsewhere.'

'That I will try to ascertain tomorrow,' I replied. 'Meanwhile, Dr Marsden, will you oblige your old friend's nephew by writing to Mr Junius Gridley, and asking him to acquaint you with the contents of the letter, and the circumstances under which I received it?'

'It seems an absurd thing to do,' he said, 'but I will if you like. What shall I say?' and he sat down at his desk to write the letter.

It was written in less than five minutes. It simply asked for the desired information, and requested an immediate reply. Below the doctor's signature I added a short postscript in these words:—

'My story about the letter and its contents is discredited. Pray answer fully, and at once.—W.F.F.'

At my request the doctor accompanied me to the postoffice, on Toronto Street, and dropped the letter into the box with his own hands. I bade him good night, and repaired to the Rossin House. I did not feel like encountering Alice again until I could place myself in a more satisfactory light before her. I despatched a messenger to her with a short note stating that I had not discovered anything important, and requesting her not to wait up for me. Then I engaged a room and went to bed.

But not to sleep. All night long I tossed about from one side of the bed to the other; and at daylight, feverish and unrefreshed, I strolled out. I returned in time for breakfast, but ate little or nothing. I longed for the arrival of ten o'clock, when the banks would open.

After breakfast I sat down in the reading-room of the hotel, and vainly tried to fix my attention upon the local columns of the morning's paper. I remember reading over several items time after time, without any comprehension of their meaning. After that I remember—nothing.

Nothing? All was blank for more than five weeks. When consciousness came back to me I found myself in bed in my own old room, in the house on Gerrard Street, and Alice and Dr Marsden were standing by my bedside.

No need to tell how my hair had been removed, nor about the bags of ice that had been applied to my head. No need to linger over any details of the 'pitiless fever that burned in my brain'. No need, either, to linger over my progress back to convalescence, and thence to complete recovery. In a week from the time I have mentioned, I was permitted to sit up in bed, propped up by a mountain of pillows. My impatience would brook no further delay, and I was allowed to ask questions about what had happened in the interval which had elapsed since my overwrought nerves gave way under the prolonged strain upon them. First, Junius Gridley's letter in reply to Dr Marsden was placed in my hands. I have it still in my possession, and I transcribe the following copy from the original now lying before me:—

Boston, Dec. 22nd, 1861.

Dr Marsden

In reply to your letter, which has just been received, I have to say that Mr Furlong and myself became acquainted for the first time during our recent passage from Liverpool to Boston, in the Persia, which arrived here Monday last. Mr Furlong accompanied me home, and remained until Tuesday morning, when I took him to see the Public Library, the State House, the Athenæum, Faneuil Hall, and other points of interest. We casually dropped into the post-office, and he remarked upon the great number of letters there. At my instigation—made, of course, in jest—he applied at the General Delivery for letters for himself. He receive one bearing the Toronto postmark. He was naturally very much surprised at receiving it, and was not less so at its contents. After reading it he handed it to me, and I also read it carefully. I cannot recollect it word for word, but it professed to come from 'his affectionate uncle, Richard Yardington'. It expressed pleasure at his coming home sooner than had been anticipated, and hinted in rather vague terms at some calamity. He referred to a lady called Alice, and stated that she had not been informed of Mr Furlong's intended arrival. There was something too, about his presence at home being a recompense to her for recent grief which she had sustained. It also expressed the writer's intention to meet his nephew at the Toronto railway station upon his arrival, and stated that no telegram need be sent. This, as nearly as I can remember, was about all there was in the letter. Mr Furlong professed to recognize the handwriting as his uncle's. It was a cramped hand, not easy to read, and the signature was so peculiarly formed that I was hardly able to decipher it. The peculiarity consisted of the extreme irregularity in the formation of the letters, no two of which were of equal size; and capitals were interspersed promiscuously, more especially throughout the surname.

Mr Furlong was much agitated by the contents of the letter, and was anxious for the arrival of the time of his departure. He left by the B. & A. train at 11:30. This is really all I know about the matter, and I have been anxiously expecting to hear from him ever since he left. I confess that I feel curious, and should be glad to hear from him—that is, of course, unless something is involved which it would be impertinent for a comparative stranger to pry into.

Yours, &c.,
Junius H. Gridley.

So that my friend has completely corroborated my account, so far
as the letter was concerned. My account, however, stood in no need
of corroboration, as will presently appear.

When I was stricken down, Alice and Dr Marsden were the only
persons to whom I had communicated what my uncle had said to me
during our walk from the station. They both maintained silence in the
matter, except to each other. Between themselves, in the early days
of my illness, they discussed it with a good deal of feeling on each
side. Alice implicitly believed my story from first to last. She was wise
enough to see that I had been made acquainted with matters that I
could not possibly have learned through any ordinary channels of
communication. In short, she was not so enamoured of professional
jargon as to have lost her common sense. The doctor, however, with
the mole-blindness of many of his tribe, refused to believe. Nothing
of this kind had previously come within the range of his own
experience, and it was therefore impossible. He accounted for it all
upon the hypothesis of my impending fever. He is not the only
physician who mistakes cause for effects, and *vice versa*.

During the second week of my prostration, Mr Marcus Weatherley
absconded. This event so totally unlooked for by those who had had
dealings with him, at once brought his financial condition to light. It
was found that he had been really insolvent for several months past.
The day after his departure a number of his acceptances became due.
These acceptances proved to be four in number, amounting to exactly
forty-two thousand dollars. So that that part of my uncle's story was
confirmed. One of the acceptances was payable in Montreal, and was
for $2,283.76. The other three were payable at different banks in
Toronto. These last had been drawn at sixty days, and each of them
bore a signature presumed to be that of Richard Yardington. One of
them was for $8,972.11; another was for $10,114.63; and the third and
last was for $20,629.50. A short sum in simple addition will show us
the aggregate of these three amounts—

$$\begin{array}{r}
\$\ \ 8,972.11 \\
10,114.63 \\
\underline{20,629.50} \\
\$\ 39,716.24
\end{array}$$

which was the amount for which my uncle claimed that his name had been forged.

Within a week after these things came to light a letter addressed to the manager of one of the leading banking institutions of Toronto arrived from Mr Marcus Weatherley. He wrote from New York, but stated that he should leave there within an hour from the time of posting his letter. He voluntarily admitted having forged the name of my uncle to the three acceptances above referred to and entered into other details about his affairs, which, though interesting enough to his creditors at that time, would have no special interest to the public at the present day. The banks where the acceptances had been discounted were wise after the fact, and detected numerous little details wherein the forged signatures differed from the genuine signatures of my Uncle Richard. In each case they pocketed the loss and held their tongues, and I dare say they will not thank me for calling attention to the matter, even at this distance of time.

There is not much more to tell. Marcus Weatherley, the forger, met his fate within a few days after writing his letter from New York. He took passage at New Bedford, Massachusetts, in a sailing vessel called the *Petrel* bound for Havana. The *Petrel* sailed from port on the 12th of January, 1862, and went down in mid-ocean with all hands on the 23rd of the same month. She sank in full sight of the captain and crew of the *City of Baltimore* (Inman Line), but the hurricane prevailing was such that the latter were unable to render any assistance, or to save one of the ill-fated crew from the fury of the waves.

At an early stage in the story I mentioned that the only fictitious element should be the name of one of the characters introduced. The name is that of Marcus Weatherley himself. The person whom I have so designated really bore a different name—one that is still remembered by scores of people in Toronto. He has paid the penalty of his misdeeds, and I see nothing to be gained by perpetuating them in connection with his own proper name. In all other particulars the foregoing narrative is as true as a tolerably retentive memory has enabled me to record it.

I don't propose to attempt any psychological explanation of the events here recorded, for the very sufficient reason that only one explanation is possible. The weird letter and its contents, as has been seen, do not rest upon my testimony alone. With respect to my walk from the station with Uncle Richard, and the communication made by him to me, all the details are as real to my mind as any other incidents of my life. The only obvious deduction is, that I was made the recipient of a communication of the kind which the world is accustomed to regard as supernatural.

Mr Owen's publishers have my full permission to appropriate this story in the next edition of his 'Debatable Land between this World and the Next'. Should they do so, their readers will doubtless be favoured with an elaborate analysis of the facts, and with a pseudo-philosophic theory about spiritual communion with human beings. My wife, who is an enthusiastic student of electro-biology, is disposed to believe that Weatherley's mind, overweighted by the knowledge of his forgery, was in some occult manner, and unconsciously to himself, constrained to act upon my own senses. I prefer, however, simply to narrate the facts. I may or may not have my own theory about those facts. The reader is at perfect liberty to form one of his own if he so pleases. I may mention that Dr Marsden professes to believe to the present day that my mind was disordered by the approach of the fever which eventually struck me down, and that all I have described was merely the result of what he, with delightful periphrasis, calls 'an abnormal condition of the system, induced by causes too remote for specific diagnosis'.

It will be observed that, whether I was under an hallucination or not, the information supposed to be derived from my uncle was strictly accurate in all its details. The fact that the disclosure subsequently became unnecessary through the confession of Weatherley does not seem to me to afford any argument for the hallucination theory. My uncle's communication was important at the time when it was given to me; and we have no reason for believing that 'those who are gone before' are universally gifted with a knowledge of the future.

It was open to me to make the facts public as soon as they became known to me, and had I done so, Marcus Weatherley might have been arrested and punished for his crime. Had not my illness supervened, I think I should have made discoveries in the course of the day following my arrival in Toronto which would have led to his arrest.

Such speculations are profitless enough, but they have often formed the topic of discussion between my wife and myself. Gridley, too, wherever he pays us a visit, invariably revives the subject, which he long ago christened 'The Gerrard Street Mystery', although it might just as correctly be called 'The Yonge Street Mystery', or, 'The Mystery of the Union Station'. He has urged me a hundred times over to publish the story; and now, after all these years, I follow his counsel, and adopt his nomenclature in the title.

HONORÉ BEAUGRAND · 1848-1906

The Miser's Ghost

All of you, old and young, know the story I'm about to tell. But the moral of this tale cannot be retold too often. Remember that behind it is the terrible lesson of an avenging God who commands the rich to be charitable.

It was New Year's Eve in the year of Our Lord 1858.

It was dry and biting cold.

The highway along the north bank of the St Lawrence River from Montreal to Berthier lay covered by a thick coat of snow, fallen before Christmas.

The roads were smooth as a Venetian looking-glass. You should have seen how the sons of the rich farmers of the river parishes loved to spur on their frisky horses, racing like the wind to the happy sound of the bells on their silvery harnesses.

I was spending the evening at the house of Old Joseph Harvieux, whom you all know. You also know that his house, which is built of stone, stands half-way between the churches of Lavaltrie and Lanoraie. There was a party at Old Harvieux's that evening, and after dining copiously, all the members of the family had gathered in the vast living-room.

It is customary for every Canadian family to have a banquet on the last day of the year, in order to greet at midnight, with all the necessary ceremony, the arrival of the unknown that brings us all our share of joy and suffering.

It was ten o'clock.

The children, heavy with sleep, dropped off one by one on the buffalo hides thrown around the immense kitchen stove.

Only the children's parents and the young folk wanted to stay up at this late hour, and wish one another a happy and prosperous New Year before retiring for the night.

A bright young girl, seeing the conversation languish, rose suddenly to her feet and, respectfully kissing the forehead of her grandfather, who was almost a hundred years old, said to him in a voice she knew was irresistible:

'Grandfather, please tell us again the story of how you met the ghost of the poor Jean-Pierre Beaudry—God have mercy on his soul—which you told us last year, at this same time. It is a sad story, I know, but it will help us pass the time until midnight.'

'Oh yes, yes, grandfather, the New Year's Eve story,' chorused the guests, who were, almost all, descendants of the old man.

'My children,' the white-haired grandfather began in a trembling voice, 'for many years now I have told you, every New Year's Eve, this story of my youth. I'm very old, and perhaps it is for the last time that I will tell you the story tonight. Pay attention, and note above all what terrible punishment God reserves for those who, in this world, refuse hospitality to a traveller in distress.'

The old man drew his chair nearer to the fire, and as his children formed a circle around him, he told his tale this way:

'It was seventy years ago today. I was twenty years old.

'On my father's orders, I had left early one morning for Montreal to buy several things for the family; among others, a magnificent demijohn from Jamaica, which we urgently needed in order to entertain our friends as they deserved on New Year's Eve. By three o'clock in the afternoon I had completed my errands and was getting ready to return on the Lanoraie road. My buggy was quite full, and as I wanted to be back home before nine, I whipped my horse briskly and he started off at a trot. At five-thirty I found myself at the shortcut across the tip of the island, and had encountered no obstacles on the way. But the sky had begun gradually to cloud over, and there was every sign that a heavy snowstorm was to be expected. I set out on the shortcut and before reaching Repentigny the storm was full-blown. I have seen some fierce snowstorms in my life, but I cannot remember any as terrible as that one. I could see neither land nor sky, and I could barely follow the highway in front of me: the signposts had not yet been set up, as winter was not far along. At dusk I passed the church of St Sulpice, but soon pitch darkness and the blizzard whipping my face made it impossible to go any further. I was not entirely certain of where I was, but thought I was in the vicinity of Old Robillard's farm. I thought that the best I could do was tie my horse to a post on the roadside and try to find a house in which to seek shelter until the storm calmed down. I wandered about for a few minutes and was beginning to despair of ever succeeding, when I noticed, to the left of the highway, a dilapidated hovel half buried in the snow, which I could not remember having seen before. With a great effort I made my way through the banks of snow towards this house, which I thought at first was abandoned. I was wrong: the door was closed, but I could see through the window the reddish glow of a roaring open fire in the hearth. I knocked and at once heard the steps of someone coming to open the door. To the traditional 'Who's there?' I answered, through chattering teeth, that I had lost my way, and immediately, to my great delight, heard my host lift the latch. He only opened the door halfway so as to prevent, as far as possible, the cold from entering, and I stepped in shaking my clothes, which were covered with a thick layer of snow.

'"Welcome," said the owner of the hovel, giving me a hand that seemed burning hot, and helping me out of my hood and bright woven belt.

'In a few words I explained to him the reason for my visit, and having thanked him for his kind hospitality and accepted a fortifying glass of brandy, I sat down on a rickety chair to which he pointed in a corner of the room. The he went out, saying that he was going to get my horse and buggy to put them under cover, safe from the storm.

'I couldn't help but cast a curious eye on the peculiar furnishings of the room in which I found myself. In a corner there was a cot over which was spread a buffalo hide, surely the bed of the big old man with stooping shoulders who had let me in. An ancient rifle, probably dating from the days of the French occupation, was suspended from the raw wooden joists that held up the thatched roof of the house. Several deer, bear, and moose heads were hung as hunting trophies from the whitewashed walls. Next to the hearth, a solitary oak log seemed to be the only vacant seat that the host could offer the traveller who, by chance, might knock on his door seeking shelter.

'I asked myself who could this person be, who lived like a savage in the very heart of the St Sulpice parish, without my ever hearing of him. I thought hard, because I knew everyone, from Lanoraie to Montreal, but in vain. Just then my host came back in and, without saying a word, sat down across from me, on the other side of the hearth.

'"I am extremely grateful for your kindness," I said, "and I wonder if you would be good enough to tell to whom I owe such gracious hospitality? I am as familiar with the parish of St Sulpice as my father is, and yet until today I never knew that there was a house in this place, and your face is unknown to me."

'Saying these words, I looked at him in the face and observed, for the first time, a strange light in the eyes of my host, like the eyes of a wildcat. Instinctively, I drew my chair backwards under the penetrating gaze of the old man, who looked at me but did not answer.

'The silence was becoming strained, and my host continued to stare at me with eyes as bright as burning coals.

'I began to feel frightened.

'Gathering all my courage, I asked him once again for his name. This time, my question had the effect of making him stand up from his seat. Slowly he walked over to me, laid his bony hand on my trembling shoulder, and in a sad voice, like the wind moaning in the chimney, he said:

'"Young man, you are not yet twenty years old and you ask how is it that you are not familiar with Jean-Pierre Beaudry, once the richest man in the parish. I will tell you, because your visit tonight has saved me from the flames of Purgatory in which I have been burning for the past fifty years, without having been able, until this very day, to fulfil the punishment that God imposed upon me. I am he who once, during a storm like this one, refused to open my door to a traveller exhausted by cold, hunger, and weariness."

'I felt my scalp prickle, my knees shake, and I began to tremble like a poplar leaf in the north wind. But the old man, paying no attention to my fear, continued in a slow voice:

'"This was fifty years ago, long before the English set foot in your native parish. I was rich, very rich, and I lived in this same house into which I have let you tonight. As now, it was New Year's Eve, and alone by my hearth I rejoiced at the thought of being protected from the storm, and was grateful for a fire to keep me from the cold that cracked the very stones of my house. There was a knock at my door, but I hesitated to open it. I was afraid it might be a thief who, knowing of my wealth, might have decided to rob and perhaps even murder me."

'"I turned a deaf ear and after a few moments the knocking ceased. Soon I fell asleep, and did not wake up until well into the next day, to the infernal racket made by two men from the village who were kicking down my door. I quickly rose to punish them for their impudence when on opening the door, I saw the inanimate body of a young man lying dead of cold and weariness on my front step. Through love of my gold I had caused the death of the man who had knocked at my door, and I was practically a murderer. I went mad with pain and regret."

'"After having a solemn mass sung for the soul of the poor unfortunate youth, I divided my fortune among the poor of the neighbour-hood, begging God to accept this sacrifice as expiation for the crime I had committed. Two years later, I was burned to death in my own house, and had to appear before my Creator and account for my behaviour on earth. I was found undeserving of the bliss of the chosen, and was condemned to return every New Year's Eve to wait for a traveller to knock at my door, so that I might offer him the hospitality I had refused during my life to one of my fellow men. For fifty winters I returned, on God's orders, to spend here the last night of the year, and never has a traveller in need knocked at my door. At last, tonight, you have come, and God has forgiven me. May you be forever blessed for having freed me from the fire of Purgatory, and believe me when I say that, whatever happens to you down here, I will pray for you to God on high."

'The ghost, for such it was, was still talking when, giving in to my fear and amazement, I lost consciousness.

'I woke up in my buggy, on the highway, in front of the church of Lavaltrie.

'The storm had calmed down and, no doubt under the guidance of my host from the other world, I had set off again on the Lanoraie road.

'I was still trembling with fright when I reached this house at one o'clock in the morning, and told the assembled guests my terrible adventure.

'My late father, may he rest in peace, made us kneel down in prayer, and we recited the rosary in gratitude for the special favour of which I had been found worthy, to allow a soul in pain to escape from Purgatory after waiting so long for deliverance. Since then, my children, we have never failed to say a prayer to the Holy Virgin for the peace of the souls of those poor travellers exposed to the cold and the storm.

'Several days later, on a visit to St Sulpice, I told my story to the parish priest. From him I learned that the church registry did indeed mention the tragic death of a certain Jean-Pierre Beaudry, whose land lay in the location now occupied by young Pierre Sansregret. A few cranks suggested that I had dreamt it all. But if that were so, where did I learn the names and facts relating to the burning of the late Beaudry's farm, which I had never heard of before? The priest of Lanoraie, to whom I told the story, had nothing to say except that the finger of God was in all things, and that we were to bless His Holy Name.'

Translated by Alberto Manguel

W.H. BLAKE · 1861-1924

A Tale of the Grand Jardin

His story comes back to me in sharp and vivid outline, though I look
across years not a few to the telling of it, and to our little tent pitched
high and lonely in the Grand Jardin des Ours. Who can say what share
time and place, the wild August storm, and my friend's emotion, had
in etching the picture so deeply on memory? Perhaps the impression
is not communicable; perhaps it may be caught, if you will consent
to make camp with us in those great barrens that lie far-stretching and
desolate among the Laurentian Mountains.

We had been fishing the upper reaches of one of the little rivers
that rise in the heart of the hills, quickly gather volume from many
streams and lakes, loiter for a few miles in dead-waters where a canoe
will float, and then plunge two thousand feet, through amazing
gorges, to the St Lawrence and the sea. An evening rare and
memorable, when the great trout were mad for the fly; more than a
dozen of these splendid fellows, a man's full load, lay on the bank,
where they rivalled the autumn foliage in crimson, orange and
bronze. This first good luck came after many barren days, the smoke-
house of bark was still unfilled,—so it happened that we did not leave
the river till the darkness, and the thunder of an oncoming storm put
down the fish. From the towering cumulus that overhung us immense
drops plumped into the water like pebbles, and the steady roar of the
advancing squall warned us to hasten. Gathering up the trout we
dashed for the tent, to find it well-nigh beaten to the ground by the
weight of the wind and the rain. Though a clump of stunted spruces
to windward gave a little shelter, we had much ado to keep the
friendly canvas roof over our heads by anchoring it with stones.

After putting on dry clothes we explored the provision sack,
discovering nothing more inviting than pork and crumbled biscuit.
Tea there was, but even an old hand could not boil a kettle, or cook
fish, in such a tumult of rain and wind. Three weeks of wandering
had brought us to the lowest ebb, and our men, who had departed
in the morning for an outpost of civilization where supplies could be

obtained, would scarcely return in such weather. We guessed, and
rightly as it turned out, that they had chosen to spend the night at La
Galette, the nerve-extremity, responding faintly to impulses from the
world of men, where the gossip of the countryside awaited them.

So were we two alone in one of the loneliest places this wide earth
knows. Mile upon mile of grey moss; weathered granite clad in
ash-coloured lichen; old *brûlé*,—the trees here fallen in wind-rows,
there standing bleached and lifeless, making the hilltops look barer,
like the sparse white hairs of age. Only in the gullies a little green-
ness,—dwarfed larches, gnarled birches, tiny firs a hundred years
old,—and always moss, softer than Persian rug,—moss to the ankle,
moss to the knee, great boulders covered with it, the very quagmires
mossed over so that a careless step plunges one into the sucking black
ooze below.

Through the door of the tent the lightning showed this endless
desolation, and a glimpse of the river forcing its angry way through
a defile.

When the sorry meal was over we smoked, by turns supporting the
tent pole in the heavier gusts. My companion was absent-minded and
restless; he seemed to have no heart for the small talk of the woods,
and to be listening for something. Breaking into an attempt of mine
at conversation, he asked abruptly:—

'Did you ever hear about the disappearance of Paul Duchêne?'

The name came back to me in a misty way, and with some tragic
association, but the man himself I had never known. Any sort of a
yarn was welcome that would take one's mind off the eeriness and
discomfort of our situation, and H— required no urging. He spoke
like a man who has a tale that must be told, and I try to give you
neither more nor less than what he said:—

'Duchêne was in camp with me years ago, in fact it was he that
brought me into this country in the old days before trails were cut,
and when no one came here but himself and his brothers, and a few
wandering Montagnais Indians. The Duchênes were trappers, and
they guarded the secrets of the place very jealously, which was natural
enough as it yielded them game and fur in plenty. Though he showed
me good sport, it was quite plain that he never told all that he knew.
The paths he followed, if indeed they were paths, were not blazed.
He seemed to steer by a sense of direction, and from a general
knowledge of the lie of the mountains, valleys, and rivers. Seldom
did we return by the way that had taken us to the feeding-grounds of

moose or caribou. Duchêne was contemptuous of easy walking, and almost seemed to choose the roughest going, but he jogged along in marvellous fashion through swamps and windfalls, with a cruel load on his back. The fellow was simply hard as nails, and, measured by my abilities, was tireless.

'Looking back to that autumn, it strikes me that there was something demonic in his energy. Food and rest did not matter to him. He was always ready to go anywhere,—leaving me to follow as best I could; and though I was a pretty stout walker, and carried but little compared to him, it was only shame that kept me from begging for mercy on the long portages.

'Only a few weeks after our trip together Duchêne went out of his mind, and took to the woods. For ten days he wandered in the mountains without food, gun, or matches, but he appears to have partially regained his senses, and made for La Galette, where he arrived in a very distressing condition. Under his father's roof he fell into a harmless, half-witted existence, which lasted for several months. With the spring the fit came upon him again and he disappeared. The brothers followed his trail for days, but lost it finally in the valley of the Enfer, nor were they ever able to discover further trace of him. No man knows what end he made, nor where in this great wilderness his bones are bleaching.

'You have heard, perhaps, the belief of the Montagnais,—strange medley of Paganism and Christianity, that those who die insane without the blessing of a priest become wendigos,—werewolves, with nothing human but their form, soulless beings of diabolic strength and cunning, that wander for all time seeking only to harm whomever comes their way. A black superstitious race these Indians are, and horribly sincere in their faith. They shot down a young girl with the beads of her rosary, because her mind was weakening, and they thought thus to avert the fate from her, and themselves. You would not doubt the truth of this, had you seen the look in the eyes of the man who told me that he had been a helpless witness of the murder.

'I have never spoken of what happened to me the following summer, because one does not like to be disbelieved; perhaps tonight, with the storm-hags abroad and the voices of the sky filling our ears, you will understand. Our tent is pitched so near that infernal spot,—the whole thing takes possession of me again. I keep listening—

'You know the Rivière à l'Enfer, but you have not seen its head-waters, and never will if you are wise. A queer lot of tales old and new, but all pointing to prodigious trout, took me past the mouth of the canyon that gives the river its name. A bold man might follow this cleft in the mountain, but he would go in peril of his life; the precipitous ascent on the left side is safer, if not easier.

'Duchêne would not guide me there, but he gave an extraordinary account of the fishing in the lake which is the source of the river. There is an Indian tradition, and these traditions usually have a foundation of some kind, that it contains trout of tremendous size. Duchêne asserted that stout lines he had set through the ice, in the morning were found broken. Trying again, with the heaviest gear, his tackle was smashed as easily. Heaven knows what the lake holds; nothing came to my fly but half a dozen ink-black trout a few inches long.

'Very little over a hundred years ago it was firmly believed that an active volcano existed not far from here, and this lake, at the very summit of one of the hills to the northwest of us, fills to the brim what looks like an old crater.

'The good fellows who were with me did not seem to like this fancy of mine to push to the source of the stream, but I cannot say whether this was due to the uncanny reputation of the place, or to the fact that we had nothing but Duchêne's vague description, and the flow of the water to guide us. It was a heavy task to get a canoe up to the lake through that difficult country, and it is very safe to say that mine was the first craft ever launched on its gloomy surface.

'I began fishing at once, but nothing stirred; this was what one might expect in water without a ripple, beneath a cloudless sky; there could be no fair trial under such conditions, before the time of the evening rise. I made some soundings, but my two lines together did not fetch bottom a hundred feet from the shore. The slope under water is very steep, and huge fragments of stone hanging there, seem ready, at a touch, to plunge into the depths. It is hard to describe the colour of the water; like neither the clear brown of the river we fished today, nor the opaque blackness of the swamp rivulets;—transparent ink comes nearest to it.

'No stream feeds the lake, but there must be powerful springs below, for the *décharge* flows strongly through a channel of boulders, with water weed moving in the current like something snaky and alive. The tent was pitched on a patch of black sand at the farther shore, the only level spot we could find, and, climbing a few feet higher, I looked out over the bleakest prospect of crag and valley, of moss and granite, till the eye met and welcomed the line of the horizon, and the blue above. Beside me three dead whitened firs, the height of a man, were held in a cleft of the rock, and some fantastic turn of the mind made of the place a wild and dreary Calvary.

'The sea is old and the wind is old, but they are also eternally young. Of the elements it is only earth that speaks of the never hasting never resting passage from life to death,—where the years of a man are an unregarded moment in the march of all things toward that end which may be the beginning. Here on this peak of the world's most ancient hills it seemed to me as though creation had long passed the flood, and was ebbing to its final low tide.

'There fell upon me that afternoon one of those oppressions of the spirit that never weigh so heavily as when they visit you in the full tide of health, under the wide and kindly sky. How shall one account for the apprehensions that crowd upon you, and seem not to have their birth within? In what subtle way does the universe convey the knowledge that it has ceased to be friendly? Even in the full sunlight, the idea of spending a night there alone was unwelcome.

'Soon after arriving I had despatched my men to La Galette for supplies, as we did today, but the distance is shorter by the old Chemin de Canot trail, and they should easily return before sunset. Although knowing this well, and that nothing but serious mischance would detain them, it was with a very definite sense of uneasiness that I watched the canoe cross the lake, saw them disembark, and in a few seconds disappear.

'The afternoon wore away in little occupations about the camp, and in fishing along the shore; later on I intended to scramble around the edge of the lake to the canoe, and try casting in the middle. Out there, quite beyond the reach of my flies, one tremendous rise showed that Duchêne's stories were not wholly fables, and when evening fell there might be a chance to prove them true. But this fortune was not for me; another must discover the secrets of that mysterious water.

'Already the barometer had shown that a swift change of weather was at hand; gradually, and scarcely perceptibly, the ever thickening veil of cirrus mist dimmed the brightness of the sun, until, pale and lifeless, it disappeared in tumultuous clouds that rose to meet it. As the storm came rapidly on, it seemed to me, in the utter stillness, that

I could hear the rush of the vapours writhing overhead. Then with a roar that fairly cowed the soul, the wind, leaping up the mountain-side, fell upon the little habitation, and would have carried it away had my whole weight not been thrown against the tent-pole. In the darkness that drew like a curtain across the sky I waited miserably, dreading I knew not what, beyond the gale and the javelins of the lightning.

'Sitting with an arm around the pole I heard, through the wind and the rain, a cry. Even answering it, I doubted that it was human; when it came again I tried to think that some solitary loon was calling to his familiar spirits of the storm. Never have I passed such an hour under canvas. The wind had the note you hear in a gale of sea. Lightning showed the surface of the lake torn into spindrift that was swept across it like rank on rank of sheeted ghosts. The thunder seemed to have its dwelling-place in both earth and sky.

'In a lull to gather force for a fresh assault, the cry again: again, and nearer, when the wind burst upon the mountain-top, as though released from some mighty dam in the heavens. This was not voice of beast or bird, and courage fell from me like a garment. The numbness of terror possessed me; I sat with nails digging into the wood, saying over and over some silly rhyme. Close at hand the cry;—heart-breaking, dreadful, unbearable . . .

'Wrenching myself free, as from the grip of a nightmare, I leaped to the door of the tent; five paces away in the howling blackness stood something in the form of a man, and in one stricken moment the lightning revealed what I would give much that is dear to blot from memory. As the creature sprang, with its hellish voice filling my ears, I flung into the water, diving far and deep. Swimming with frantic strokes for the farther shore, I did not, in the greater fear, bethink me that this indeed was the Lake of Hell. The pursuing cry; rising ever and anon above all other sounds, kept nerve and muscle strung in the agony of the desire to escape. Crawling out exhausted and breathless, but stopping no instant, I plunged down the mountain-side;—staggering, falling, clutching, somehow I reached the bottom, and pitched into a bed of moss, like an animal shot through the neck.

'When I could breathe and feel and hear again, my ears caught only the sounds of the retreating storm and of a rapid on the river. Stumbling painfully towards it, I saw with inexpressible joy the light of a fire, where my men had camped when overtaken by darkness and the tempest.

'The next day I went out of the woods, the men returning to bring in tent and canoe. They met with nothing, but I don't believe that their heart was in the search.'

'And what in God's name was it?'

'Pray Him it was not poor Duchêne in the flesh.'

GILBERT PARKER · 1862-1932

The Flood

Wendling came to Fort Anne on the day that the Reverend Ezra Badgley and an unknown girl were buried. And that was a notable thing. The man had been found dead at his evening meal; the girl had died on the same day; and they were buried side by side. This caused much scandal, for the man was holy, and the girl, as many women said, was probably evil altogether. At the graves, when the minister's people saw what was being done, they piously protested; but the Factor, to whom Pierre had whispered a word, answered them gravely that the matter should go on: since none knew but the woman was as worthy of heaven as the man. Wendling chanced to stand beside Pretty Pierre.

'Who knows!' he said aloud, looking hard at the graves, 'who knows! . . . She died before him, but the dead can strike.'

Pierre did not answer immediately, for the Factor was calling the earth down on both coffins; but after a moment he added: 'Yes, the dead can strike.' And then the eyes of the two men caught and stayed, and they knew that they had things to say to each other in the world.

They became friends. And that, perhaps, was not greatly to Wendling's credit; for in the eyes of many Pierre was an outcast as an outlaw. Maybe some of the women disliked this friendship most; since Wendling was a handsome man, and Pierre was never known to seek them, good or bad; and they blamed him for the other's coldness, for his unconcerned yet respectful eye.

'There's Nelly Nolan would dance after him to the world's end,' said Shon McGann to Pierre one day; 'and the Widdy Jerome herself, wid her flamin' cheeks and the wild fun in her eye, croons like a babe at the breast as he slides out his cash on the bar; and over on Gansonby's Flat there's—'

'There's many a fool,' sharply interjected Pierre, as he pushed the needle through a button he was sewing on his coat.

'Bedad, there's a pair of fools here, anyway, say I; for the women might die without lift at waist or brush of lip, and neither of ye'd say,

"Here's to the joy of us, goddess, me own!"'

Pierre seemed to be intently watching the needle-point as it pierced up the button-eye, and his reply was given with a slowness corresponding to the sedate passage of the needle. 'Wendling, you think, cares nothing for women? Well, men who are like that cared once for one woman, and when that was over—but, pshaw! I will not talk. You are no thinker, Shon McGann. You blunder through the world. And you'll tremble as much to a woman's thumb in fifty years as now.'

'But the holy smoke,' said Shon, 'though I tremble at that, maybe, I'll not tremble, as Wendling, at nothing at all.' Here Pierre looked sharply, then dropped his eyes on his work again. Shon lapsed suddenly into a moodiness.

'Yes,' said Pierre, 'as Wendling, at nothing at all? Well?'

'Well, this, Pierre, for you that's a thinker from me that's none. I was walking with him in Red Glen yesterday. Sudden he took to shiverin', and snatched me by the arm, and a mad look shot out of his handsome face. "Hush!" says he. I listened. There was a sound like the hard rattle of a creek over stones, and then another sound behind that. "Come quick," says he, the sweat standin' thick on him; and he ran me up the bank—for it was at the beginnin' of the Glen where the sides were low—and there we stood pantin' and starin' flat at each other. "What's that? and what's got its hand on ye? for y' are cold as death, an' pinched in the face, an' you've bruised my arm," said I. And he looked round him slow and breathed hard, then drew his fingers through the sweat on his cheek. "I'm not well, and I thought I heard—you heard it; what was it like?" said he; and he peered close at me. "Like water," said I; "a little creek near, and a flood comin' far off." "Yes, just that," said he; "it's some trick of wind in the place, but it makes a man foolish, and an inch of brandy would be the right thing." I didn't say No to that. And on we came, and brandy we had with a wish in the eye of Nelly Nolan that'd warm the heart of a tomb. . . . And there's a cud for your chewin', Pierre. Think that by the neck and the tail, and the divil absolve you.'

During this, Pierre had finished with the button. He had drawn on his coat and lifted his hat, and now lounged, trying the point of the needle with his forefinger. When Shon ended, he said with a sidelong glance: 'But what did *you* think of all that, Shon?'

'Think! There it was! What's the use of thinkin'? There's many a trick in the world with wind or with spirit, as I've seen often enough in ould Ireland, and it's not to be guessed by me.' Here his voice got a little lower and a trifle solemn. 'For, Pierre,' spoke he, 'there's what's more than life or death, and sorra wan can we tell what it is; but we'll know some day whin—'

'When we've taken the leap at the Almighty Ditch,' said Pierre, with a grave kind of lightness. 'Yes, it is all strange. But even the Almighty Ditch is worth the doing: nearly everything is worth the doing; being young, growing old, fighting, loving—when youth is on—hating, eating, drinking, working, playing big games: all is worth it except two things.'

'And what are they, bedad?'

'Thy neighbour's wife. Murder.—Those are horrible. They double on a man one time or another; always.'

Here, as in curiosity, Pierre pierced his finger with the needle, and watched the blood form in a little globule. Looking at it meditatively and sardonically, he said: 'There is only one end to these. Blood for blood is a great matter; and I used to wonder if it would not be terrible for a man to see his death advancing on him drop by drop, like that.' And he let the spot of blood fall to the floor. 'But now I know that there is a punishment worse than that . . . *mon Dieu!* worse than that,' he added.

Into Shon's face a strange look had suddenly come.

'Yes, there's something worse than that, Pierre.'

'So, *bien?*'

Shon made the sacred gesture of his creed. 'To be punished by the dead. And not see them—only hear them.' And his eyes steadied firmly to the other's.

Pierre was about to reply, but there came the sound of footsteps through the open door, and presently Wendling entered slowly. He was pale and worn, and his eyes looked out with a searching anxiousness. But that did not render him less comely. He had always dressed in black and white, and this now added to the easy and yet severe refinement of his person. His birth and breeding had occurred in places unfrequented by such as Shon and Pierre; but plains and wild life level all; and men are friends according to their taste and will, and by no other law. Hence these with Wendling. He stretched out his hand to each without a word. The hand-shake was unusual; he had little demonstration ever. Shon looked up surprised, but responded. Pierre followed with a swift, inquiring look; then, in the succeeding pause, he offered cigarettes. Wendling took one; and all, silent, sat down. The sun streamed intemperately through the door-

way, making a broad ribbon of light straight across the floor to
Wendling's feet. After lighting his cigarette, he looked into the sunlight for a moment, still not speaking. Shon meanwhile had started
his pipe, and now, as if he found the silence awkward,—'It's a day
for God's country, this,' he said: 'to make man a Christian for little or
much, though he play with the Divil betunewhiles.' Without looking
at them, Wendling said, in a low voice: 'It was just such a day, down
there in Quebec, when it happened. You could hear the swill of the
river, and the water licking the piers, and the saws in the Big Mill and
the Little Mill as they marched through the timber, flashing their teeth
like bayonets. It's a wonderful sound on a hot, clear day—that wild,
keen singing of the saws, like the cry of a live thing fighting and
conquering. Up from the fresh-cut lumber in the yards there came a
smell like the juice of apples, and the sawdust, as you thrust your
hand into it, was as cool and soft as the leaves of a clove-flower in
the dew. On these days the town was always still. It looked sleeping,
and you saw the heat quivering up from the wooden walls and the
roofs of cedar shingles as though the houses were breathing.'

Here he paused, still intent on the shaking sunshine. Then he
turned to the others as if suddenly aware that he had been talking to
them. Shon was about to speak, but Pierre threw a restraining glance,
and, instead, they all looked through the doorway and beyond. In the
settlement below they saw the effect that Wendling had described.
The houses breathed. A grasshopper went clacking past, a dog at the
door snapped up a fly; but there seemed no other life of day.
Wendling nodded his head towards the distance. 'It was quiet, like
that. I stood and watched the mills and the yards, and listened to the
saws, and looked at the great slide, and the logs on the river: and I
said ever to myself that it was all mine; all. Then I turned to a big
house on the hillock beyond the cedars, whose windows were open,
with a cool dusk lying behind them. More than all else, I loved to
think I owned that house and what was in it. . . . She was a beautiful
woman. And she used to sit in a room facing the mill—though the
house fronted another way—thinking of me, I did not doubt, and
working at some delicate needle-stuff. There never had been a sharp
word between us, save when I quarrelled bitterly with her brother,
and he left the mill and went away. But she got over that mostly,
though the lad's name was never mentioned between us. That day I
was so hungry for the sight of her that I got my field-glass—used to
watch my vessels and rafts making across the bay—and trained it on

the window where I knew she sat. I thought it would amuse her, too, when I went back at night, if I told her what she had been doing. I laughed to myself at the thought of it as I adjusted the glass. . . . I looked. . . . There was no more laughing. . . . I saw her, and in front of her a man, with his back half on me. I could not recognize him, though at the instant I thought he was something familiar. I failed to get his face at all. Hers I found indistinctly. But I saw him catch her playfully by the chin! After a little they rose. He put his arm about her and kissed her, and he ran his fingers through her hair. She had such fine golden hair; so light, and lifted to every breath. . . . Something got into my brain. I know now it was the maggot which sent Othello mad. The world in that hour was malicious, awful. . . .

'After a time—it seemed ages: she and everything had receded so far—I went . . . home. At the door I asked the servant who had been there. She hesitated, confused, and then said the young curate of the parish. I was very cool: for madness is a strange thing; you see everything with an intense aching clearness—that is the trouble. . . . She was more kind than common. I do not think I was unusual. I was playing a part well,—my grandmother had Indian blood like yours, Pierre,—and I was waiting. I was even nicely critical of her to myself. I balanced the mole on her neck against her general beauty; the curve of her instep, I decided, was a little too emphatic. I passed her back and forth before me, weighing her at every point; but yet these two things were the only imperfections. I pronounced her an exceeding piece of art—and infamy. I was much interested to see how she could appear perfect in her soul. I encouraged her to talk. I saw with devilish irony that an angel spoke. And, to cap it all, she assumed the fascinating air of the mediator—for her brother; seeking a reconciliation between us. Her amazing art of person and mind so worked upon me that it became unendurable; it was so exquisite—and so shameless. I was sitting where the priest had sat that afternoon; and when she leaned towards me I caught her chin lightly and trailed my fingers through her hair as he had done: and that ended it, for I was cold, and my heart worked with horrible slowness. Just as a wave poises at its height before breaking upon the shore, it hung at every pulse-beat, and then seemed to fall over with a sickening thud. I arose, and, acting still, spoke impatiently of her brother. Tears sprang to her eyes. Such divine dissimulation, I thought;—too good for earth. She turned to leave the room, and I did not stay her. Yet we were together again that night. . . . I was only waiting.'

The cigarette had dropped from his fingers to the floor, and lay there smoking. Shon's face was fixed with anxiety; Pierre's eyes played gravely with the sunshine. Wendling drew a heavy breath, and then went on.

'Again, next day, it was like this—the world draining the heat. . . . I watched from the Big Mill. I saw them again. He leaned over her chair and buried his face in her hair. The proof was absolute now. . . . I started away, going a roundabout, that I might not be seen. It took me some time. I was passing through a clump of cedar when I saw them making towards the trees skirting the river. Their backs were on me. Suddenly they diverted their steps towards the great slide, shut off from water this last few months, and used as a quarry to deepen it. Some petrified things had been found in the rocks, but I did not think they were going to these. I saw them climb down the rocky steps; and presently they were lost to view. The gates of the slide could be opened by machinery from the Little Mill. A terrible, deliciously malignant thought came to me. I remember how the sunlight crept away from me and left me in the dark. I stole through that darkness to the Little Mill. I went to the machinery for opening the gates. Very gently I set it in motion, facing the slide as I did so. I could see it through the open sides of the mill. I smiled to think what the tiny creek, always creeping through a faint leak in the gates and falling with a granite rattle on the stones, would now become. I pushed the lever harder—harder. I saw the gates suddenly give, then fly open, and the river sprang roaring massively through them. I heard a shriek through the roar. I shuddered; and horrible sickness came on me. . . . And as I turned from the machinery, I saw the young priest coming at me through the doorway! . . . It was not the priest and my wife that I had killed; but my wife and her brother. . . .'

He threw his head back as though something clamped his throat. His voice roughened with misery:—'The young priest buried them both, and people did not know the truth. They were even sorry for me. But I gave up the mills—all; and I became homeless . . . this.'

Now he looked up at the two men, and said: 'I have told you because you know something, and because there will, I think, be an end soon.' He got up and reached out a trembling hand for a cigarette. Pierre gave him one. 'Will you walk with me?' he asked.

Shon shook his head. 'God forgive you!' he replied; 'I can't do it.'

But Wendling and Pierre left the hut together. They walked for an hour, scarcely speaking, and not considering where they went. At last

Pierre mechanically turned to go down into Red Glen. Wendling stopped short, then, with a sighing laugh, strode on. 'Shon has told you what happened here?' he said.

Pierre nodded.

'And you know what came once when you walked with me. . . . The dead can strike,' he added.

Pierre sought his eye. 'The minister and the girl buried together that day,' he said, 'were—'

He stopped, for behind him he heard the sharp, cold trickle of water. Silent they walked on. It followed them. They could not get out the Glen now until they had compassed its length—the walls were high. The sound grew. The men faced each other. 'Good-bye,' said Wendling; and he reached out his hand swiftly. But Pierre heard a mighty flood groaning on them, and he blinded as he stretched his arm in response. He caught at Wendling's shoulder, but felt him lifted and carried away, while he himself stood still in a screeching wind and heard impalpable water rushing over him. In a minute it was gone; and he stood alone in Red Glen.

He gathered himself up and ran. Far down, where the Glen opened to the plain, he found Wendling. The hands were wrinkled; the face was cold; the body was wet: the man was drowned and dead.

DUNCAN CAMPBELL SCOTT · 1862-1947

Vengeance Is Mine

I

'And God said, Let the dry land appear, and it was so.' But as yet the waters alone seemed gathered together into one place. There they lay, vast, unmoving, lustreless, of the same grey colour as the sky. And the land, which had risen without violence, pressed from beneath the surface of the waters, lying a little above them, but clearly as yet the bottom of a sea, extended on all sides, the mere essential earth without the form of hill or valley.

So thought Evan McColl as he gazed at the surface of James Bay from the shore, a little above its level, and remembered the first chapter of Genesis. This was the famous bay he had dreamed about as a boy, until it had become a land of fairy, which, if he could only reach it, would render up adventure as the very spirit of its shores and waters.

This was the reality! Behind him were the buildings of the Hudson's Bay Company trading-post at Winisk—low, rude structures crouching on the shore; before him was the waste of waters, lightened here and there by patches of dirty yellow, where lay the shifting sand-banks, and clouded by vast marshy beds, the haunt of the wild fowl.

If he had not long ago wrung his heart dry so that there were in it no more tears he would have wept aloud. But where his heart was there was a feeling of ache and terror; and where his soul should have animated him there was deadness. He had been only two years in that land, but it was enough. To one sensitive and subject to the longing for things home-like, and with comfort at the core of them, two years of that land were equal to ten of strange cities. He had signed for five years, and three of them lay before him. Suddenly a voice smote him:

'What are ye gaupin' at there, ye loon? Have ye naught to do but look at the water as if it was going to bite ye?'

Evan's shoulders drew together as if a scourge had fallen on him. Without looking behind him he turned and walked toward the storehouse, and the trader, Ian Forbes, scowled after him.

'God be feared,' he muttered to himself, 'that they should have put an idiot upon me when I have enough to bear!'

A gull that seemed to have no power of flight flopped awkwardly near him. He called out to it:

'Gabriel, ye loon, ye have more sense in your bit of a feathered body than he has in his whole carcass.'

Evan unlocked the door with a ponderous key and plunged into the gloom of the interior and the heavy smell of dried fish and strong tobacco, leather, and rancid tallow. It was a dreariness and an odour like unto that of Whale River, where he had spent eighteen months of his two years on the bay, and where his soul and body had been broken.

Here at Winisk he had hoped all things would be changed; at Whale River, Winisk seemed to be in the old magic zone of his dreams. Surely no other place in the world would be so sunk in loneliness and squalor as Whale River! The voyage across the bay had some trembling of romance about it—the breezes seemed fortunate; there beyond the tawny line of the horizon lay—fabulous, secret, and full of lustre—a new province, and surely a new life. It was a recrudescence of hope.

When he first sighted the post it was transfigured by a mirage and gleamed in the morning light. Held high above a long silver strip of water, the white buildings looked like things fashioned of crystal, around them the sheen that is upon the breasts of doves. A large content took hold upon him; no intoxication of pleasure could equal this lull of all earthly passion into peace, absolute and virginal. Two miles nearer the coast the vision was snatched away and the low, grey shoreline, with dull, small buildings, dwelt in its place—the reality.

When he landed, the trader, Ian Forbes—'Black Ian', as he was called—looked him over from crown to foot, looked him through from breast-bone to shoulder-blade, and with never a word turned on a grinding heel and spat upon the ground contemptuously. Yet at first glance Ian was rather engaged with the tall, red-haired Highland lad; but his experience of clerks and helpers had been a long one, varied with bitterness, and he would begin by crushing and humiliation; if any human relations were to follow, they would be allowed to creep up by a process of reconstruction. He expected nothing of God or man. The country and the trade, loneliness and disappointment, had seared his heart, and having met with kindness nowhere for years and years, he paid his debt by hardness, studied and determined. But he was ready for comradeship in the midst of all his cruel perversity, was in very truth longing for it, and his first glance at Evan revealed possibilities to him. The reception, so wilfully brutal, was not lost upon the newcomer. With one look of terror at the averted shoulder, the strong, round head with its Kilmarnock bonnet, and the short, powerful figure, Evan busied himself extracting his few belongings from the miscellany of the cargo.

His hope fell dead, but in a day or two, taking an inventory of his new situation, he found himself with some items of privilege. It was, to be sure, a fine thing to be free of the filthy Eskimos of Whale River. Here his quarters were roomy, if nothing great to boast about, and, moreover, clean. There was some pretence at Christian cooking of such coarse food as was to be had.

The Indians, all but a few, had left for their hunting-grounds, and the permanent staff of the post was, in addition to himself, Luke Contrecœur, his Cree wife, and his daughter Julie. There was another member of the group with an individuality of his own—the seagull, a resident by compulsion since Ian had captured him and clipped his wings. They called him Gabriel, and he seemed to love the warmth of the house and the easy fare, of which he was monstrous greedy. You might say he was tamed, for Ian in his idleness, and by a certain measure of cruelty, had taught him a few odd tricks. But his chief use was as a foil for his master, to curse when he was in a raging temper, and to apostrophize with remarks which were intended to apply to other people. Many a hard saying had been delivered over the gull's wing.

Evan had to admit that there was society. His mind very quickly governed his body, and his lassitude and the physical weakness which had been upon him receded and his heart gladdened a little. Ian noticed the change and, although he made no sign, was pleased enough. There would be plenty of time for the amenities when he has shown the lad the extent of his power. So he was a heavy taskmaster, and Evan bore it without a word, for something was at work upon his heart.

II

'It's a fine thing to be here with you, Luke,' he would say, as he filled his pipe by the light of Contrecœur's fire. 'A better place than that heathen Whale River. I should have died there this winter.'

'Yes, surr,' Luke would reply; 'and you don't look right strong yet, surr.' He was a huge, kindly fellow, with a low, soft, rumbling voice.

'Oh, I'm all right. Say, Luke, doesn't Julie ever speak to anybody?'

'Yess, surr. Speak to him, Julie.'

'Yess, surr,' Julie whispered, her eyes fixed on the floor.

She was about seventeen, with a shapely figure and a grave, oval face, and her eyes, when she showed them, were brown. It was an innocent game of Evan's in these days to catch a full sight of her eyes. But her glance was like a young bird learning to fly; its perch was somewhere in Evan's face, but it fluttered off and fell back to the ground constantly. He wooed her shyness and tried to gain her confidence by most boyish wiles, and was happy without reasoning about happiness. Ian was unobservant of what was going on between Julie and the lad, as he called him in his mind, but he was glad enough to hear his high voice flourishing amid the roundelays of some good old song.

'Call me Evan, Julie.'

'Yes, surr,' she would drawl in her most musical voice—with a laugh beginning in her mind.

'Well, the, say it—Evan.'

'Evan, surr.' She pronounced it Eevan, with a long stress on the first 'E'.

The glance almost fluttered up to its perch; then followed two or three liquid sounds, the end notes of her laughing melody, the first of which had only run through her mind.

Ian spoke almost kindly to him one day. 'Lad,' he said, 'I'm thinking we'll have to make some new skidways afore we haul up the boats for the winter, and you and Luke had better edge up the axes in a way.'

'Of course, Mr Forbes,' he said lightly, and Ian did not like the manner of his reply. He thought his first mildness should have received more consideration. He was sensitive, this broad-breasted Highlander, as quickly proud and sensitive as a fine lady, and the advances he had already made in his liking for Evan were now so many causes for self-reproach. 'Tut! He's but like the rest o' them, and I was fair to make a fool o' myself.'

But Evan was indifferent now to the trader's tone, whether rough or smooth. The next day Ian stumbled upon the reason. Julie had come up to the store for some flour, and Evan had caught her hands. Then, timidly as a lover may, and not breathing for very ecstasy, he drew her toward him. Her shawl fell back from her dark, lustrous hair—her bright eyes dwelt upon his face, her breast rose in one short sigh. He clasped her close, and long and shudderingly he kissed her lips. Then, just as his face left hers, she pursued it timidly and her lips met his cheek somewhere, fugitively, with the lightest of caresses; then, frightened at this disclosure of her heart, she swiftly covered her head.

Forbes, who just then came down from the fur-loft, saw this play. The little new-born humanity of the man was blighted. He had never before considered Julie—she had been as a child; but if any one thought her a woman, no one but himself would own her. His temper of jealousy grew two days, then he sent Evan down the shore on a wild-goose chase, and called Luke.

'Take the women away to Albany!'

'Yes, surr.'

Luke was fairly stupefied and stared like an ox. Forbes struck him full in the face.

'Will ye go?' he said in a frenzy. 'Be around the point before McColl comes back, or 'twill be the worse for ye.'

'Yes, surr,' said Luke patiently.

III

When Evan went down to Luke's house that evening it was dark; there was no fire on the hearth. He came back with a great misgiving. Ian sat in a huge timber chair filled with cushions, a grim look on his face. He watched the boy, who was excited by apprehension. Gabriel was wedged in among the cushions in a warm corner.

'We'll find out who is the master here, Gabriel,' said the trader. 'We'll all find out sooner or later, songsters, and high and mighty lovers, and all.'

Six days later Luke came back. Evan burst in upon him.

'Luke, for God's sake, tell me what has happened! Where is Julie?'

'Gone to Albany, surr.'

'A hundred miles! Luke, I shall die here; there is no help for it.'

'Better not do that, surr.'

'Who sent them away? Tell me, quick.'

'Him.'

'What right has he over *your* wife and daughter?' he said, passionately.

'He has the saying,' said Luke simply. Surely they were all in the trader's hand; his power was close over them.

By and by they began to build the skidways. They were flattening long cottonwood logs and pinning them together. The labour was too heavy and exasperating for Evan, who was wasted with longing and many sleepless nights. His old lassitude had come upon him; he felt weary as death; he would look long upon the heavy waters and hate his life. He longed to kill Ian with his broadaxe; to lay him low in the midst of some cruel jibe. Once, when the trader was bending over the chalk-line adjusting it, Evan swung back the axe with a sudden passionate impulse—but Ian looked up. When he saw the gleaming blade hanging over him he showed his teeth in a smile; but he never turned his back on the boy again. After that they were pitted against each other, and Ian was the more savage because he had had those inner drawings which were now, he thought, all proved to be false.

The winter was now close upon them, though as yet it held off wondrously. A chief item of their provender was the wild fowl which they salted. The birds came in flocks among the reed-fringes of innumerable small islands, and they shot them from stands set for the purpose. Grey daylight would find the men hidden and ready with their huge fowling-pieces. One morning Evan came away without his great coat—for he could hardly now collect his thoughts upon any subject—and it was bitterly chill. A breeze which stung to the very bone with cold moved the reeds.

'Ye young donkey, ye're here without your coat. Ye'd leave yer head if it was any particular use to ye.'

'Luke will go back for it when he comes out.'

'Listen to that, now!—the young lord! Luke has better to do than fetch and carry for such as you.' He was feeling in his pocket for his flint and steel to make a light for his pipe.

'You've forgotten something yourself,' said Evan impudently, at a hazard.

'You're over-quick to guess. You've thieved it yourself, you young devil. I see it in your face.' He whipped himself into an awful rage. 'It's my fire-box I want, d'ye hear? and I'm going to find it, and you'll wish ye had even such a wee spark of fire before anybody remembers to come out for ye'.

He seized the boat and put off through the reeds. Luke was kept busy by Ian all that day while he nursed his raging heart, but toward sundown, in a passion, he ordered him to go for the lad, as if the delay had been one of his faults. Evan was lying unconscious on the soggy marsh grass in the half-frozen water. Luke rowed him to the shore and carried him to the post. He had been all day without food. He had shot some geese, and in trying to reach them had fallen into the water.

All that night Luke laboured to get some of the warmth and breath of life into the lad's body, and all the next day he lay in a raging fever, with Luke alone ministering to him, as tenderly and with such rude comforts as might be. Ian, if he thought of him, betrayed no sign of it. He was warring against the demon within him. Ashamed to be solicitous for the life he had nearly taken, he argued it out with Gabriel.

'When he is well. I'll make it up with him. I'll forgive him. I'll not be ungenerous with the laddie. But he stole my fire-box, do you know that, Gabriel—reived it away, the black-hearted young devil, to think on't!'

With a heavy, desperate face he went about his business, but he did not once sit down in the house that day, not even to eat his meals. He took his food standing over against the window and gazed upon the parchment covering as if he could see through it, out upon the immensity of the waters beyond. When night came he slept in his clothes, if he slept at all, sitting in the large chair, his hands extended upon the arms and his head fallen down upon his breast.

Luke was faithful all night to the fire and to Evan, and only murmured to him when he replaced his blanket or moistened his lips with a little oatmeal-water. As the room was warmer than usual, Gabriel sat close under his master's chair and did not seek his usual haunts; occasionally he would stretch his wings, snap his bill, and move his feet restlessly. Once he was aware of something which dropped from the cushions of the chair, struck him softly on the back, ran lightly over his plumage, and fell upon the floor beside him. He opened one eye wisely and blinked at the firelight.

Toward morning Luke must have slept, for when he awoke the room was filled with equivocal daylight and Ian was gone. Evan's fever had left him, but he could barely move his limbs, so weak was he. The ordinary coarse nourishment of the post he refused when Luke prepared it for him.

'Oich! I'm done for,' he said heavily. 'I can't swallow the stuff, and I'm a long way from home. I wish you'd bring over my casette, Luke.'

He carried the box and set it by his side, and Evan made him rummage for a certain book of which he was fain. When he found it, at intervals all day he pored upon it, searching for something. Suddenly he said:

'Luke, bring me here a coal from the hearth.'

Luke brought it in his naked fingers, which could stand fire like steel. In his excitement the boy took it from him and burned the page opposite a certain text. The live coal ate his flesh, the page, and the blanket. He sank back exhausted. In a quarter of an hour he was up again, leaning against the strength of Luke.

'I want to tell you, Luke, that I loved Julie. But there was nothing wrong; I loved her in the way men love women in God's country. I want you to give her this to be minded of Evan, who loved her in the true way.'

He unwound a heavy gold chain that went three times about his neck, and gave it in Luke's hand. He was quiet for a space.

'Luke, I want you to show Ian Forbes this book, where I have burned it with the coal. At the right time—you will know—show him that, as from me. He was mightier than I, but another shall deal with him. Show it to him.'

IV

'He's gone, surr,' said Luke to Ian, humbly, as if he were in some way responsible.

'Who's gone?'

'Master Evan, surr.'

'Where?'

'He's dead, surr.' Ian was convicted.

'My God! He did it to spite me. Luke, the fellow crossed me from the first. It was like him to slip away—never to say where he hid the fire-box.'

But Ian was filled with an awful dread; after they buried the body, for a week he never took off his clothes. He was buried himself, deep, deep in his own mind. He never spoke. He had all the superstitious feeling of his race. Every moment he was aware of the long white body in the shallow grave, covered so lightly that he expected any moment to see it stand in the doorway.

One day as he stood before the table in a dream he saw Gabriel flounder along, pushing something from under the chair. He stooped mechanically and picked up—the fire-box!

A peculiar smile came upon his face. He launched a kick at Gabriel, and turned away, trembling. What was he to do? He leaned upon the table, which shook with his trembling. Murdered, and accused falsely! He could not escape from the impeachment. He was consumed of it, as by a slow fire.

One afternoon he must have dozed in his chair. At dusk he half awoke. Mysteriously he saw the door open without a sound. An appearance stood there, gaunt, grey, fearsome, and passed like a mist into the room. It had the weird look of the boy in the grave.

With a scream Ian threw himself against the door. There was something on the floor moving strangely about. Gabriel! Then he knew. Sometimes when the bird was outside he would open the door himself by fluttering as high as the big oak latch, which extended six inches beyond the door. He would perch upon it, over-balancing it by his weight, and the heavy door would swing inward. Then some one would get up and shut it. Ian began to laugh a wild, half-mad laugh, and laughed until he was faint and covered with cold sweat.

Some days after this his mind was quieter, and Luke, who was ever watching his opportunity, heard him half-whimpering to Gabriel:

'Ye know I really loved the lad. There was that about him that I liked—ye ken? But he would not let me, he was that quick with me, and ye mind he tried to hit me with the broadaxe. But I wanted to love him, Gabriel.'

Then Luke brought forth the Book.

'What's this?'

'The lad told me to show it to you, there—where he burned it with a coal of fire.'

Ian say down with his head in his hands and studied the page. He read before and after. Suddenly his face turned grey. He was in the hand of God. A judge rising from the grave had placed him there. He knew his crime now: he had killed the lad he loved, as, in his heart, he had restrained and killed his love for him. What would his sentence be?

Day after day he paced the shore and knew he would go mad. But he wondered how God would visit him. Gazing sometimes at the water, he thought it would rise and sweep him away; sometimes that the wind would drive him into the wilderness like a dry leaf; sometimes that the earth would open and that he would fall, fall, fall forever.

'Luke, go to Albany and tell the factor that I'm going mad. Bring him back, bring the women, bring everybody, and be as sudden as ye can.'

There had been no deep cold as yet, and the ice had barely formed, but Luke obeyed. The danger, and it was great, meant nothing to him.

v

Three days after that Ian, exhausted with frantic watching and overcome with dread, slept in his chair. The fire went low on the hearth. A change of which he was all unconscious was abroad in the world. It was the beginning of one of those periods of intense and awful cold which strangle life and make callous the very earth itself. There was no stir in the air, but it seemed to tighten as from some enormous pressure.

Ian slept. Then, mysteriously, the door opened without a sound. Gabriel fluttered in. But there was no one to shut the door.

Ian slept on. The bird flew upon the chair and nestled close behind him, eager for the warmth of his body. Time passed silently; the cold grew deeper and deeper.

Ian slept on. His breath fell in little regular showers of rime on his beard and breast.

Swiftly a shade of white flew across the back of his bare hands, extended on the arms of his chair. His face grew blanched, white as a leper's. The last of the frost fell lightly down upon his beard. His face, clouded no longer by his breath, shone out upon the dusk with a grim, terrible distinctness. There was he fixed, ice to the core, rigid and unchangeable. Over the Book was his right hand, frozen down upon the words in Romans which had been marked with the coal of fire—'Vengeance is mine; I will repay, saith the Lord.'

STEPHEN LEACOCK · 1869-1944

Buggam Grange: A Good Old Ghost Story

The evening was already falling as the vehicle in which I was contained entered upon the long and gloomy avenue that leads to Buggam Grange.

A resounding shriek echoed through the wood as I entered the avenue. I paid no attention to it at the moment, judging it to be merely one of those resounding shrieks which one might expect to hear in such a place at such a time. As my drive continued, however, I found myself wondering in spite of myself why such a shriek should have been uttered at the very moment of my approach.

I am not by temperament in any degree a nervous man, and yet there was much in my surroundings to justify a certain feeling of apprehension. The Grange is situated in the loneliest part of England, the marsh country of the fens to which civilization has still hardly penetrated. The inhabitants, of whom there are only one and a half to the square mile, live here and there among the fens and eke out a miserable existence by frog fishing and catching flies. They speak a dialect so broken as to be practically unintelligible, while the perpetual rain which falls upon them renders speech itself almost superfluous.

Here and there where the ground rises slightly above the level of the fens there are dense woods tangled with parasitic creepers and filled with owls. Bats fly from wood to wood. The air on the lower ground is charged with the poisonous gases which exude from the marsh, while in the woods it is heavy with the dank odours of deadly nightshade and poison ivy.

It had been raining in the afternoon, and as I drove up the avenue the mournful dripping of the rain from the dark trees accentuated the cheerlessness of the gloom. The vehicle in which I rode was on three wheels, the fourth having apparently been broken and taken off, causing the fly to sag on one side and drag on its axle over the muddy ground, the fly thus moving only at a foot's pace in a way calculated to enhance the dreariness of the occasion. The driver on the box in front of me was so thickly muffled up as to be undistinguishable, while the horse which drew us was so thickly coated with mist as to be practically invisible. Seldom, I may say, have I had a drive of so mournful a character.

The avenue presently opened out upon a lawn with overgrown shrubberies and in the half darkness I could see the outline of the Grange itself, a rambling, dilapidated building. A dim light struggled through the casement of a window in a tower room. Save for the melancholy cry of a row of owls sitting on the roof, and croaking of the frogs in the moat which ran around the grounds, the place was soundless. My driver halted his horse at the hither side of the moat. I tried in vain to urge him, by signs, to go further. I could see by the fellow's face that he was in a paroxysm of fear and indeed nothing but the extra sixpence which I had added to his fare would have made him undertake the drive up the avenue. I had no sooner alighted than he wheeled his cab about and made off.

Laughing heartily at the fellow's trepidation (I have a way of laughing heartily in the dark), I made my way to the door and pulled the bell-handle. I could hear the muffled reverberations of the bell far within the building. Then all was silent. I bent my ear to listen, but could hear nothing except perhaps the sound of a low moaning as of a person in pain or in great mental distress. Convinced, however, from what my friend Sir Jeremy Buggam had told me, that the Grange was not empty, I raised the ponderous knocker and beat with it loudly against the door.

But perhaps at this point I may do well to explain to my readers (before they are too frightened to listen to me) how I came to be beating on the door of Buggam Grange at nightfall on a gloomy November evening.

A year before I had been sitting with Sir Jeremy Buggam, the present baronet, on the verandah of his ranch in California.

'So you don't believe in the supernatural?' he was saying.

'Not in the slightest,' I answered, lighting a cigar as I spoke. When I want to speak very positively, I generally light a cigar as I speak.

'Well, at any rate, Digby,' said Sir Jeremy, 'Buggam Grange is haunted. If you want to be assured of it go down there any time and spend the night and you'll see for yourself.'

'My dear fellow,' I replied, 'nothing will give me greater pleasure. I shall be back in England in six weeks, and I shall be delighted to put your ideas to the test. Now tell me,' I added somewhat cynically, 'is there any particular season or day when your Grange is supposed to be specially terrible?'

Sir Jeremy looked at me strangely. 'Why do you ask that?' he said. 'Have you heard the story of the Grange?'

'Never heard of the place in my life,' I answered cheerily, ''till you mentioned it tonight, my dear fellow, I hadn't the remotest idea that you still owned property in England.'

'The Grange is shut up,' said Sir Jeremy, 'and has been for twenty years. But I keep a man there—Horrod—he was butler in my father's time and before. If you care to go, I'll write him that you're coming. And since you are taking your own fate in your hands, the fifteenth of November is the day.'

At that moment Lady Buggam and Clara and the other girls came trooping out on the verandah, and the whole thing passed clean out of my mind. Nor did I think of it again until I was back in London. Then by one of those strange coincidences or premonitions—call it what you will—it suddenly occurred to me one morning that it was the fifteenth of November. Whether Sir Jeremy had written to Horrod or not, I did not know. But none the less nightfall found me, as I have described, knocking at the door of Buggam Grange.

The sound of the knocker had scarcely ceased to echo when I heard the shuffling of feet within, and the sound of chains and bolts being withdrawn. The door opened. A man stood before me holding a lighted candle which he shaded with his hand. His faded black clothes, once apparently a butler's dress, his white hair and advanced age left me in no doubt that he was Horrod of whom Sir Jeremy had spoken.

Without a word he motioned me to come in, and, still without speech, he helped me to remove my wet outer garments, and then beckoned me into a great room, evidently the dining-room of the Grange.

I am not in any degree a nervous man by temperament, as I think I remarked before, and yet there was something in the vastness of the wainscotted room, lighted only by a single candle, and in the silence of the empty house, and still more in the appearance of my speechless attendant which gave me a feeling of distinct uneasiness. As Horrod moved to and fro I took occasion to scrutinize his face more narrowly. I have seldom seen features more calculated to inspire a nervous dread. The pallor of his face and the whiteness of his hair (the man was at least seventy), and still more the peculiar furtiveness of his eyes, seemed to mark him as one who lived under a great terror. He moved with a noiseless step and at times he turned his head to glance in the dark corners of the room.

'Sir Jeremy told me,' I said, speaking as loudly and as heartily as I could, 'that he would apprise you of my coming.'

I was looking into his face as I spoke.

In answer Horrod laid his finger across his lips and I knew that he was deaf and dumb. I am not nervous (I think I said that), but the realization that my sole companion in the empty house was a deaf mute struck a cold chill to my heart.

Horrod laid in front of me a cold meat pie, a cold goose, a cheese, and a tall flagon of cider. But my appetite was gone. I ate the goose, but found that after I had finished the pie I had but little zest for the cheese, which I finished without enjoyment. The cider had a sour taste, and after having permitted Horrod to refill the flagon twice, I found that it induced a sense of melancholy and decided to drink no more.

My meal finished, the butler picked up the candle and beckoned to me to follow him. We passed through the empty corridors of the house, a long line of pictured Buggams looking upon us as we passed, their portraits in the flickering light of the taper assuming a strange and life-like appearance as if leaning forward from their frames to gaze upon the intruder.

Horrod led me upstairs and I realized that he was taking m to the tower in the east wing in which I had observed a light.

The rooms to which the butler conducted me consisted of a sitting room with an adjoining bedroom, both of them fitted with antique wainscotting against which a faded tapestry fluttered. There was a candle burning on the table in the sitting room but its insufficient light only rendered the surroundings the more dismal. Horrod bent down in front of the fireplace and endeavoured to light a fire there. But the wood was evidently damp, and the fire flickered feebly on the hearth.

The butler left me, and in the stillness of the house I could hear his shuffling step echo down the corridor. It may have been fancy, but it seemed to me that his departure was the signal for a low moan that came from somewhere behind the wainscot. There was a narrow cupboard door at one side of the room, and for the moment I wondered whether the moaning came from within. I am not as a rule lacking in courage (I am sure my reader will be decent enough to believe this), yet I found myself entirely unwilling to open the cupboard door and look within. In place of doing so I seated myself in a great chair in front of the feeble fire. I must have been seated there for some time when I happened to lift my eyes to the mantel above and saw, standing upon it, a letter addressed to myself. I knew the handwriting at once to be that of Sir Jeremy Buggam.

I opened it, and spreading it out within reach of the feeble candle light, I read as follows:

My dear Digby,

In our talk that you will remember I had no time to finish telling you about the mystery of Buggam Grange. I take for granted, however, that you will go there and that Horrod will put you in the tower rooms, which are the only ones that make any pretence of being habitable. I have, therefore, sent him this letter to deliver at the Grange itself. The story is this:

On the night of the fifteenth of November, fifty years ago, my grandfather was murdered in the room in which you are sitting, by his cousin Sir Duggam Buggam. He was stabbed from behind while seated at the little table at which you are probably reading this letter. The two had been playing cards at the table and my grandfather's body was found lying in a litter of cards and gold sovereigns on the floor. Sir Duggam Buggam, insensible from drink, lay beside him, the fatal knife at his hand, his fingers smeared with blood. My grandfather, though of the younger branch, possessed a part of the estates which were to revert to Sir Duggam on his death. Sir Duggam Buggam was tried at the Assizes and was hanged. On the day of his execution he was permitted by the authorities, out of respect for his rank, to wear a mask to the scaffold. The clothes in which he was executed are hanging at full length in the little cupboard to your right, and the mask is above them. It is said that on every fifteenth of November at midnight the cupboard door opens and Sir Duggam Buggam walks out into the room. It has been found impossible to get servants to remain at the Grange, and the place—except for the presence of Horrod—has been unoccupied for a generation. At the time of the murder Horrod was a young man of twenty-two, newly entered into the service of the family. It was he who entered the room and discovered the crime. On the day of the execution he was stricken with paralysis and has never spoken since. From that time to this he has never consented to leave the Grange where he lives in isolation.

Wishing you a pleasant night after your tiring journey,
I remain,
Very faithfully,
JEREMY BUGGAM.

I leave my reader to imagine my state of mind when I completed the perusal of the letter.

I have as little belief in the supernatural as anyone, yet I must confess that there was something in the surroundings in which I now found myself which rendered me at least uncomfortable. My reader may smile if he will, but I assure him that it was with a very distinct feeling of uneasiness that I at length managed to rise to my feet, and, grasping my candle in my hand, to move backward into the bedroom. As I backed into it something so like a moan seemed to proceed from the closed cupboard that I accelerated my backward movement to a considerable degree. I hastily blew out the candle, threw myself upon the bed and drew the bed clothes over my head, keeping, however, one eye and one ear still out and available.

How long I lay thus listening to every sound, I cannot tell. The stillness had become absolute. From time to time I could dimly hear the distant cry of an owl and once far away in the building below a sound as of someone dragging a chain along a floor. More than once I was certain that I heard the sound of moaning behind the wainscot. Meantime I realized that the hour must now be drawing close upon the fatal moment of midnight. My watch I could not see in the darkness, but by reckoning the time that must have elapsed I knew that midnight could not be far away. Then presently my ear, alert to every sound, could just distinguish far away across the fens the striking of a church bell, in the clock tower of Buggam village church, no doubt, tolling the hour of twelve.

On the last stroke of twelve, the cupboard door in the next room opened. There is no need to ask me how I knew it. I couldn't, of course, see it, but I could hear, or sense in some way, the sound of it. I could feel my hair, all of it, rising upon my head. I was aware that there was a *presence* in the adjoining room, I will not say a person, a living soul, but a *presence*. Anyone who has been in the next room to a presence will know just how I felt. I could hear a sound as of someone groping on the floor and the faint rattle as of coins.

My hair was now perpendicular. My reader can blame it or not, but it was.

Then at this very moment from somewhere below in the building there came the sound of a prolonged and piercing cry, a cry as of a soul passing in agony. My reader may censure me or not, but right at this moment I decided to beat it. Whether I should have remained to see what was happening is a question that I will not discuss. My one idea was to get out and to get out quickly. The window of the tower room was some twenty-five feet above the ground. I sprang out through the casement in one leap and landed on the grass below. I jumped over the shrubbery in one bound and cleared the moat in one jump. I went down the avenue in about six strides and ran five miles along the road through the fens in three minutes. This at least is an accurate transcription of my sensations. It may have taken longer. I never stopped till I found myself on the threshold of the Buggam Arms in Little Buggam, beating on the door for the landlord.

I returned to Buggam Grange on the next day in the bright sunlight of a frosty November morning, in a seven cylinder motor car with six local constables and a physician. It makes all the difference. We carried revolvers, spades, pickaxes, shotguns and a ouija board.

What we found cleared up forever the mystery of the Grange. We discovered Horrod the butler lying on the dining-room floor quite dead. The physician said that he had died from heart failure. There was evidence from the marks of his shoes in the dust that he had come in the night to the tower room. On the table he had placed a paper which contained a full confession of his having murdered Jeremy Buggam fifty years before. The circumstances of the murder had rendered it easy for him to fasten the crime upon Sir Duggam, already insensible from drink. A few minutes with the ouija board enabled us to get a full corroboration from Sir Duggam. He promised moreover, now that his name was cleared, to go away from the premises forever.

My friend, the present Sir Jeremy, has rehabilitated Buggam Grange. The place is rebuilt. The moat is drained. The whole house is lit with electricity. There are beautiful motor drives in all directions in the woods. He has had the bats shot and the owls stuffed. His daughter, Clara Buggam, became my wife. She is looking over my shoulder as I write. What more do you want?

Portrait of a Wife

César Barbet was a young painter of great promise though he had not yet accomplished much in a material way. He had never yet had the good fortune to paint the portrait of a person of wealth or distinction. His subjects had been models or his own friends. His picture of his friend Paul Chassel, his last achievement, had created something like a stir, and he waited, almost breathlessly, for some recognition from the public.

Chassel, himself, did not encourage him.

'The critics', he said, 'found the picture interesting. It is unusual. It is alive. But with what a melancholy and disintegrating life! You have captured in it all the bitterness and disillusion of my past. No one looking at it would desire to have his—or more especially her—portrait painted by an artist with a so evident flair for the cruel and mordant.'

César's elation dropped a little. There was truth in what his friend said. Of those who had the intention of having their features immortalized, how many would seek out an artist, to describe whose work, the critics had searched for the most macabre words in their vocabulary?

He had succeeded thus brilliantly with Chassel because Chassel had had a melancholy life, and his strength lay in depicting the melancholy, even the horrible.

He went over in his mind the subjects of his best portraits. . . . Yes, in every one of them was the taint of tragedy. And, unconsciously, his art had been exercised in portraying this rather than beauty. Yet, tragedy was beauty. The woof of the canvas of life was tragedy, and no amount of paint could obliterate it.

Yet in spite of his philosophy, he was depressed. Two weeks passed after the chorus of praise which had greeted his portrait of Chassel, and he had had not one enquiry from a prospective client. He began to wonder if he should be driven to commercial art in order to exist. His sensitive spirit shrank at the very thought of such a possibility.

Then, one morning, the first clear day after several of depressing fog, he was called to the telephone. A low sweet feminine voice enquired:

'Is that Monsieur César Barbet?'

After his answer in the affirmative, which he had tried to make not too eager, the voice went on:

'I wish to interview you in regard to having my portrait done by you. Could you come to my house this morning?'

She gave an address in a fashionable quarter, and César promised to wait on her there inside of the hour.

As he was whirled through the streets in a taxi, his mind was filled with delightful speculations. This sudden change in his fortune seemed almost too good to be true. A woman, young by her voice; beautiful, his florid imagination assured him; rich, or she would not have lived in such a locality! He wished he had had the time to call up his friend Chassel, and crow over him a little. What time had been to spare he had spent in changing into another suit, a well-fitting morning suit of an English cut which showed to advantage his slender supple figure.

He glanced down over himself with satisfaction as he rang the bell of the tall imposing house with its air of detached reserve.

He was at once admitted and shown up an impressive stairway by a servant who knocked at a door at the end of a dim hallway.

Inside the room, he was startled to find the furnishings those of a luxurious bedroom. The blinds were drawn but a clear light like sunlight was diffused by several tall electric lamps. One of these stood by the bed, and there his attention was at once held in an emotion approaching horror.

Propped up beneath the splendour of the silken canopy was a young woman about thirty, apparently in the last stage of some devastating disease. She was swathed in a brilliantly hued dressing-robe which only intensified the deathly pallor of her emaciated face. Her long hair, so richly black and luxuriant that it seemed like some tropic growth which had sapped the last drop of her vitality for its own nourishment, hung in a heavy cloud over her shoulders and the embroidered pillows. Her hands, palms upward, the fingers curled like the petals of dying flowers, lay limply on the bright coverlet. Her grey eyes, lighted, as though from some transcendent emotion from within were fixed on him in burning concentration from the moment he entered the room.

'Monsieur Barbet?' she asked, in the same musical voice that had spoken over the telephone.

He bowed, quite unable to speak.

'Please sit down.' She indicated a chair near the bedside with a movement, not of the pallid hand which seemed too feeble ever to stir again, but of the strong brilliantly grey eyes.

'I have been reading the comments of the critics on your portrait of Monsieur Chassel with interest,' she went on. 'I only wish that I were able to see the picture itself. But as you see, I am tied to my bed.'

César murmured words of thanks and commiseration.

'However,' the even voice proceeded, 'I saw a really excellent reproduction of it, and that, combined with the enthusiasm of the critics, has inspired me to have my own portrait done by you.'

'I am indeed honoured,' murmured César.

The intensity of her gaze deepened, as though she would search his very soul. 'You must have a very unusual mind for so young a man to paint as you do.'

'Isn't melancholy, disillusion, a characteristic of youth?' he asked, attempting an ironic smile.

'Ah, but not such melancholy, not such disillusion as you put into the face of your portrait of Monsieur Chassel!'

'It is there in the face of Chassel, himself!' cried César.

'That may be! But only one with a genius for the mordant could have so depicted the hollow heartbreak of his life. . . . I have a friend who knows something of Monsieur Chassel's past. She says you have immortalized it. What is your secret? Ah, I must not ask you that. It lies in your own soul. In the hidden places of your soul, where the light of cold reason never penetrates.'

César began to feel more at ease as he talked about himself.

'Madame de Mauriac, I am not at all an extraordinary young man. My life is so normal that I am sure if you knew the events, aside from the excitement of creative art, you would find it intolerably stupid. But while my outward life is serene, I have a strange febrility of imagination which impels me to add a certain extravagance of horror to whatever I paint. I have tried to keep it out of my portraits but I have, as you know, not succeeded, since you were attracted to them by that very quality. It was the same when I was a young child. They bought me pretty drawing-books with pictures in them to copy, but under my hand they became grotesque, horrible. I used to weep at the sight of them, and I would tear them up and bury the fragments rather than that my parents should see them. Then I would be punished for destroying my pretty book.'

He had declared that he was not extraordinary but now he glowed in the light of this bizarre confession.

'It is what I should expect,' said Madame de Mauriac, her face lighting with an expression of such cruel satisfaction that César involuntarily shuddered. He thought he had never seen so ferocious a mouth. It was the mouth of some small evil animal—a rat, a weasel, at bay.

She smiled.

'You find me repulsive, Monsieur.'

'No, no—' he stammered, his face reddening.

'Never mind. It is but natural. You see the bitterness and cruelty in my face. Lean closer and look. Tell me, what else do you see?'

He bent and looked into her eyes, heavy with passions brooded on in secret. Seductive, strangely disturbing eyes, the memory of which was always to remain with him.

'I see great pain,' he said, slowly, 'cruel jealousy, and love turned to hate.'

She drew a long, quivering sigh. 'Ah, how clever you are!'

For one instant she closed her eyes, as though there were depths in them which she would curtain from a gaze so penetrating. César leaned back in his chair, almost faint from the heavy perfume that rose from her couch, as from a bed of exotic flowers.

After a silence, she said in the voice still so surprisingly full of vitality:

'You will wonder, Monsieur Barbet, why I should wish to preserve on canvas feature which are so soon to decay. I will explain. This portrait is to be a legacy. A last gift to a husband, on whom I poured many gifts, not the least of which was the whole store of my love.'

'But, madame—' stammered César.

'I know what you are thinking. What a terrible picture! Unbearable to have in one's home. Horrible to own. That is true. . . . Well, he may destroy it if he will after one glance. But—if this portrait is as it should be—that one glance will sear his soul.' She lifted her lip in the smile that César found so repulsive, and added—'I want him to see what he has done to me.'

'Oh, Madame, do you think he deserves to be so hurt?'

Her eyes blazed up at him, but her head did not turn, nor did a finger stir of those wilted flower hands.

'Nothing that might be done to him could possibly repay him for the agony he has caused me. It is because of him that I lie here. He is a murderer. He has killed me.'

Her tense and vibrant tones rising from her immobile body were like the bursting into protest of a stone.

'Will you paint my portrait or will you not?' she demanded.

For a moment César hesitated. The thought of this commission was repellent to him. Then his febrile fancy asserted itself. To let himself go with such a subject! To present on canvas, embellished by his own mordant imagination, that face, the very throne of hatred and despair!

He bowed his head, but he could not meet her eyes. It was as though they had conspired to a crime together.

The portrait progressed day by day. Day by day César became more absorbed in his work. He thought of little else. He avoided his friends, excepting Chassel, in whom he had confided the story of the commission, begging him to find out if he could something about Madame de Mauriac and her husband.

Chassel found out she was the daughter of a wealthy banker, and had Polish blood. That de Mauriac, two years younger than she, was of a poor but aristocratic family, and that they had been separated for three years, some said owing to his infidelities, and others because of her unreasoning jealousy and exacting temper. No one knew where de Mauriac was. He had gone off with some other woman it was believed.

Madame de Mauriac talked little during the sittings. Obviously she was too weak for the effort of conversation. Frequently during the rest periods she would close her eyes and ignore him, but sometimes, her brilliant gaze would fasten upon his face, and she would tell with astonishing vigour some incident of her married life, trivial maybe, but always calculated to show de Mauriac in an evil light. She would watch catlike, the effect of her words on César. The expected expressions of sympathy were always ready on his lips but in reality he scarcely heard her. The face on the canvas held him with an hypnotic power. It rose between him and everything he saw. He had horrible dreams at night, and, waking, clammy with sweat, could scarcely wait till morning came when he might go on with his work. Once Madame de Mauriac was too ill to allow of his presence. For two days he wandered about, deeply disturbed. What if she should die, leaving the picture uncompleted?

When he was called to resume the sittings he found her much

worse. She looked more dead than alive and scarcely seemed to recognize him. But, when he carried the picture to her bedside, the sight of it put fresh life into her. The smile of satisfaction that curled her lip had something godlike about it.

The fever of his imagination unrestrained, that very fever fanned to intensity, knowing that the picture was not to be exhibited but might be as shocking as his perverse fancy and her pitiless spirit willed, César produced a portrait, unique in its horror.

When the last lines had been drawn about the mouth with its look of animal ferocity, the last luminous stroke accenting the eyes, César stepped back and looked at his work. . . . He was almost afraid to show it to Madame de Mauriac. But she asked in a low clear voice:

'Is it finished?'

'Madame, I cannot add another stroke.'

'Let me see it.'

Already propped on the pillows, she raised herself still higher. He had never seen her move before.

'It is the face of a dying woman,' she said.

'Madame—'

'Yes it is. . . . The face of a woman horribly murdered. . . . But I shall live on in it. . . . He may destroy it, but once he has seen it he can never forget. . . .'

She fell back with a gasp that was almost a cry. César thinking she had fainted returned the picture to its easel and flew to her side. She was perfectly conscious, and repeated the words 'never forget'. She was still smiling but the bitterness, the cruelty had gone out of her face, a faint colour had spread over it, her eyes had darkened with a strange tenderness. For a fleeting instant César saw her as she might once have been.

She asked him to call her nurse, and when the curious woman who had never seen the picture entered, he gathered up his materials and carried them to a small room assigned to him. This room was kept locked.

The next day he went early to look at the picture. He was told that Madame de Mauriac had taken a sudden turn for the worse. She could not see him, but he was handed a cheque for a much larger amount than he had asked for his work.

Curiously, the money meant nothing to him. He stuffed the cheque into his pocket, avoiding the eyes of the companion who brought it to him. He had a feeling that the entire household was seething with curiosity about the picture. All these dependents were conscious of the mystery surrounding it. He went into the room where it was and locked the door after him.

He stood before the picture and tried to put himself in the place of the husband who would see it only after his wife's death. What a shock it would be! Enough almost to unhinge a man's reason; that ghastly mask from which looked out those terrible eyes. Those eyes held him as so often the eyes from the bed had held him. That husband who had seen them glow up at him from her pillow where she lay flushed, adoring him. . . . Now these awful hollows, these shiny projections of bone almost through the parchment flesh! What thoughts for that man! What torture, the agony in those eyes, that crucified smile!

César pictured him standing before the picture bathed in an icy sweat of horror, remorse. He pictured him rising in the night unable to sleep because of the torture of it, standing before it in the stillness of the night, recalling the past. Even if he destroyed it, it was as she had said, he could never destroy the image of it, bitten into his soul by the acid of remorse. . . . It was not a sinister soul, César felt sure of that. He recalled certain incidents Madame de Mauriac had related to him. Even at the moment he had felt a kind of pity for de Mauriac. Now that pity rushed over him in a warm flood. What had the poor devil done that he should prepare such a torture for him? Besides he disliked Madame de Mauriac. She had the feminine qualities he found the most hateful—she was feline, relentless, self-centred, without imagination. He hated her.

The atmosphere in the room was dead. He flung open the window and let the fresh morning air sweep in. It was Autumn, and from a tree outside golden-tinted leaves were whirling on every gust. One of them blew in at the window and fluttered across the floor to his feet. He picked it up and laid it on his palm. A dead leaf, but beautiful in its death. Leaves . . . they were all leaves . . . soon to be blown away . . . an immense tenderness towards mankind possessed him . . . even towards that woman in the bedroom. He felt that the terrible terrors of his own imagination were in reality a form of pity. . . .

He took up his palette and a brush. For a long time he stood motionless before the picture. Then, like one in a dream, he began to change, very delicately, the expression of the face. Across the brow he laid the smooth brush strokes like soothing fingers. The frozen eyes he softened into pools of yearning and love, and the horrible smile of complacent cruelty he changed to a smile of forgiveness and pity. The emaciation, the pallor were still there, it was still the face of a dying woman, but in place of terror it now inspired—ah, what feeling would it inspire in Paul de Mauriac?

As César gazed into the face he had re-created, at the heavy locks framing the emaciated head, at the the hands lying like withered flowers on the embroidered counterpane, he felt that he should never again paint anything so beautiful, so disturbing. He would return to painting portraits that repelled rather than attracted patrons. But this time, gentleness, pity for de Mauriac like Autumn rain, had quenched the fever of his fancy.

Two days later Madame de Mauriac died. But to César she did not seem dead at all. For him she lived in the little locked room on his canvas. His mind dwelt constantly there brooding on the picture that changed from its second phase back to its first, and back again, with torturing rapidity. Not only that, it developed new phases. It was never still. It had a hundred moods like a perverse and wilful woman. It ogled him, it cajoled him, it glared at him with horror and with hate. He came to wish that he had never heard of Madame de Mauriac.

One day he was called over the telephone by de Mauriac himself.

'I am told by my wife's executors', said the voice of the man for whom César had endured so much, 'that I have been left a portrait painted by you. I have permission to go and get it. I wish very much that you would accompany me. I should like to ask you some questions.'

They arranged to go to the picture together that evening before dinner. In the car with which de Mauriac had called for César, the young painter tried to make out the features of the other. He saw only a slender figure, a pointed face, a sensitive compressed mouth. The eyes were hidden, shadowed by a drooping hat brim.

'I wish you would tell me something about this portrait of my wife,' said de Mauriac. 'How did you come to do it?'

'Madame de Mauriac had heard certain criticisms of my work, after an exhibition, which interested her.'

'I see. And she sent for you?'

'She was very ill then, wasn't she?'

'Very ill, indeed.'

'Yet she was determined to have this picture of herself before—the end?'

'Yes.'

'Monsieur Barbet, how did you find her as a subject? A woman, would you say who had suffered much in her life?'

'Yes,' said César, cautiously. 'But we all suffer, is it not so?'

'True, we all suffer,' returned de Mauriac and he added with apparent effort—'Do you know, Monsieur, I find the idea of looking at this portrait very difficult . . . almost unbearable. My wife and I could not get on. We had been apart for more than two years. It is with the greatest dread that I think of looking on this picture, painted just before she died. I dread to think what it may show me.'

'You need not dread looking at it,' said César. 'It is a very beautiful picture.'

De Mauriac cast a strange beseeching look at him from under the drooping brim. 'I could not come alone to look at it,' he said, with a shiver. 'I wanted you who had painted it to be with me. Thank you for coming.'

They scarcely spoke again till they reached the house. As they passed the door of the bedroom de Mauriac said—

'In there she died?'

César nodded. He took the key of the room which he for some reason had not wished to relinquish and unlocked the door.

'Ah, you have a key also,' said de Mauriac, surprised. 'The executors gave me this,' and he drew a second key from his pocket.

'They probably had forgotten the existence of this one,' returned César, his eyes already fixed on the portrait.

Slanting rays of sunshine touched the face into a divine radiance. The deep eyes seemed to glow with love, the dying lips to smile forgiveness, the pale flower hands to have fallen helpless after giving all. Only the strong rich hair, tossed over the embroidered pillow seemed to breathe perfumed sensuous recollections of bygone hours.

De Mauriac stood transfixed.

César thought: 'Thank God I saved him from the horror of what he might have seen.'

But, even as he was thinking this, he saw de Mauriac's cheeks bleach, and he felt a sinking in his own heart. A sense of foreboding crept over him, as though an unseen presence had glided into the room, a presence powerful for evil, animated by hate. A weakness came over him. He clutched de Mauriac's arm, and they stood like two children trembling before the picture.

Stronger than his pity for de Mauriac was her hatred for him. Had César absorbed it into his being during those long hours of the sittings, and now in spite of himself, irradiated it, as a kind of luminosity, that transfigured the portrait to its original horror, or had she indeed returned in spirit and looking through the painted eyes, leering through the painted lips, registered finally and terribly her loathing for her husband?

It was there, the cruel face, the very throne of hate, as César had seen it day after day, not to be denied. It was there but with something new—triumph at having overcome the laws of death.

De Mauriac turned a frozen face to César. 'What an abomination to put on canvas,' he said.

'You see it that way, too?' groaned the artist.

'What way?'

'This new way—no, the old—oh, I cannot explain! But has it changed since you came into the room?'

'Changed?'

'Yes, I tried . . . I did my best, but . . . she was stronger . . . even in death.'

'You are mad,' said de Mauriac. 'Only a madman could have painted such a picture. For Christ's sake, let me away from here before I too lose my reason!'

Without daring to look again on the portrait, he turned and fled through the house. César heard his footsteps echoing through the dismantled halls, and then he heard the hollow clang of the heavy front door.

He turned his eyes fearfully towards the picture. In the last dark flush of the sunset the illumined features faintly smiled at him in the expression of tender forgiveness which he had imposed on them.

ETHEL WILSON · 1888-1980

Mr Sleepwalker

During the time that Mary Manly's husband was in Australia, Mrs
Manly had an experience that was peculiar. I should like to say that
up to the time that her husband went to the war, Mrs Manly had never
shown any tendency to undue imagination, nervousness, hysteria,
nor to any of those weaknesses which are supposed to be the
prerogative of her sex, but are not—any of which might have been
considered responsible for the mounting episodes which culminated
in her nearly killing Mr Sleepwalker. Let us begin with Mary Manly,
because we do not know very much about the past of Mr Sleepwalker.
It would be provocative, but not fair, to speculate about Mr Sleepwalker's past, but, unless we knew something about his origin and
his history, the speculations would be useless, and disturbing.

Mary Davidson married Hugh Manly who was a forester in the
government service of British Columbia, and so able a man was Hugh
Manly in the matter of conservation of forests, marketing of lumber—
especially as these things applied to the province of British Columbia
whose forests are among her noblest treasures—that his government
began to send him on long journeys to foreign countries where export
trade might be developed, and it became no great surprise—but a
source of something like grief—to Mary when Hugh walked in for
dinner, and said later on in the evening as he often did, 'Well, it looks
as though I'm off again,' and Mary would learn that Hugh was being
sent by his government to South Africa, or to the United Kingdom, or
to Sweden, and so it was that Mary had to gear herself—as they
say—to these absences which became to her a mounting sorrow,
because she loved her husband beyond expression, and he loved
only her. Each time that Hugh left he said something like this, 'Next
time, darling, we'll see if you can't come too,' and Mary would say,
'Yes, next time, Hugh.' But next time Hugh might go to Hyderabad,
and how can a young wife whimsically accompany her husband to
Hyderabad, when there is a future to look to? I mention all this
because it is possible that the unhappiness of repeated separation, in

a world whose essential limit is bounded by the life and love of two people closely united, may have done something to Mary's otherwise calm and extroverted nature, and may have made her susceptible to outside influence of an esoteric, suprahuman, or even subhuman kind.

Just at the time when it seemed that Hugh had approached the point in his chosen profession at which he could say, 'Come with me and be damned to everything and hang the expense,' there came the war. Hugh went to the war, and Mary's sense of separation became exacerbated to the point where it was anguish. Are we who love each other so dearly, she said to herself, always to be deprived of our greatest joy, and have I to accustom myself to the theory that we belong to each other *in absentia* only, for it is an actual fact that the woman in the next apartment and I have lived for seven years with only one wall dividing us, and we do not belong to each other; while Hugh and I, who belong to each other, have lived for seven years with half the world between us most of the time. And now this war!

She busied herself at once, but in spite of being daily involved in responsibility and detail, her other life—that is to say, her absent life with Hugh—gradually became more real to her than the life of meetings, administration, billeting, in which her body was engaged, especially after Hugh left for overseas. ('Onlie the body's busy, and pretends.') Again I say that this other-worldness, which developed in Mary, and in many other young women like her during those years, but more in Mary Manly, because absence and frustration had already made some mark on her before the war began, may have been responsible for many queer things, one way and another. Directly the war was over, Hugh came home (fortunately) and was placed at once at the head of his department; and before the two had spent a month together, Hugh was sent to Australia. 'You're coming this time, Mary, and no nonsense about it,' said Hugh, and Mary with rapture prepared to go, broke her left elbow, and Hugh went without her.

To go now to Mr Sleepwalker.

Before Hugh went overseas he was stationed for a while in Winnipeg. Mary camp-followed him to Winnipeg, and it was in Winnipeg that she first saw Mr Sleepwalker. It was in a streetcar. The streetcar swinging along Portage Avenue was full, and Mary stood, holding onto a strap. She looked idly about her, and the swaying of the streetcar so determined that her eyes fell upon this person and that sitting in the row of seats immediately beside the entrance to the streetcar. She saw a small slim man sitting in this seat, with people on either side of him. Mary's whole attention was taken by this man, although no one else seemed to observe him, and as the body of someone swaying beside her interposed between her and the small man seated, she did not see him, and then she saw him again.

She became violently curious about the small man, and began to speculate about him. He appeared unaware of people around him, and certainly unaware of Mary's scrutiny. If I were accustomed to menservants, thought Mary, or if we lived in a different age, I should think that this man is, or has been, a 'gentleman's gentleman'. He is drilled in some precision of thought and action, and he hides behind that soft and deferential pose and immobility some definite and different entity. The small man sat erect, looking straight ahead of him, servile yet proud, his hands—in worn black gloves—folded on the head of his walking-stick which rested between his knees. His hat was a kind of square obsolete bowler. He wore a wing collar, and a small black tie of the kind known as a string tie. His black suit was old, worn, and very neat. Below the anachronistic hat was the face that so attracted and repelled Mary Manly. The features were neat and of a prissy femininity. The eyes were a warm stealthy reddish brown. His hair descended in reddish brown sideburns; otherwise he was clean-shaven. The hair was soft and unlike the hair of a man; in fact it resembled a soft fur. His mouth was set—so, with gentility. He is a mixture, thought Mary, as she watched the little man, now and again obscured from her, of gentility—a fake product of civilization—and of something feral, I do not know what. I seem to have seen those russet eyes, she continued to herself, in some animal. Is it a fox? No, I know no more about foxes than about gentlemen's gentlemen, and yet it seems like a fox. Or a watching hawk. Or some red-eyed rodent. And why is he in the middle of Canada, in Winnipeg, new city of grain, utility, and railroads, looking like this, dressed like this? He is as much a phenomenon in his dreadful respectability, riding on an unlikely streetcar in the city of Winnipeg, as if he wore a crown, or a grey topper, or a sarong. What life does he lead, and why is he here? The small man sat alone, it appeared, in his personal and genteel world, politely apart from those who rubbed shoulders with him or crowded his neatly brushed worn buttoned boots, and he looked straight ahead of him. Mary now avoided looking at the small man, because, so lively had been her interest in his peculiarities, she was afraid that he might become aware of her, and she did not want this to happen; so she turned her back, and faced in the other direction. Then she got off the streetcar and, for the moment, forgot him.

On the next evening, Hugh came in from the barracks, and they had dinner together. Mary tried to tell Hugh about the small man on the streetcar, but found that she was unable to describe him in such a way as would interest Hugh; and when Hugh told her, as he did, that he was ordered east and that he thought that embarkation would be the next step, this drove other thoughts from Mary's mind and she determined at once to move east also, because, as she said, 'We may as well continue living together, Hugh, in our own peculiar hap-hazard fashion. I have really loved it in Winnipeg, and who knows but that they may keep you in the east longer than you think. So I shall not go back to Vancouver. I shall go east, too.' Mary then prepared to go east, following Hugh, who left at a day's notice.

She had by this time attained (she thought) a fairly philosophic regard for things as they have to be, realizing of course that she was only one of the millions of persons—friends and enemies—whose lives were dislocated by war; that she could expect no special privilege because she was Mary Manly, wife of Hugh Manly (usually *in absentia*); and that she could and must assume the matter-of-fact-ness which is necessary in the successful conduct of life, which other people achieve so admirably, and which passes very well for courage. So she took life as it came, allowing herself to hope, as was natural, that her husband would be kept in Canada, although a part of each of them wished that he would be sent away and would see action, but safely, with everybody else, and no favours sought or granted. Mary said good-bye to her friends in Winnipeg, many of whom, like herself, were also in motion one way or another, and then, late one night, she boarded the eastbound train.

Because Mary was what is called a good train traveller, she soon bestowed her things neatly away and settled down for the remainder of the night in her lower berth. She slept at once, and only in a half-conscious and comfortable way was she aware of the stopping, starting, moaning, creaking of the great train. Suddenly she was awakened by a quiet. The train was standing still, perhaps in a siding, because there seemed to be no noise, or it may have been in the night-time stillness of the railway station of a town. Mary was half awake, and did not care. She was sleepily aware of stillness, of time and place suspended—and then of persons passing quietly, almost stealthily, in the aisle outside her curtain . . . the porter . . . perhaps

. . . passenger . . . porter . . . a murmur . . . a smell . . . earth . . . rotted wood . . . an animal . . . in the sleeping-car . . . impossible . . . a smell . . . earth . . . rotted wood . . . an animal . . . it passed. She fell asleep.

When day broke, the train had left Manitoba and was speeding into the vast western wooded lake-strewn regions of Ontario. The train stopped at Chapleau for twenty minutes. Mary got out, and wandered, as she always did at Chapleau station, to the small stone memorial that bears the name of Louis Hémon. Why, she wondered, did Louis Hémon come to Canada, write his book which, although unknown to most young Canadians, had already dimmed to a reputation faintly classic, and die? And why did Louis Hémon die, still young, at Chapleau, straggling rawly beside its railway station and its forests? A young man stood beside her and studied the carved words. Mary looked up at him and spoke tentatively. 'Do you know why Louis Hémon came here?' she asked.

'Sawry,' said the young man awkwardly, 'I never heard of him. I was kinda wondering myself who he was,' and he strolled away.

Mary turned and walked briskly up and down the platform, with the breeze and against the breeze that blew refreshingly through Chapleau. She heard the cry 'All aboard'. She turned towards her own porter at her own car. As she waited to mount the steps, she saw walking down the platform the small man in black whom she had seen in the Winnipeg streetcar. She was startled to see the small figure in motion. He walked, one might say, with as much stillness as he sat, regarding no one. He walked with his arms at his sides, guarded, genteel, like a black-suited doll. She climbed on the train, entered her car, and found her seat. She did not see him again.

When she joined Hugh in Halifax, there were many urgent things to think about without recalling to mind the small man whose hair was like fur, and so it seemed that he had never been. Hugh's convoy sailed, and Mary Manly went back to Vancouver and put herself at once to work.

It was months later that Mary Manly and Thérèse Leduc went to a movie together. At the end of the first picture, the two people who were sitting beside Mary went out, and, in the dark, another occupant took the seat beside her. Suddenly Mary's attention was taken from the screen by the scent, slight at first, then stronger, of, perhaps, an animal, or, perhaps, rotted wood, thick and dank (but how could it be rotted wood?). This smell was not at first heavy, but pervasive, and was very unpleasant to her. It became at last heavy in the air, and made her uneasy. It recalled to her a journey . . . a what? . . . some smell . . . not train smell . . . something that passed by. She tried to look at the person next to her without appearing to do so. This was difficult. She murmured to Thérèse Leduc, 'Do you smell anything queer?'

'No,' whispered Thérèse. 'What kind of thing?'

'I don't know,' answered Mary.

'I smell nothing,' said Thérèse.

The smell persisted. Suddenly the skin on the back of Mary's neck seemed to prickle. The man (it was a man) who sat beside her was small, and say very still. Mary sat still too, and thought, 'I want to get up and leave. I can't. That is unreasonable.' But at last she whispered to Thérèse, 'I'm sorry, Terry, but the man beside me *does* smell. Let's get out . . . perhaps we can move. Let's go your way.'

The two women got up and shuffled out of the long end of the row.

'How disgusting!' expostulated Thérèse.

'Yes, wasn't it? It really *was*,' said Mary, but she did not explain that the smell was not what Terry thought it was. Not dirt. Nothing like dirt. Something animal. Something wild. They found other seats, but Mary could not give her attention to the play. After the movie, she discovered also that she could not tell Thérèse about the small man, and about this animal smell which she had begun to associate with him. The thing was fanciful, and Mary did not like to be thought fanciful. Most of all, she did not like to admit to herself that she was fanciful. But there it was. She put her mind to other things, and that was not very difficult.

Some time later, as Mary rose from her knees in church, she did not need to look in order to see who it was that had come into the pew and had now dropped on his knees beside her. The feral scent wafted and then hung heavy. The small man in black drew himself up to his seat, and sat, doll-like, prim, just as (Mary knew) she had seen him sit in the streetcar on Portage Avenue. She saw him as plainly now as though her physical eyes observed the genteel shape, the russet fur of the sideburns, the prissy set of the mouth. He sat beside her, she knew, correct, genteel, yet vulpine, if it was vulpine. Mary's head began to spin. My imagination plays tricks, or does it? she asked herself. . . . Soon, of course, I shall see the two people in front of me move, turn slightly, disturbed by the smell that disturbs me. It cannot be to me, me alone, that it comes. He carries it round with him. Others *must* smell it—always. He is horrible, horrible. But now I can't leave

... I must stay ... he can never have observed me (for we never think, do we, that we are the observed ones; always we are the observers), I shall sit here. I shall stay for the service, and outstay him. But he is horrible. And a revulsion at the proximity of this small being almost overcame her, and she felt faint.

The little man sat still; his worn-gloved hands were on his knees, she could see. He took his Prayer Book and found his place, following the service respectfully, and in an accustomed manner. Mary's mind worked obliquely, directed, in spite of herself, towards the small man.

But the two people in front of her did not turn round, disturbed by the alien smell of rotted wood, of something animal, unknown.

Mary outsat the service. Then, with elaborate negligence, while the small man was leaving and after he had left, she put on her gloves, leaned back in her pew, and awaited the end of the slowly drifting columns of church-goers moving with slightly rocking inhibited motion down the aisles. Then she joined the departing stream at its end, went out into the open air, felt refreshed and, by a foolishly roundabout way, returned home.

I shall tell Hugh, she thought. It's very silly. I take this too seriously, and if I tell Hugh, I'll get rid of it. The thing bothers me out of all proportion. What concerns me is the war, and Hugh, and my jobs of work to do, and my life that I have always had; and a small being that smells like—perhaps—a weasel or a muskrat has no part and does not matter. So she wrote, but when she read the letter that she had written to Hugh, her story seemed idiotic. She tore the letter up, and wrote again and did not mention the small man. Hugh, she thought, would not in any case be amused. She could not make the story amusing. She could just make it sound silly. Hugh might be interested in a man that smelled like an animal (she had seldom smelled an animal), but she would not be able to conceal from him the fact that something was being established that affected her unreasonably and unpleasantly; it seemed to her that the small man, in spite of his apparent immobility and unawareness, was in some peculiar way aware of her also. This, of course, was possible, yet unlikely and very unpleasant. She neither saw the small man, nor did the strange scent reach her, for a long time.

One night it rained. Mary drove carefully in her little car. She picked up her cousin, Cora Wilmot, and drove through the lashing rain, and through the lights and reflections of lights, cross-hatched in the early dark in splashing pools and pavements, lighted by and left behind by the beams of her own headlights, onto Granville Street Bridge. She drove carefully in the late dinner-time traffic, peering through the rainstorm. She drove rather slowly. Cora, beside her, peered too. Then the thing nearly happened.

Just before Mary reached the narrow span of the bridge, Cora cried out, and stifled her cry. Off the slightly raised platform-like sidewalk of the bridge, into the light of the headlights of Mary's slowly moving car, stepped a small man. He faced the lights of the car, and seemed to look through the windshield of the car, and at, or into, the occupants. The lights showed all in one flash the white face (and Mary could see the lighted russet eyes), the intolerable propriety of mouth and chin, dark lines of hair framing the almost rectangular face. The man threw up his arms with the stiff gesture of a marionette. Mary swerved sharply to the left into whatever cars there might be, into the span, if need be, rather than touch or become involved in any way with the man who had stepped in front of her car. She did not touch him. She touched neither cars nor span. She did not speak. She drove to the end of the bridge, up Granville Street hill, through lights, darkness, and rain, and then she pulled up at the side of the road. She was trembling violently. Cora was voluble.

'That horrible little man!' she said, ' *What* was he doing? *Why* did he do it? He did it on purpose! No one crosses the bridge there! There's nothing to cross for! Oh Mary, what a narrow shave! Let's sit here a while. What a face! He looked as if he could see us, as if he was looking at us! I'll never forget him, will you? Do you feel like driving now? Let's get there, and then they'll give us a drink before dinner, and that will help us both.'

'Yes,' said Mary, and she drove on. He saw me, she thought, as I drove so slowly in the lights, and then stepped out.

Before the end of the year, Hugh came home, the war being incredibly over. And then, as I said, Hugh went to Australia, and Mary, with the complicated fracture of her left arm in a sling, stayed at home.

Many and many a time, towards the end of the war, and now, when alone, when sleeping, and at waking, she seemed to see the doll-like figure of the small man with her motor lights full on his white face. She saw a marionette's gesture—two dark arms flung stiffly upwards, she swerved, she drove on in her dream. And then, the obsession became less frequent. Nevertheless, within herself, she knew that she had begun to be afraid of something.

Hugh wrote from Melbourne, 'I'm going to be here longer than we thought. Just as soon as the elbow is better enough cable me. I'll advise you, and you get a passage by air. And at last. . . .' The load of aggravation lifted from Mary, and she began to lie about her elbow in order to get away and to join Hugh in Australia. However, their friend the doctor, Johnny Weston, put her off for a week.

One afternoon she returned from John's surgery with the permission that she might now make arrangements for her flight to Australia, and so she cabled to Hugh. Such a thing as this had never happened to Mary Manly before. She went home, and in her ecstasy, her rapture, she telephoned Thérèse Leduc and Cora, and anybody else that came to mind, to tell them that she was flying to Australia to join Hugh.

There came a ring at the door of the flat. Still careful of her clumsy left arm, Mary went lightly to the door and opened it. A feral smell entered the apartment, followed by the small respectable man who had stood outside Mary's door and had rung her doorbell. The man was dressed as usual in black. As he stepped humbly but without question into the hall, he took off his obsolete square-shaped bowler hat, laid it upon a table, turned and shut the door in a serviceable manner, and then advanced obsequiously on Mary. In his hand he carried a small black valise. Scent hung heavy and it was the smell of fear.

Mary was aghast. Her right hand flew to her mouth. She pressed the back of her hand to her mouth and gazed at the small man over her hand. She did not think, I am alone in this apartment with this unpleasant little creature. She did not think at all. The air was full of the dank wild earthy smell of something old and unknown. She backed, and obsequiously the small man advanced upon her. She saw the russet animal eyes, the reddish animal fur. She saw the prissy gentility of the lips. She smelled the smell.

'Sleepwalker,' said the man softly, looking at her.

Mary snatched up a small bronze vase, and hit the man hard upon the side of the head. He looked at her with infinite surprise and reproach, swayed, and sank to the floor. He lay there like a large black-garbed doll, and blood began to flow from the wound on his head. His eyes were closed and he was very pale.

Mary stood looking down upon him, and tried to measure what she had done. 'Three minutes ago,' she thought, 'I was mad with joy because I was going to Hugh, and now perhaps I have killed a man who is a stranger.' She now felt curiously hard and not at all frightened. She went to the telephone and called John Weston at his surgery.

'John,' she said, 'this is Mary Manly. I am at home. I think I have killed a man. Please come.' And she hung up the telephone and went back to the small man who lay as she had left him.

I am very stupid, thought Mary, because I do not know whether he is unconscious or whether he is dead, and I don't know how to find out such things. At least I will bathe his head, and perhaps if he is unconscious he will rally a bit. She got water and a cloth, and although it was repugnant to her, she knelt down and bathed the wound which she had inflicted on the small respectable man. He stirred. He opened his eyes and looked steadily at her. She rose to her feet and looked down at him.

'Dear lady,' whispered the man, still prostrate on the floor, 'whatever made you do that to me?' and his eyes were indeed the eyes of an animal.

Well, thought Mary, I can see that this is going to be a very odd conversation. She could not answer his question, and so she said, 'I am very, very sorry that I have done this to you, but why are you here? And why did you walk into my flat like that? And what was that you said to me when you came in?' It gave her satisfaction that John Weston would soon come, and would act as some kind of solvent to this situation.

The man sat up slowly, and felt his head. He looked at his red hand with surprise, and again looked up at Mrs Manly.

'Name of Sleepwalker,' he said, 'carrying a line of ladies' underwear samples of special buys in rayon, silk, crêpe, also ladies' hosiery put out by the Silki-Silk Company with agents in all major cities of Canada,' and he looked at the black valise which lay where it had fallen.

'Oh,' said Mary, feeling very silly indeed. 'And do you really mean that your name is Sleepwalker?'

'Name of Handel Sleepwalker,' said Mr Sleepwalker, and subsided again into a faint on the floor.

The doorbell rang, and Mary opened the door to Dr Weston. Because Dr Weston was ruffled, and had—unwillingly—left his patients when Mary summoned him so imperatively and strangely, he had, since leaving his consulting-room, built up a genuine and justified annoyance mixed with real uneasiness, and because he could find no other object for his annoyance, he had hung it upon Mary Manly. Therefore by the time Dr Weston arrived at Mary's apartment he was very angry indeed with her for having killed a man at a quarter past five in the afternoon, for having taken him forcibly from his consultations, and for having chosen to do this at a time when Hugh was not at home and therefore was unable to take the matter in hand. Although a very good friend of Hugh and Mary, Dr Weston was not at that moment in the frame of mind to shoulder the results of murder. This is why, when Mary opened the door with a sense of relief, John Weston dismayed her by a complete absence of sympathy; he turned on her an angry face, and roared at her in an injured manner, 'What on earth *have* you been doing?' as if she were guilty. Well, so she was.

Mary, aware of all that had gone before that was so ridiculously unexplainable at that very instant, realized that she had to cope with her own emotions, to attend—in the first place—to Mr Sleepwalker who lay inert on the living-room floor, and to manage Dr Weston either by returning anger for anger, innocence for anger, or by disregarding anger. This latter she decided to do.

'Come,' she said. She turned and indicated Mr Sleepwalker with an air quite sublime. 'You see!'

When Dr Weston saw the actual body of Mr Sleepwalker lying on the floor of the room in which Dr Weston and his wife had so often enjoyed a cocktail, and saw Mr Sleepwalker's blood upon the carpet, and saw Mary standing there pale, helpless, bandaged, and gentle, other feelings began to take possession of him. He kneeled down and examined the prostrate one. Then he looked up and said to Mary in a fretful tone, 'He's not dead at all!'

Well, really, thought Mary, this is too much! Does John expect that one should make sure of *killing* someone before disturbing him! John is going to be aggravating, I can see. But she said simply, 'Oh, John, I am so thankful. This has been very alarming.'

'Did *you* hit him?' asked Dr Weston, scrambling to his feet.

'Oh yes, I hit him.'

'Why. . . ?'

'He *terrified* me,' said Mary, 'He stole into the room when I opened the door, and followed me up, and did not explain his business, and then he said something that frightened me very much. And here I was with my bad arm and alone, and before I realized what I was doing, John, I hit him with that little vase.'

'What did he say to you?' asked Dr Weston.

Mr Sleepwalker spoke from the floor. His eyes were closed. He said softly, 'I did not indeed desire to frighten the dear lady; I merely told the dear lady my name.'

Dr Weston shot a very baleful look at Mary; he became suspicious of her again (and there were all those patients in the waiting-room).

'And what *is* your name?' asked Dr Weston.

'Sleepwalker,' said Mr Sleepwalker, opening his eyes.

'And where do you live?' asked Dr Weston.

Mr Sleepwalker closed his eyes again. 'I am afraid', he said, 'that for the moment I am unable to remember.'

'Well, where would you like us to take you?' asked the doctor.

'Yes, where would you like us to take you?' asked Mary, eagerly.

Mr Sleepwalker paused for a moment. Then, 'I would like to stay ere,' he said.

'That is impossible, quite impossible,' said Dr Weston crossly. 'You can take him to the hospital, Mary. He's all right to move, and a day or two will be all that's needed.'

'John,' said Mary, taking the doctor aside, 'do you notice a very queer smell in this room?'

'No, I don't,' said the doctor. 'Do you?'

She did not answer. 'I will get an ambulance if you will arrange with the hospital,' she said.

'I would much prefer,' said a silky voice from the floor, 'if the dear lady would take me to the ospital erself. Far be it indeed to go in an ambulance.'

Mary scowled at the doctor, who said at once, 'No, we'll get an ambulance. See if you can sit up now.'

Mr Sleepwalker obediently sat up, a little black figure with legs outstretched on the floor. The doctor supported him.

'Now into this chair.'

'I am a poor man,' said Mr Sleepwalker, sitting up straight and stiff in the chair, with his disfigured head.

'I will pay for your ambulance, Mr Sleepwalker, and I will pay for your days in the hospital as long as Dr Weston says that you must stay,' said Mary.

'Oh, ow kind, dear lady,' said Mr Sleepwalker humbly, and Mary thought, What a brute I am, I've never abased myself and really apologized for hitting him! 'I shall get you some tea,' she said. Meanwhile, the doctor was busy at the telephone. He looked at his watch. 'Don't leave me!' murmured Mary as she brushed past him in the hall, and Dr Weston gave her an unaffectionate look. She took a tray in to Mr Sleepwalker, who gazed round the room as though he were memorizing it.

'I shall burn this tray, break the cup and saucer, give away the chair, and send the carpet to the cleaners, or we can sell it—in fact, we might leave the flat. I can't bear to have had this little horror in the room,' Mary said to herself unfairly, forgetting that she was very lucky.

Mr Sleepwalker coughed. 'One thing may I hask,' he said.

'What?' said Mary.

'I should like to hask,' he said, 'that the dear lady will visit me in the ospital.'

Mary considered. That was the very least she could do.

'Yes, of course I will,' she said, trying to sound hearty.

'Oh, thank you, *thank* you,' said Mr Sleepwalker. The doctor came out of the hall.

'I have arranged for the bed and the ambulance,' he said, looking again at his watch. 'Some time I will hear more about this.' He had one leg out of the door.

'You will stay!' besought Mary with agitation, seizing his arm.

The doctor put down his overcoat again. 'Very well, I will stay,' he said irritably, and thought of his waiting-room. He did not like Mary Manly at all just now, whether because she had or had not killed Mr Sleepwalker (although on the whole he was relieved that she had not); but chiefly he disliked Mary because she had behaved in an irrational manner—he disapproved of people being irrational—and had called him away from his surgery in the middle of the afternoon. He whirled to the telephone, and Mary heard him say brusquely, 'I'll be back. Keep Mrs Jenkins, and tell Mr Howe I'll see him tomorrow, and explain to the two others that I'll see them tomorrow, and give them a time, and tell Mrs Boniface that I'll drop in on the way home, and don't let the Jackson boy go home till I've seen him, and. . . . '

'Oh Lord,' thought Mary, contrite, 'what have I done to all these people! Poor Johnny!' and she tried to look pathetic, but it was no good.

The ambulance arrived, and Dr Weston sped away. Two burly ambulance men helped Mr Sleepwalker; he walked between them in his still fashion. One big man carried his absurdly small valise. The other one took charge of the obsolete hat. Mary stood.

At the door Mr Sleepwalker made as if to turn.

'I do hask, dear lady, that you will recollect your promise?' he said, with a question.

'I will indeed,' said Mary heartily and with the greatest repugnance.

She heard the door close. She turned and opened all the windows, and did what she could to the room. Then she telephoned Cora. 'Cora,' she said, 'a very peculiar thing has happened. I won't tell you over the telephone, but here, but for the grace of God, sits your cousin, the famous murderess . . . ' a thought checked her, 'or,' and she laughed, 'the famous huntress.'

'What *do* you mean!' asked Cora.

'Well,' said Mary slowly, 'you remember the night we nearly ran that man down on the bridge?'

'Yes, yes,' said Cora.

'Well,' continued Mary slowly, 'it's the same man. Coincidence, of course, of the most extraordinary kind' (was it coincidence?) 'and it's left me rather shaken.'

'Too much happens to you. Come at once and have dinner,' said Cora.

'I will,' said Mary gratefully.

As Mary Manly went to her cousin's house, she asked herself some questions. If I wished to go the bottom of the queerness of this, if I had any scientific curiosity and not just a detestation of the whole affair, I would take up a notebook and pencil, and question that . . . that . . . person (she avoided even his name). I would say to him, Was your aunt a fox, or was your grandmother a weasel, and of course, he would say no, and where should I find myself then? I could ask him if he seeks me in particular, and how, and why. But I am such a coward that I don't want to know. Then I would say, My good sir, do you know that you smell? And if he said yes, I should have to ask him, Do some people (such as I) and not other people, recognize this animal (yes, I should have to say 'animal') scent? I can see how totally impossible such a conversation is, and so I shall leave it alone, and shall admit, to myself, and not to others, only the fact that this man frightens me. . . .

When Mary left Cora the next morning (for Cora easily persuaded her to stay the night), she knew that the talk of her attack upon Mr Sleepwalker would spread among her friends and acquaintances, and that it would be well and properly launched by Cora. She realized that she would be the object of universal pity ('Poor Mrs Manly, wasn't it dreadful for her! The man, my dear, walked straight into the flat, and there was Mary all alone, with a broken arm. . . . I think she's very good not to prosecute! And so brave. The most extraordinary coincidence my dear! Cora Wilmot says. . . . ') and that this was not quite fair to Mr Sleepwalker who, after all, was the one who had been hit on the temple with a bronze vase and was now in hospital. She knew that she would be decried as soft, foolish, too kind because she had provided the ambulance and was about to pay the hospital bill. However, she had to choose between all or nothing, and the section of the story which was in Cora's possession, and which Cora would launch on all their acquaintances with her well-known energy, approximated to nothing, and that was best.

The following afternoon Mary said to herself as she alighted clumsily with parcels at the hospital, This (calling on this man, I mean) is the most unpleasant thing that I have deliberately done in my whole life. I don't call hitting . . . Mr Sleepwalker . . . deliberate. It was instinctive. If only Hugh were with me it would be easier. However, as she had that afternoon received a cable from Hugh which read: 'Cheers and cheers take first passage and cable me', she felt more carefree than she would have thought possible. I can tell this . . . individual . . . she thought, that I am going to Australia (that seems far enough way)—which is true—that I'm going tomorrow, which is not true, but it is true enough. And she entered the hospital.

She found Mr Sleepwalker propped up a little on his pillows, looking very pale. His head was bandaged, and when she saw the bandage, she felt much more guilty than when, in the storm of terror, she had struck down Mr Sleepwalker and had seen him lying on the floor, with blood flowing upon the carpet.

Patients in the adjacent beds regarded her apathetically. Mr Sleepwalker looked earnestly, too earnestly, at her. I should, of course, give him my hand, she said to herself, this hand which has struck him down. But she did not wish to do so. She found that her feelings were strangely involved. In order to avoid touching Mr Sleepwalker's hand, and for no more altruistic reason, Mary had filled her good hand with flowers, and carried magazines and a box of chocolates under her arm. As she disposed these articles awkwardly about Mr Sleepwalker's bed, the handshaking moment passed, as she had intended it should. A nurse, seeing her arm in a sling, brought forward a chair. Mary smiled at her, thanked her, and sat down.

'I hope you are not too uncomfortable,' she said.

'Oh, no, thank you, dear lady,' said Mr Sleepwalker, 'this is a very nice ospital, nicer than what I was in in England that time the dogs bit me.'

'Dogs. . . !' said Mary.

'Ounds,' said Mr Sleepwalker.

Mr Sleepwalker's bandages really afflicted Mary. They made her feel more guilty even than her own conscience. However, she could not afford to get soft about Mr Sleepwalker, even though she had hit him with a vase.

'I am sorry that I cannot have a nice long chat,' she said untruthfully, 'but the fact is that I am flying to Australia tomorrow to join my husband.'

'Come a little closer, dear lady,' said Mr Sleepwalker. His reddish eyes were fixed upon her. Mary made hitching noises with her chair, but she was near enough. She began to feel faint. 'I should like to go to Australia,' he said. 'Oh, ow I should like!'

'Australia is, I am sure, a very nice country,' replied Mary with considerable idiocy. I must keep this impersonal, she thought, and proceeded to talk about Australia, of which she knew very little. 'So you see I cannot stay any longer; in fact, I must go. Everything will be arranged, the bill, you know. I am so very sorry for what I did to you. It was really some terrible misunderstanding.'

The little man in the bed continued to look earnestly at her.

'It as been a pleasure indeed to meet you, dear lady,' he said in his soft voice. (What an extraordinary statement! thought Mary.) 'May I thank you indeed for your kindness, and may I tell you, dear lady, ow grateful I ave always been to you, and ow I ave frequently and in oh ever so many places enjoyed your delicious smell . . . fragrance, I *should* say.'

'My. . . ! my. . . !' stammered Mary, and sprang to her feet. She stood for one moment looking down at Mr Sleepwalker. Then she turned and the patients saw her running like a hare out of the ward.

A.M. KLEIN · 1909-1972

No Traveller Returns . . .

I stepped into my roadster, and began swallowing miles. The car agglutinated strip after strip of ribboned road. The engine throbbed like the heart of a dissected frog.

Yesterday I had said: I will carry my nostrils away from the smell of fried flesh. I will escape the ratty whisper in the ear. I will avoid the apothecary taste upon the tongue.

And now I was swallowing miles. Into a long highwayed vista, flanked by overhanging elms, I shot, like one motoring through a framed picture. Now and again, I crossed a wooden bridge whose broken boards rattled under the wheels, a rustic xylophone. I clung to the side of mountains; I leaped into the valleys. The car sped like an electric current.

Suddenly I came upon a stretch of road, with clovered meadowland on either side. It was a scented Paisley shawl before my eyes. But the odour always and ever became the odour of ether, and the noise of the machine was the noise of pestle in mortar.

Then I stepped on the gas. I seemed to feel a traffic cop behind me. A ghost on a motorcycle. I looked into the mirror. It was not Dr Constantine Nekrovivos. I saw nothing, nothing except scenery.

Yesterday the doctor was alive. Then at twelve o'clock of the night they sat him down on a seat. Professor Constantine Nekrovivos, holding the chair of electro-dynamics. Then they pulled a switch. The power of eight hundred ordinary sized electric bulbs raced through his Greek body. Professor emeritus. A doctor pronounced the doctor dead.

But I knew better. Himself he told me that he knew the formulae for life. He could mix poisons for death; and he could brew a broth of eternal wakefulness.

When they sat him down upon the seat, he surely hated me.

It was not my fault. They said, Your name is Armstrong, and you are a press-agent. I said yes. They said, You also used to insure your friends. I said yes. They said, You had many friends. I said yes. They said, Then your friends would fall sick, and Dr Nekrovivos would come, always Dr Nekrovivos, and he would prepare a prescription, and your friends would die, and you would travel to a new city where you had more friends, and you would insure them, and the doctor would come, always Dr Nekrovivos, and the friends would die. I said, Yes, yes, yes, yes.

Then they let me go.

At the trial, the prosecutor made me repeat what he said. Then Constantine's lawyer got up and called me a rat. He lifted his hand in the air, between finger and thumb dangled something and shouted, His own sweet hide. Twenty-four nostrils curled and seemed to snort squealer. Twenty-four eyes looked sorry that I had been given the protection of the Court.

When they led the doctor away, he stuck out his tongue, made with his fingers as if scissoring it, and then pointed at me.

So I didn't want to be around the place any longer; and on the following morning set out to put as many miles as possible between myself and the professor, his potions, and his upholstered seat.

The sun was a hot brasier. Clouds hung in the sky like an ad for featherbeds. On hill and valley, the grass was verdant with the varying shades of green. Now and again, a wind sallied forth from nowhere, and thither disappeared. It was a beautiful day. I sped along, only occasionally hearing the crackle of voltaged copper, only occasionally smelling a nostalgic grain of poison.

Suddenly the sky went dark. Black clouds rolled in the heavens, like barrels. The wind stevedored them one against the other, making thunderous noise. Their metal bands snapped lightning. Raid poured down, a million broken casks.

I flew along in my motorized shell. But the storm was so wild, I had to stop. I noticed that I was near a railway station. I looked at the name. Once, on an envelope, I had seen it before. Then I remembered that the doctor's brother sold banana-splits in this town.

The unspigoted barrels continued to drench the world. Thunders roared in their cages. Lightnings shot across the sky like erratic lines on a blueprint chart. I crawled along the road. A half-a-mile away, a stranger, issuing from the woods, hailed me. I said, Hop in.

We drove on. Through the corner of my eye, I regarded him. He had a crescent-shaped scar upon his forehead. He moved in his clothes as if they were too big for him. When he spoke, his voice was anaemic. His fingers looked earthy, like roots recently torn from the ground. He smelled as if he had slept with worms.

He told me that he was a herbalist. He always went out to the woods before a storm. That was the best time to pluck out roots, mysterious roots which he called by a Greek name. And shriek like mandrakes torn out of the earth, he said, and smiled with totally black teeth. The corners of his mouth curled, like the fretwork of a violin. It seemed to me that I once knew a white smile like that.

The thunder was rolling over on its belly. Soon the storm would be dead. The crescent-scarred stranger talked much, using botanical terms. Once he leaned over from his side of the seat, and whispered in my ear . . . I am about to make a great discovery. That whisper was familiar; it was the shadow of an echo of a voice that I had heard a long time ago, I thought.

We became very friendly. I will confide in you, he said. I trust you. You look like one who wouldn't spill a secret. I have unearthed, unearthed great wisdom. I have found the formula for life. Somewhere someone had said that to me. I looked again at the crescent-scarred stranger. It was not Dr Constantine Nekrovivos. He caught my look, and said: *Similes similibus curant.* Poison fought with poison; bane with bane battled; electricity shocked by electricity. He smiled his sable smile.

I drove into the courtyard of an inn. I invited the stranger. He opened his mouth so that I expected *Yes, only too pleased, certainly,* to issue forth, curtseying; but instead, he closed his mouth slowly, as if retracting a yawn, and said nothing.

At the table I noticed that he wore neither tie nor collar. I don't dress formal to go out into a storm, he said. I am much too preoccupied with herbs to worry about a cravat.

He spoke unremittingly. I did not notice that he touched no food. I have peeped through a knot-hole in the fence around hell, he said. Then he spoke about the fine furnishings in the inn. I have clutched, he said, roots; and I have heard the gossip of the worms. Herbs, he said, there are many miracles that happen underground.

Where do you live, I asked. I hoped incidentally that he would tell me who he was, precisely.

I live in a place in the woods where nobody can find me, he said. Then he went on to talk about plants, and their souls, especially carnivorous plants. Hylozoic, he said with his anaemic voice. Even a man, lying six fathoms deep beneath the sod, was a plant. A creeper, he said. His mouth was a humorous slit.

Then he bent over the table, his scarred forehead almost touching mine, and said, In fact I am interested also in the herbs which grow downwards from the sky. Such as lightning. He began to tell me about a most refreshing massage which he had once enjoyed from a lightning bolt, when a wet voice was heard in the courtyard.

The innkeeper was greeting a friend. What's this new style, he was saying. Evidently the man was naked, except for shorts. In staccato gasps, the friend was telling, like a courier returned from hot pursuit, of how a man, dressed only in winter underwear, had rushed out of the woods, in the rain, and had ordered him to undress, and had robbed him of his coat and trousers.

I turned to my guest at the table to make some comment upon these strange doing. He had melted away, as if swallowed by some carnivorous invisibility.

Upon the menu-card before me was written, with the waiter's pencil I later discovered, as part of the dessert: *I will be back to pay the bill.*

Then I realized who he was. The handwriting was familiar. I had seen it on prescriptions, and now I saw it on my menu. The voice was a recognizable echo. Even the face was a clay mask of a face I had known. Only it had had no crescent-shaped scar on its forehead.

I stepped into the roadster, and sped back to the city. The car vomited forth all the miles it had so hastily swallowed. I rushed into the warden's well-appointed cell.

He is after me, I said. Who, he said. The doctor, Dr Constantine Nekrovivos, I said.

The warden laughed a routine laugh. Calm yourself, he said. The doctor passed away last night at seven minutes after midnight. His brother, the confectionery man, called for his body early this morning. He wanted to bury it in the family plot. We dressed it in winter underwear,—tuxedoes are not included in the services here—and I sent it along with some guards. I presume he was buried this afternoon. He's dead, as dead as if he had taken his own prescriptions.

I saw him this afternoon, I said. I saw him, I spoke to him this afternoon.

The warden looked at me, measuring me for a straitjacket.

Do me a favour, I said. Phone the local sexton and ask him to go to the cemetery. Please, I said, he's after me.

Alright, the warden said.

When he put the receiver down he said, The sexton says he was covering the coffin with earth, when the storm broke, and he left the grave temporarily unfilled. He's going back now. He will phone again.

What will I do, I said. Where can I run away?

Travel, the warden said. Europe.

Greece, maybe, I said.

We both waited for the telephone ring to shred the air.

He said he would be back to pay the bill, I said.

You've got the jitters, the warden said. If you wish, I could give you accommodation here.

He was humouring me. A giggle jangled in the warden's throat, like keys.

Then the telephone rang. The warden stepped into an adjacent room. He came back. Looked as if he had spent a week in the hole. That's strange, he said.

What did he say, I said. What did he say.

Lightning struck the coffin, the warden said, went right through the coffin lid, and the coffin is empty.

I told you, I said. He's going to get me. Then my voice choked.

ROBERTSON DAVIES · b. 1913

Dickens Digested

In this, the centenary of his death, I should like to speak well of
Charles Dickens; the literary world has united to do him honour as
one of the half-dozen foremost geniuses of our great heritage of
poetry, drama and the novel. That I should have to stand before you
tonight and direct at that Immortal Memory a charge of—the word
sticks in my throat, but it must be given voice—a charge of Vampirism,
repels and disgusts me, but when Dickens has cast this hateful
shadow across the quadrangle of Massey College, I have no other
course.

This is what happened.

It was the best of times, it was the worst of times, it was the age of
wisdom, it was the age of foolishness, it was the epoch of belief, it
was the epoch of incredulity—in short, it was the beginning of the
autumn term, and the year was 1969. I met the incoming group of
Junior Fellows, and among the thirty-five or so new men were some
who immediately attracted my attention—but the subject of my story
was not one of these. No, Tubfast Weatherwax III had nothing about
him to draw or hold one's interest; he was a bland young man, quite
unremarkable in appearance. Of course, I was familiar with his
dossier, which had been thoroughly examined by the Selections
Committee of the College. He came to us from Harvard, and he was
a young American of distinguished background—as the dynastic
number attached to his name at once made clear. His mother, I know,
had been a Boston Winesap. But young Weatherwax bore what one
politely assumed to be—in republican terms—a noble heritage lightly, and indeed unobtrusively.

He was a student of English Literature, and he sought a Ph.D. When
I asked him casually what he was working at, he said that he thought
perhaps he might do something with Dickens, if he could get hold of
anything new. I considered his attitude rather languid, but this is by
no means uncommon among students in the English graduate school;
hoping to encourage him I said that I was certain that if once Dickens

thoroughly took hold of him, he would become absorbed in his subject.

Ah, fatal prophetic words! Would that I might recall them! But no—I, like poor Tubfast Weatherwax, was a pawn in one of those grim games, not of chance but of destiny, which Fate plays with us in order that we may not grow proud in our pretension to free will.

I saw no more of him for a few weeks, until one day he came to see me, to enquire about Dickens as a dramatist. I am one of the few men in the University who has troubled to read the plays of Charles Dickens, and relate them to the rest of his work, so this was normal enough. He knew nothing about the nineteenth-century theatre, and I told him I thought Dickens' drama unlikely to yield a satisfactory thesis to anyone but an enthusiastic specialist. 'And you, Mr Weatherwax,' I said, 'did not seem very much caught up in Dickens when last we spoke.'

His face changed, lightening unmistakably with enthusiasm. 'Oh, that's all in the past,' he said; 'it's just as you said it would be—I feel that Dickens is really taking hold of me!'

I looked at him more attentively. He had altered since first I saw him. His dress, formerly that elegant disarray that marks the Harvard man—the carefully shabby corduroy trousers, the rumpled but not absolutely dirty shirt, the necktie worn very low and tight around the loins, in lieu of a belt—had been changed to extremely tight striped trousers, a tight-waisted jacket with flaring skirts, and around the throat what used to be called, a hundred and fifty years ago, a Belcher neckerchief. And—was I mistaken, or was that shadow upon his cheeks merely the unshavenness which is now so much the fashion, or might it be the first, faint dawning of a pair of sidewhiskers? But I made no comment, and after he had gone I thought no more about the matter.

Not, that is, until the Christmas Dance.

There are many here who remember our Christmas Dance in 1969. It was a delightful affair, and, as always the dress worn by the College men and their guests ran through the spectrum of modern university elegance. I myself always wear formal evening clothes on these occasions; it is expected of me; of what use is an Establishment figure if he does not look like an Establishment figure? But somewhat to my chagrin I found myself outdone in formality, and by none other than Tubfast Weatherwax III. And yet—was this the ultimate in modern fashion, or was it a kind of fancy dress? His bottle green tail coat, so tight-waisted, so spiky-tailed, so very high in the velvet collar and so sloping in the shoulders; his waistcoat of garnet velvet, hung all over with watch-chains and seals depending from fobs; his wondrously frilled shirt, and the very high starched neck-cloth that came up almost to his mouth; his skin-tight trousers, and—could it be? yes, it certainly was—his varnished evening shoes, were in the perfection of the mode of 1836, a date which—it just flashed through my mind—marked the first appearance of *Pickwick Papers*. And his hair—so richly curled, so heaped upon his head! And his sidewhiskers, now exquisite parentheses enclosing the subordinate clause which was his innocent face. It was—yes, it was certainly clear that Tubfast Weatherwax III had got himself up to look like the famous portrait of the young Dickens by Daniel Maclise.

But his companion! No Neo-Victorian she. I thought at first that she was completely topless, but this was not quite true. Braless she certainly was, and her movement was like the waves of ocean. As for her mini, it was a *minissima*, nay, a *parvula*. She was a girl of altogether striking appearance.

'Allow me to present Miss Angelica Crumhorn,' said Weatherwax, making a flourishing bow to my wife and myself; 'assuredly she is the brightest ornament of our local stage. But tonight I have tempted her from the footlights and the plaudits of her ravished admirers to grace our academic festivities with beauty and wit. Come, my angel, shall we take the floor?'

'Aw, crap!' said Miss Crumhorn, 'where's the gin at?'

I knew her. She was very widely known. Indeed, she was notorious, but not as Angelica Crumhorn, which I assume was her real name, but as Gates Ajar Honeypot, star of the Victory Burlesque. She was the leader of an accomplished female group called the Topless Tossers.

If there is one point that has been made amply clear by the university revolt of the past few years, it is this: students will no longer tolerate an educational institution which professes to stand *in loco parentis*; good advice is absolutely *out*. Therefore I did not call young Weatherwax to me the following morning and tell him that he stood on the brink of an abyss, though I knew that this was the case. It was not that, at the dance, he had eyes for no one but Gates Ajar Honeypot; in that he was simply like all the rest of us, for as she danced, Miss Crumhorn gave a stunning exhibition of the accordion-like opening and closing of her bosom by means of which she had won the professional name of Gates Ajar. No, what was wrong was that when he looked at her he seemed to be seeing someone else— some charming girl of the Regency period, all floating tendrils of hair, pretty ribbons, modest but witty speech, and flirtatious but essentially chaste demeanour. I saw trouble ahead for Tubfast Weatherwax III, but I held my peace.

I thought, you see, that he was trying to be like Charles Dickens. This happens very often in the graduate school; a young man chooses a notable literary figure to work on, and his subject is so much more vital, so infinitely more charged with life than he himself, that he begins to model himself on the topic of his thesis, and until he has gained his Ph.D.—and sometimes even after—he acts the role of that great literary man. You notice it everywhere. If you were to throw an orange in any English graduate seminar you would hit a foetal Henry James, or an embryo James Joyce; road-company Northrop Fryes and Hallowe'en versions of Marshall McLuhan are to be found everywhere. This has nothing to do with these eminent men; it is part of the theopathetic nature of graduate students; the aspirant to academic perfection so immerses himself in the works of his god that he inevitably takes on something of his quality, at least in externals. It is not the fault of the god. Not at all.

Very well, I thought. Let Tubfast Weatherwax III take his fair hour; he has heard of Dickens' early infatuation with Maria Beadnell; let him try on Dickens' trousers and see how they fit.

This meant no small sacrifice on my part. Whenever I met him, I said, as I should, 'Good-day, Mr Weatherwax;' and then I had to listen to him shout, 'Oh, capital, capital! The very best of days, Master! Whoop! Halloo! God bless us every one!' Or if perhaps I said, 'Not a very fine day, Mr Weatherwax,' he would reply: 'What is the odds so long as the fire of soul is kindled at the taper of conviviality, and the wing of friendship never moults a feather!' I began to avoid encounters with Weatherwax. The only Dickensian reply to this sort of thing that I could think of was, 'Bah! Humbug!' but I shrink from giving pain.

But I saw him. Oh, indeed, I saw him crossing the quad, his step as light as a fairy's, with that notable strumpet Gates Ajar Honeypot upon his arm. 'Angelica' he insisted on calling her, poor unhappy purblind youth. I longed to speak, but my Wiser Self—who is, I regret to tell you, a cynical, slangy spirit whom I call the Ghost of Experience Past, would intervene, snarling, 'Nix on the *locoparentis*,' and I would refrain.

Even when he came, last Spring, to ask permission to marry Angelica Crumhorn in the Chapel, late in August, I merely gave formal assent. 'I shall fill the little Chapel with flowers,' he rhapsodized; 'flowers for her whose every thought is pure and fragrant as earth's fairest blossom.' I repressed a comment that a bridal bouquet of Venus' fly-trap would be pretty and original.

I prepared the required page in the College Register, but August came and went, and as nothing had happened I made a notation—Cancelled—on that page, and waited the event.

Poor Weatherwax pined, and I ceased to avoid him and began to pity him. I enquired how his Dickens studies went on? He asked me to his rooms in the College and when I visited him I was astonished to find how Victorian, how like chambers in some early nineteenth-century Inn of Court he had contrived to make them. He even had a bird in a cage: inevitably it was a linnet. The most prominent objects of ornament were a large white plaster bust of Dickens—very large positively dominant—and a handsome full set of Dickens' Works in twenty-five volumes. I recognized it at once as the Nonesuch Dickens, a very costly set of books for a student, but I knew that Weatherwax had money. He languished in an armchair in a long velvet dressing-gown, his hair hanging over his face, the picture of romantic misery. I decided that—prudent or not—the time had come for me to speak.

'Rally yourself, Mr Weatherwax,' cried I; 'marshal your powers, recruit your energies, sir!' I started to hear myself give utterance to these unaccustomed phrases, but with that bust of Dickens looking at me from a high shelf, I could not speak in any other way. So I told him, in good round Victorian prose that he was making an ass of himself, that he was well quit of Gates Ajar Honeypot, and that he must positively stop trying to be Charles Dickens. 'Eating your god,' I cried, raising my hand in admonition, 'cannot make you into your god. Stop aping Dickens, and read him like a scholar.'

To my dismay, he broke down and wept. 'Oh, good old man,' he sobbed, 'you come too late. For I am not eating my god; I fear that my god is eating me! But bless you, bless your snowy locks! You have sought to succour me, but alas, I know that I am doomed!'

I rose to leave him, and as I did so—I tell you this knowing how incredible it must seem—the bust of Dickens seemed to smile, baring sharp, cruel teeth. I shrieked. It was a mental shriek, which is the only kind of shriek permitted to a professor in the modern university, but I gave a mental shriek, and fled the room.

Of course I returned. I know my duty. I know what I owe to the men of Massey College, to the spirit of university education, to that sense of decency which is one of the holiest possessions of our changing world. And as autumn wore on—it was this autumn just past, but as I look back upon it, it seems far, far away—the conviction grew upon me that Weatherwax's trouble was greater than I had supposed; it was not that he thought he was Dickens, but that he thought he was one of Dickens' characters, and by that abandonment of personality he had set his foot upon a shadowed and sinister path. One of Dickens' characters? Yes, but which? One of the doomed ones, clearly. But which? Which? For me this past autumn was a season of painful obligation, for not only had I to care for Weatherwax—oh yes, it reached a point where I took him his meals, and fed him such scant mouthfuls as he could ingest, with my own hands—but I had to adapt myself to the only kind of language he seemed now to understand.

One day—it was in early November—I took him his usual bowl of gruel, and found him lying on his little bed, asleep.

'Mr Weatherwax,' I whispered, 'nay, let me call you Tubfast; arouse yourself; you must eat something.'

'Is it you, Grandfather?' he asked, as he opened his eyes, and across his lips stole a smile so sweet, so innocent, so wholly feminine, that in an instant I had the answer to my question. Tubfast Weatherwax III thought he was Little Nell.

His decline from that moment was swift. I spent all the time with him I could. Sometimes his mind wandered, and seemed to dwell upon Gates Ajar Honeypot. 'I never nursed a dear Gazelle, to glad me with its soft black eye, but when it came to know me well and love me, it was sure to prefer the advances of a fat wholesale furrier on Spadina Avenue,' he would murmur. But more often he talked of graduate studies, and of that great Convocation on High where the Chancellor of the University confers Ph.D.s, *magna cum* angelic *laude*, on all who kneel before his throne.

When I could not longer conceal from myself that the end was near, I dressed his couch here and there with some winter berries and green leaves, gathered in a secluded portion of the parking-lot. He knew why. 'When I die, put me near to something that has loved the light, and had sky above it always,' he murmured. I knew he meant our College quadrangle, for though the new Graduate Library will shortly throw upon our little garden its eternal pall of shadow, it had been while he knew it a place of sunshine and of the laughter of the careless youths who play croquet there.

Then, one dreary November night, just at the stroke of midnight, the end came. He was dead. Dear, patient, noble Tubfast Weatherwax III was dead. His little bird—a poor slight thing the pressure of a finger would have crushed—was stirring nimbly in its cage; and the strong heart of its child-owner was mute and motionless for ever.

Where were the traces of his early cares, the pangs of despised love, of scholarly tasks too heavy for his feeble mind? All gone. Sorrow was dead indeed in him, but peace and perfect happiness were born; imaged in his tranquil beauty and profound repose. So shall we know the angels in their majesty, after death.

I wept for a solitary hour, but there was much to be done. I hastened to the quad, lifted one of the paving stones at the north-east end, where—until the Graduate Library is completed—the sun strikes warmest and stays longest. For such a man as I, burdened with years and sorrow, the digging of a six-foot grave was heavy work, and it took me all of ten minutes. With the little chisel in my handy pocket-knife it was the work of an instant to inscribe the stone—

Hic jacet
STABILIS WEATHERWAX TERTIUS

and then, as my Latin is not inexhaustible, I continued—

He bit off more than he could chew

It was my intention to place the stone over the grave, with the inscription downward, so that no unhallowed eye might read it. Now all that remained was to wrap the poor frail body in the velvet dressing-gown and lay it to rest. Or rather, I should be compelled to stand it to rest, for the grave had to be dug straight down.

It was only then I raised my eyes toward the windows of Weatherwax's room, which lay on the other side of the quad. What light was that, which flickered with an eerie effulgence from the casement? Had I, stunned by my grief, forgotten to turn off the electricity? But no; this light was not the bleak glare of a desk-lamp. It was a bluish light, and it seemed to ebb and flow. Fire? I sped up the stairs, and threw open the door.

Oh, what a sight was there revealed to my starting eyes? My hair lifted upward upon my head, as if it were fanned by a cold breath. The bust of Charles Dickens, before so white, so plaster-like, was now grossly flushed with the colours of life. The Nonesuch Dickens, which had hitherto worn its original binding of many-coloured buckram was—Oh, horror, horror!—bound freshly in leather, and that leather—would that I had no need to reveal it—was human skin! And that smell—why did it so horribly remind me of a dining-room in which some great feast had just been completed? I knew. I knew at once. For the body—the body was gone!

As I swooned the scarlet lips of the Dickens bust parted in a terrible smile, and its beard stirred in a hiccup of repletion.

It was a few days later—last Friday, indeed—when a young colleague in the Department of English—a very promising Joyce man—said to me, 'It is astounding how Dickens studies are picking up; quite a few theses have been registered in the past three months.' I knew he despised Dickens and all the Victorians, so I was not surprised when he added, 'Wonderful how the old wizard keeps life in him! Upon what meat doth this our Charlie feed, that he is grown so great?'

He smiled, pleased at his little literary joke. But I did not smile, because I knew.

Yes, I knew.

BRIAN MOORE · b. 1921

The Sight

Benedict Chipman never took a drink before five and never drank after midnight. He ate only a light lunch, avoided bread and potatoes, and drank decaffeinated coffee. These self-regulations were, he sometimes thought, the only set rules he observed. Otherwise, he did as he liked.

Yet on the morning he returned to his eight-room apartment on Fifth Avenue after four days in hospital, his first act was to tell his housekeeper to bring some Scotch and ice into the library. When she brought it, he was standing by the window, looking out at Central Park. He did not turn around.

'Will that be all, sir?'

'Yes, thanks, Mrs Leahy.'

Chipman was fifty-two and a partner in a New York law firm. A few weeks ago, during his annual medical check-up, his doctor had noticed a large mole on his back and had recommended its removal. The operation was minor but, for Chipman who had never been in hospital before, the invasion of his bodily privacy by doctors, nurses, and attendants had been humiliating and vaguely upsetting. Then, to complicate matters, while the biopsy showed the mole to be probably benign, the pathologist advised that 'to be completely sure', the surgeon should repeat the procedure but, this time, make a wider incision. The second biopsy had been scheduled for the end of the month. 'There's nothing to worry about,' the surgeon said. 'Just relax and come back ten days from now.'

But Chipman did not feel like relaxing. He felt nervous and irritable. As he poured the Scotch, he looked at the tray containing his mail. The first letter on the pile was postmarked Bishopsgate, NH. He had been born in Bishopsgate and for some reason he could not explain the sight of the postmark disturbed him. The letter was from his brother, Blake, who wrote that he and his wife were coming to New York to visit their son Buddy, a journalism major at Columbia. Buddy, it seemed, had learned that his uncle had been in hospital and Blake wrote that all three of them would like to call tomorrow afternoon. The letter irritated Chipman. He had no wish to see Blake and his family. He thought of his brother as a man who had never in his life owned a hundred dollars he didn't know about and whose relations with himself were sycophantic rather than fraternal, largely because of loans which Blake had not repaid.

At the library door, Mrs Leahy announced herself with a small prefatory cough. 'Mrs Kirwen is here, sir.'

'Show her in. And ask if she'd like something to drink.'

As he put his brother's letter down and rose to greet Geraldine, he heard her chatting with Mrs Leahy in the front hall.

'Is *he* having one? Oh, well then, a sherry, I think. By the way, how's your nephew, Mrs Leahy?'

'He still has the pleurisy, ma'am. But he'll be all right.'

'Good, that's good news.'

'Thank you, Mrs Kirwen.'

I never knew Mrs Leahy had a nephew, Chipman said to himself. But, come to think of it, he didn't know much about Mrs Leahy, although she had been with him for almost ten years. Lately, he had decided that his interest in other people was limited to the extent of their contributions to his purse, his pleasure, or his self-esteem. He had a weakness for such aphoristic judgements. But in this instance he also remembered another aphorist's warning: lack of interest in others is a first sign of age.

'Ben, darling, how are you? Shouldn't you have your feet up or something? You mustn't overdo it on your first day home.'

'Stop fussing.'

'I'm not fussing. Dr Wilking told me you should take it easy.'

'When was Wilking talking to *you?*'

'I met him in the corridor yesterday. Remember, he thinks I'm your wife.'

The surgeon, who did not know Chipman, had come in on them unexpectedly the night after the biopsy and found Geraldine, the buttons of her dress undone, lying on the hospital bed with Chipman. The surgeon had tactfully assumed she was Chipman's wife and had addressed her as such in the subsequent conversation. No one had contradicted him. 'That was a mistake,' Chipman said now, remembering. 'I should have said something.'

'Oh, what's it matter?'

'Well, my own doctor, Dr Loeb, know I'm not married.'

'Oh, Ben. Who cares nowadays?'

At that point Mrs Leahy brought Geraldine's sherry. Geraldine, sipping it, put her long legs up on a yellow silk footstool. In this posture her skirt fell back, revealing her elegant thighs. Although impromptu erotic views normally pleased Chipman, this morning he was not pleased: he was irritated. 'Why can't you sit properly?'

'That's not a very nice thing to say when I've given up an important job to be with you today.'

'What job?'

'Remember I tried out for the Phil Lewis show last week? Well, my agent called and said they want me for a second audition this afternoon. He says that usually means you've got the job. But, I'm not going.'

'Why not?'

'Because if I got the job it would mean I'd be on the coast for the next seven weeks. I'm not going to be three thousand miles away while you're in and out of hospital.'

'I'm not in and out of hospital. I'm just going back for a couple of days, that's all. Now, be a good girl. Phone and say you'll be glad to audition this afternoon.'

'No,' she said, suddenly looking as though she might begin to cry.

'But why not?'

'Because I've realized something, Ben. I'm in love with you. I don't want to be separated from you.'

In love with him? He remembered La Rochefoucauld's maxim that nothing is more natural or more mistaken than to suppose that we are loved. He knew Geraldine did not love him. She was an unsuccessful young actress, divorced from a television producer and in receipt of a reasonable alimony. His own role in her life was that of a suitable escort, an older man capable of providing presents and a good time, a friend who was good for a small loan and might not expect to see his money again. This sudden protestation of love was, he decided, no more than the familiar feminine need to justify having gone to bed with him. Geraldine would not give up her alimony: he did not want her to. The present arrangement suited him perfectly.

Nevertheless when she said that she loved him, for one moment he felt strangely elated. Then put his glass back on the silver tray and in its surface saw his face, which seemed distorted, white, old. This foolishness must stop. 'Now, don't talk nonsense. Go and phone those people.'

'Are you trying to get rid of me?'

'Of course not. But if you go out to Hollywood this week it might work out very well. I was thinking of going to Puerto Rico. I thought I'd take a vacation. Lie in the sun until I have to go back into the hospital.'

'Do you know people in Puerto Rico, is that it?'

'No. No. Look, Geraldine, you're *not* in love with me. My God, I'm twenty years older than you.'

'Age has nothing to do with being in love with someone.'

'Maybe not at your age. But at my age it has everything to do with it. Now go and make that phone call. Then I'll take you out and buy you lunch.'

She stood and picked up the otter coat he had helped pay for, trailing it behind her on the carpet as she moved across the room. At the door, she turned. 'So that's what you want? To go to Puerto Rico alone?'

'Yes.'

'Okay.'

She went into the hall. He listened to hear the tinkle as she picked up the phone, but instead heard the front door slam. He started across the room, thinking to go after her and bring her back, but stopped. He realized that he was close to the almost forgotten sensation of tears. Dammit, he'd just invented Puerto Rico to help her make up her mind about the audition. But now, as he felt himself tremble with anger—or was it weakness?—he decided a short vacation in the sun might be the ideal way to wait out the next ten days. Maybe with Geraldine. He decided to suggest it at the office when he went in tomorrow.

There might be a little ill-feeling, though. He had already had a long vacation this summer. But what could they do? In the seventeen years he had been a member of the firm he had frequently demonstrated that his interests were not the law or the success of the partnership, but women, music, and his collection of paintings. However, on the day he joined the partnership he brought with him, as a wedding present from his father-in-law, an insurance company which dwarfed all other clients the firm did business with. And although his marriage had subsequently broken up (his wife died eight years later in an alcoholic clinic, driven there, some said, by Chipman's behaviour with other women) his father-in-law had not held it against him. He still represented the insurance company and this power, coupled with his disregard for the firm's other clients, had driven his partners to revenge themselves on him in the only way they knew. They no longer invited him to their homes or, indeed, to any social function. Their boycott amused him: they bored him. They knew that he was amused and bored. Their dislike of him, he guessed, had long ago turned to hatred.

Yet on the following morning when he went to the office he was surprised to see George Geddes, the senior partner, come in at his doorway, eager, out of breath, and smiling like a job applicant. 'Ben, how are you, how're you feeling?'

'Hello, George.'

'So, how did it go?'

Directly behind Geddes, Chipman's secretary was at her desk in the outer office. He did not want her to hear what he had to say and so beckoned Geddes in and shut the door. 'Matter of fact, George, I wanted to have a word with you about that. Everything went very well, but they want me to go back, just as a precaution, and have a wider excision made. They've scheduled it for the thirty-first. I don't know. I'm feeling a little knocked out. I thought, if you don't mind, I might go and lie in the sun for a week. Not really come back to the office until next month.'

As he spoke he noticed that Geddes was already nodding agreement as though helping someone with a speech impediment. 'Of course, Ben, of course. No sense sitting around here. Good idea.'

'Well, thanks. Of course there are a few things I can clear up before I go.'

'No, no,' Geddes said. 'Let the juniors do some work for a change. Get on your feet again, that's the main thing.'

After Geddes had left, Chipman phone a travel agency. He booked a double room with patio and pool in a first-class Puerto Rico resort hotel, starting the following Monday. He called in his juniors and reviewed their current handling of his clients' affairs. At noon he told his secretary that he was leaving and would not be back until the first week in December. Then he took a taxi to his apartment and for the second morning in a row broke his rule and made himself a drink.

But now his reason was celebratory. What a relief it had been to find Geddes agreeable for once. And there was a note saying Geraldine had telephoned. Obviously, her temper tantrum had not lasted. After pouring a Scotch he picked up the phone and dialled her number.

'Geraldine? Ben. First of all, I'm sorry about yesterday.'

'No, darling, it was my fault. Why shouldn't you go on a trip if you want to? When are you going, by the way?'

'No, tell me first, how was your audition?'

'I didn't go. It's a long story, I won't bore you with it.'

'Does that mean you might be free to join me in Puerto Rico?'

'Ben, do you mean it?'

'Of course. I booked a double room with patio and pool in the Caribe Imperial. Or would you rather I got you a room of your own?'

'No, no.'

'Good. And what about the weekend? Are you free?'

'Do you mean now? Yes. Completely.'

'Well, so am I. Or, almost. I have to be here tomorrow afternoon when my brother and his family are coming. But that shouldn't take more than an hour.'

'Are we thinking of the same thing?'

'I hope so.'

'All right, darling. Come on down. I'll be waiting.'

'I'll be right there.'

His brother's hand, tentative at first, went out to finger the Steinway's polished surface, then boldly stroked the wood. His brother's head turned, afternoon sunlight merciless on the thin grey hair, the pink skull-cap of skin beneath. His brother smiled, ingratiate and falsely intimate. 'Beautiful piano, eh, Ben?' his brother said. 'You must play something for us before we go. I mean, if you feel up to it.'

'Oh yes, Ben, you must,' said his brother's wife who, he knew, did not care at all for music.

If he felt up to it. What would they say if they knew he had come up from the village two hours ago after a night of screwing that would exhaust anyone? Perhaps it would not exhaust Blake's wife, though. One summer, when their son Buddy was still a brat in rompers, Chipman had gone to visit them at their summer cottage on Cape Cod. He was sunbathing in the dunes when Blake's wife came up from the beach, drying her hair on a towel, her shoulder-straps undone, her swimsuit wet from the sea. She did not see him until she stumbled on him and when he reached up and pulled her down she did not say a word. Later they walked hand in hand over the dunes towards the cottage. Blake was sitting on a deck-chair on the lawn, reading a book, and the child was on the porch playing with an old inner tube.

Man and child looked up and his brother's wife at once let go of his hand and ran to kiss her child. She avoided Chipman for the rest of that evening and the following morning he thought it wise to pretend a business engagement in Boston. He had not been to stay with them since.

'Let Buddy play something,' he said, knowing that Buddy's atrocious playing would please them much more than his own. And so Buddy obediently flopped down on the piano bench, looked disdainfully at the music scores in front of him, then poised his large hands over the keys. 'What'll it be, Uncle Ben?'

'You choose,' Chipman said. Years ago, prodded by Blake's wistful hints about the child's musical inclinations, he had paid for a series of piano lessons for Buddy. The money had been wasted for Buddy's musical talents were a myth, the first of a long series of efforts on his parents' part to make Chipman feel a special affection for the boy. All had failed. Buddy's only effect on his uncle was to relieve him of any regrets about not having had a son of his own.

But now he pretended to listen as Buddy stumbled through some Cole Porter tunes, noticing as he mimed attention that Buddy's parents seemed nervous as though they had quarrelled before coming and were now trying to cover it up by a surfeit of polite remarks to each other. Chipman was uninterested. He simply wanted them to go and so, when Blake glanced at last in his direction, he pretended drowsiness. It worked. As his son thumped to a pause in the music, Blake stood up. 'Thanks, Bud, but we'd better not overtire your uncle. Besides, your mother and I want to catch that Wyeth show at the Met before our train leaves.'

Then he turned to Chipman. 'Ben, could I have a word with you?'

As on signal both Buddy and his mother left the room. It was, Chipman knew, the usual prelude to Blake's asking for money, but today a loan seemed well worth it to get rid of them. He went to his desk, aware that Blake, if left to his own devices, would take at least five minutes to come to the point. He opened a drawer and took out his cheque-book.

'What's that for?' Blake asked sharply.

'Nothing.'

'Put that away, will you,' Blake said. 'I'm ashamed that I owe you so much. As a matter of fact, Ben, it wasn't that at all. It was just that we wondered if you'd like to come up to Bishopsgate to convalesce until you go back into the hospital.'

'Thanks, but I'm going to Puerto Rico.'

'Oh. Puerto Rico?'

'Yes, I thought I'd like to lie in the sun for a few days.'

'Oh, that's a pity, we were looking forward to the thought of having you. You and I haven't spent much time together these last years.'

'I know. Well, maybe some other time.'

'Any time,' Blake said. 'I'd like us to go for walks around the old place and have talks and all that. I'd like that a lot.'

And then, abruptly, Blake took hold of his hand and squeezed it. 'I'd really like it, Ben.'

'Well, we'll do it,' Chipman said, uneasily, beginning to move towards the hallway where the others waited. As they came out he saw Blake's wife glance at her husband and saw Blake give a small, almost imperceptible shake of his head. Buddy came forward, hand out, smiling. 'Good-bye, sir.'

'Good-bye,' Chipman said. 'Good-bye, Blake.'

His sister-in-law came towards him. He held out his hand. She ignored it and reached up to kiss him on the cheek. He was astonished. 'Good-bye,' his sister-in-law said. 'Take care of yourself.'

The elevator came. They went down.

Confused, Chipman closed the door of his apartment. It was as though he had found an interesting passage in a dull book and had seen it snatched away before he had time to finish it. Why had Blake's wife kissed him, she who had so carefully avoided kissing him ever since that summer on the beach? And why had Blake come up with this unprecedented invitation to visit them at Bishopsgate? Why were they being so kind all of a sudden? Come to think of it, everyone had been abnormally kind these past two days—Geraldine, Geddes, Blake. It was irritating, dammit, to be treated as though, all of a sudden, he were made of glass. How did La Rochefoucauld put it? *Pride does not wish to owe, nor vanity to pay.* He didn't want favours from anyone. So, why did they try?

He had reached the library door before the thought and the answer came to him. He was going to die. That was why they were all being so gentle. They knew something he didn't know. A wider excision, that was what the surgeon said. 'To be completely sure,' the pathologist said. They hadn't told him the truth, that was it. 'Just relax,' the surgeon said.

He must not panic. He must call Dr Loeb, his internist, and put the question to him quite casually, implying that he already knew all about it. He must go to the phone now and clear things up.

He went into his bedroom and closed the door so that Mrs Leahy would not overhear him. He phoned Dr Loeb but the answering service said Dr Loeb was out of town for the weekend and a Dr Slattery was taking his calls. So that was no use. The surgeon's name was Wilking. He looked up the number. The answering service said Dr Wilking wasn't in, but would he leave a message. He left his name and number and lay down on the bed, worrying. After five minutes he telephoned again and said it was an emergency. He must reach Dr Wilking at once. This time, the answering service gave him a number to call. Dr Wilking answered.

'Dr Wilking, this is Benedict Chipman speaking. Now, I know this may sound silly to you, but was there anything about that operation of mine that I should know about?'

'Why do you ask, Mr Chipman?'

'I just want to know the truth. It's important, doctor.'

'Well, look, Mr Chipman, it's pretty much as I told you. I don't think you have anything to worry about.'

'Is that the truth? I want the truth.'

'Yes, what can I say? Look, Mr Chipman. The best thing you can do now is relax. Your wife mentioned you might go off for a short vacation. I think that's a good idea.'

'How the hell can I take it easy? For God's sake, doctor, that's like telling a man to take it easy in the condemned cell while you decide whether or not he's to be reprieved.'

'Oh, come on now, Mr Chipman, I wouldn't say that.'

'Of course, you wouldn't,' Chipman shouted. 'And that girl isn't my wife, do you hear? So anything you have to say, just say it to me!'

He put the receiver down without waiting to hear the surgeon's reply. He looked at his bed. This was the bed he might die in. He turned from it and went into his library. Small picture-lights lit his collection of Krieghoff landscapes. When he died these pictures would be sent to the Bishopsgate Art Gallery to be exhibited in a special room with a brass plaque over the door, identifying him as their donor. They would arrive after his body, which would be buried under a plain headstone in the episcopal cemetery, next to his parents' grave. How many people ever read donor's plaques or the names on headstones? A year from now he would be forgotten.

But wasn't that jumping the gun, giving in to a bad case of jitters unsupported by any evidence? How could they know he was going to die when they hadn't even done the second biopsy yet? What were they keeping from him? Whatever it was had frightened Geraldine into suddenly declaring her love. But she doesn't love me, Chipman decided, she pities me. Pity is what everyone feels for me now: Geraldine, Geddes, Blake, Blake's wife. Yet how could they all know this thing about me? Geraldine has never met Geddes. Or Buddy. Who told Buddy, for instance?

Chipman went to his desk, searched it, and then went to the telephone table in the hall. He knew he had a number for Buddy someplace, and when he found it and dialled it, it was a fraternity house. No one answered for a long time and then some boy told him Buddy wasn't in, and that he didn't know when he would be back. As Chipman replaced the receiver, Mrs Leahy passed him in the hall, going down the corridor to her own room. Only one person might have spoken to Buddy, to Geddes, to Geraldine. One person who would answer the phone when people called here to ask how he was. He went down the corridor to the far end of the apartment and stopped outside Mrs Leahy's door. He almost never came into this part of the apartment, near the pantry and wine cellar, and past the kitchen. He stood for a moment and then, without knocking, he opened the door.

He had not seen the inside of Mrs Leahy's room for years. Sometimes he heard the television sound, turned low, and sometimes she would leave the door open, at night, when she went to answer the phone. Now, his eyes went from the television set to the horrid rose and green curtains, the cheap coloured lithograph of some saint, to the crucifix, entwined with fading palm, which hung over what seemed to be a sewing-table. It was the sort of room he used to glimpse through upper-storey windows, years ago, when he still rode the subways, a room which screamed a sudden mockery of all other rooms in his elegant apartment. And its occupant, her back to him, unaware of his presence, was the perfect figure in this interior. In her pudgy fingers, the surprise of a cigarette: on her lap, inevitably, the garish headlines of the *Daily News.*

'Mrs Leahy?'

She turned. Her grey head was that of a stranger's, utterly changed by the absence of her uniform cap. 'Oh, did you ring, sir? Is the bell not working?'

'No, I didn't ring.'

'Can I get you something, sir? Are you all right?'

By this time she had stubbed her cigarette and had pinned on the familiar housemaid's cap. 'A little whisky?' she said. 'Or, are you hungry, sir? Would you like a sandwich?'

'Whisky,' he said. 'And I want to talk to you.'

'Yes, Mr Chipman.' Swiftly she moved past him going down the corridor to the monastic neatness of her kitchen. She did not, of course, expect him to follow her into the kitchen and looked up, surprised, when he did.

'A little water with it, sir? I'll bring it into the library, will I?'

'No. Sit down, Mrs Leahy. Please.'

As she placed the bottle of Scotch, ice, and a glass and pitcher of water on a tray, he drew out one of the chrome and leather kitchen chairs, indicating that she should sit in at the table. As she did, he saw a red rash of embarrassment rise from her neck to her cheeks. They had never been informal together. He sat opposite her and poured himself a Scotch. 'Now,' he said. 'Let me ask you something. Are you the person who's been telling people I have cancer?'

'Me, sir?'

'Yes, you.'

She did not answer him at once. She put her veiny old hands on the table, joined them as in an attitude of prayer, then looked at him with the calculating, ready-to-bolt caution of a rodent. He had never before noticed this animal quality of hers. Why, she's a hedgehog, he decided. She's Mrs Tiggy-winkle.

'Yes, sir. It was me.'

He must keep calm. He must not let her know that he was ignorant of all the facts of his illness. 'I see. And who told *you* that I might have cancer?'

'Mrs Kirwen, sir.'

'And what did she say, exactly?'

'Ah, she didn't say you had cancer, she said they were going to operate on you again just to be sure. There was always the chance, she said. And I said to her I thought I should let Mr Buddy know. On account of your brother, sir. And then Mr Geddes rang up about you. And I told him. To let him know, like.'

'Oh, you did, did you? Well, I like the way you let them know. They think I'm going to die. I could see it on my brother's face this afternoon. He thinks I'm going to die.'

'I'm very sorry, now, Mr Chipman.'

'Mrs Kirwen *didn't* say to you I had cancer, did she? She didn't say the doctors had told her something they hadn't told me. Or, did she?'

'Ah, no, sir. Mrs Kirwen never said you were going to die. 'Tis not Mrs Kirwen's fault at all. 'Tis my fault, and I'm very sorry now.'

'Tell me, Mrs Leahy. Do you dislike me?'

'Oh, no, sir.'

'Then why did you tell these people that I'm going to die?'

'Ah, well, sir, that's a long story. And I'm very sorry to be bringing you news like that. But them doctors don't know everything, now do they?'

'What do you mean?' He was shouting, but he could not stop himself. 'Just exactly what the hell do you mean, Mrs Leahy?'

Mrs Leahy, avoiding his eye, stared down at her joined hands. 'Well, sir, you see, I have something now, something not many people have. And there's times I wish I didn't, let me tell you.'

'Didn't what? Didn't have what?'

'I have the sight, sir. The second sight.'

'Second sight?' Chipman repeated the words with the joy of a man repeating the punch line of a joke. 'Well. And there I was. . . .' Beginning to shake with amusement, he lifted his glass and drank a great swallow of whisky. 'You mean you dreamed it, or something like that?'

'Yes, sir. Last Monday, the night before your operation.'

'Now let me get this straight,' Chipman said. 'Mrs Kirwen told you nothing except what you've told me. The truth is nobody *knows* I have cancer. There's absolutely no proof of it at all.'

'That's right, sir.'

'My God, do you realize the mischief you've caused?'

'I'm very sorry, now. I see I shouldn't have said anything. I beg your pardon, sir.'

'It was a disgraceful thing to do!'

'Yes, sir. I'm sorry, sir. Maybe I should give you my notice?'

'No, no.' Chipman poured himself a second drink. Suddenly, he felt like laughing again. 'Well, now,' he said. Unconsciously, and for the first time in their acquaintance, he found himself slipping into an imitation of her Irish brogue. 'And how long have you had this "sight"?'

'Ah, a long time, now. I noticed it first when I was only fourteen.'

'You dream about things and then they happen, is that it?'

'In a way, sir.'

'What do you mean. Tell me.'

'I'd rather not, now, sir. I'm sorry about speaking to those people. I only meant it for your sake, sir.'

'Now, wait. I'm just interested in this premonition of yours. Now, what happened in my case? You had a dream?'

'Yes, just the dream, sir. Nothing else.'

'What do you mean, nothing else?'

'Well you see, first there's the dream. And then, later on, you see, there's a second sign.'

'And what's the second sign?'

'It's a look I do see on the person's face.'

'A look?'

'Yes. When the trouble is very close.'

Chipman, in the act of downing his second Scotch, looked at her over the rim of his glass. Ignorant, stupid old creature with her hedgehog eyes and butterfat brogue. Some primitive folk nonsense, typically Irish, he supposed; it was their religion that encouraged these fairy-tales. 'When it's close,' he said. 'What does that mean?'

'When it's close to the time, sir.'

'So, I take it you haven't seen this look on my face. Not yet.'

'That's right, sir.'

'When do you think you'll see it?'

'I don't know that, sir. Better not be asking me things like that. It's no pleasure to me to be seeing the things I do see. That's the God's own truth, sir.'

'But how do you know you'll see it? Do you always see it after you have this dream?'

'I'd say so, sir.'

'Give me an example.'

'Well, I saw it on my own sister, sir, the night before she died. I had a dream and saw her in the dream, and when I woke up she was sleeping in the bed with me and I lit the lamp and looked at her face. I saw it in her face. And the very next night she was killed by a bus on her way home. I was fourteen at the time.'

'Tell me about another time.'

'Ah, now, what's the use, sir?'

'No, you started this, Mrs Leahy. I want to hear more.'

'And I don't want to tell you, sir.'

'But you told Mrs Kirwen and Mr Geddes and my nephew. You weren't afraid to tell them this fairy-tale.'

'Ah, I didn't tell them that at all, sir. Sure they wouldn't believe it. I just said I had information, I couldn't say more. But that the doctors were very worried about you.'

'*Did* you?' Again, he felt furious at her. 'How dare you, Mrs Leahy!'

'I'm sorry, sir. I wanted to be a help to you, sir. I mean I wanted Mrs Kirwen, and your family and all, to be good to you now in your time of trouble.'

I must *not* lose my temper with a servant, Chipman told himself. 'All right,' he said. 'You told me about your sister. Give me another example.'

'My husband, sir, God rest his soul. I dreamed about him June second, 1946, and he was took on the second of November, the same year. And on the first of November I saw the look on his face. I begged him not to go to work the next day, but he didn't heed me. He fell off a scaffolding. He never lived to see a priest.'

'Wait,' Chipman said. 'Both these deaths were from accidents, not illnesses.'

'Yes, sir.'

'Well, have you have any premonitions about deaths from illness?'

'Well, Jimmy, one of the doormen in this building. I saw him in a dream four months before he died of heart disease. And on the day he was taken I went to see him in the hospital. And I saw the look on him.'

'Indeed.' Slowly, Chipman finished his Scotch.

'Of course, 'tis not always departures. Deaths. Sometimes I do see arrivals. Do you remembers, sir, the night you came home from Washington, last New Year's it was? I had your dinner waiting for you. I dreamed the night before that you would come at nine, wanting your dinner. And you did.'

As a matter of fact, Chipman thought, I remember it well. I remember thinking she'd prepared that roast of lamb for herself and some crony. Extra-sensory perception, premonition: of course all that was only one jump away from teacup reading, table turning, spiritualistic quacks. But she dreamed of my death.

'So, Mrs Leahy. You dreamed of me, again, the other night. But this time it wasn't about my arrival?'

She nodded.

'Tell me the dream.'

'Ah, don't be asking, sir.'

'But I am asking. If you go around telling false stories to people about my death, you have the obligation to tell me the truth about what prompted you to do it. Now, what did you see in this dream?'

'I saw the shroud, sir. You came in the room and you were wearing the shroud.'

'A shroud. That means death.'

'Yes, sir.'

'When?'

'Ah, now, I don't know that, sir.'

'But you will know, as soon as you see this look on my face, is that it?'

'Yes, sir. I'd know the time, then.'

'I see,' Chipman said. 'And now I suppose you'd like me to cross your palm with silver, so that you'll tell me when I must make my funeral arrangements. Well, Mrs Leahy, I'm going to disappoint you. A few minutes ago, when I thought of the mischief you've done and the worry you've caused my family and friends, I was quite prepared to let you go. But, believe me, I wouldn't let you go now for all the gold in Fort Knox. A year from now, Mrs Leahy, you and I will sit here together. We'll have a drink together, this time, this date, one year from now.'

'God willing and we will, sir.'

He stood up, suddenly feeling his drink, his chair making a screeching noise on the linoleum floor. 'And now,' he said, 'I'd better phone Mrs Kirwen and those other people and explain what's really happened.'

'Yes, sir. I'm very sorry.'

He went back into the library. There was no point in being angry with her, it was a joke really. He should be celebrating. The doctors weren't alarmed, and even if they found some malignancy, there are all sorts of treatments, cobalt bombs, chemotherapy and so on. To think that stupid old hedgehog had set all this in motion—Geddes, Buddy, even Geraldine. Poor Geraldine.

He went to his shelves, took down a volume of the *Encyclopaedia Britannica* and read the entry under *cancer*. He then read the entry under *clairvoyance*. When he had finished, he replaced the books and rang the bell.

'Yes, sir.'

She stood at the door, her uniform cap on straight, the perfect housekeeper, a treasure, his women friends said. 'I'd like some ice and water,' he said.

She nodded and smiled. Mrs Tiggy-winkle. When she came back

with the tray, he tried to affect a bantering tone. 'Now, just in theory, mind you, just for curiosity's sake. When you do think you'll see that look on my face?'

'I don't know, sir. I hope it will be a long, long time off. Was there anything else, sir?'

'No.'

'Goodnight, sir.'

She bobbed her head in her usual half-curtsey of withdrawal. When she had gone he made himself a fresh drink, then went to the window and stood looking down at Fifth Avenue. People in evening dress were getting out of rental Cadillac limousines in front of his building, laughing and joking, going to some function.

An hour later, he was still standing there. The room behind him was quite dark. He heard no sound in the apartment. He walked into the lighted hallway and went towards the kitchen. She was not there. He went past the kitchen, going towards her room. He stood in front of her door, trembling with excitement. He knocked.

'Yes, sir.'

She was sitting in her armchair, stitching the hem of an apron. The television set had been turned off.

'You were waiting for me, weren't you.'

'No, sir. Would you be wanting dinner, sir?'

'You should know I don't want dinner. I thought knowing things like that was one of your specialties.'

She bent to her sewing.

'Mrs Leahy, I want to ask you something. What if I fired you tonight? You'd never see the look, would you?'

'I suppose not, sir.'

'Then you'd never know if you'd been right. I mean supposing you never saw my death in the paper. You wouldn't know, would you?'

She bit the edge of the thread.

'Well, answer me.'

'Yes, sir, I'd know.'

'Look at me!' Even to himself, his voice sounded strange. 'You haven't looked at me since I came into the room.'

She folded the apron, placed it on the sewing-table and turned around. He went towards her, his face drained. As her eyes met his, he thought again of an animal. An animal does not think: it knows or it does not know. He say on the edge of a worn sofa, facing her.

'Well?' His voice was hoarse.

'Well what, sir?'

'You know what. Am I still all right?'

'Yes, sir.'

'Mrs Leahy,' he said. 'You wouldn't lie to me, would you? I mean you'd tell me if you saw it.'

'I suppose so, sir. I might be afraid to worry you, though.'

His hands gripped hers. 'No, no, I want to know. You must tell me. Promise me you'll tell me when the time comes?'

Tears, the unfamiliar tears of dependence, blurred his vision: made the room tremble. Gently, she nodded her head.

FARLEY MOWAT · b. 1921

The Snow Walker

I am Ootek, and my people are the people of the River of Men. Once they were many and the land was good to them, but now it is my time and we have almost forgotten how it was in the old days when the deer flooded the tundra and gave us life. Hunger comes often now, and the deer but seldom. No one now lives by the big lakes to the north although when my father was young the tents of the people stood everywhere along those shores. I have travelled down the River to the big lakes but when I reached them I turned back from an empty land.

Only the spirits who remain in those places remember the times when a man might stand on a hill as the deer passed by and though he looked to the east or the west, the south or the north, he would see only their brown backs and hear only the clicking of antlers and the grumbling of their full bellies.

The great herds have gone . . . and so we who lived by the deer must follow the Snow Walker even as my father followed him in the spring of the year.

After the ice had grown thick on the lakes last winter there came a time of storms and for many days we stayed in our igloos. The children grew quiet and did not play and the old people sometimes looked toward the door tunnels with shadowed eyes. The snows mounted over the top of the igloos until we could not even venture out to look for willow twigs to burn. The igloos were cold and dark for we had long since eaten the deer fat that should have burned in the lamps. So little food remained to us from the few southbound deer we had been able to kill in the autumn that the dogs were beginning to starve, and we ourselves were not much better off.

One day Belikari, who was my closest neighbour among the seven families living in the camp, came to tell me that a mad fox had run into the tunnel of his snowhouse where his dogs lay and had bitten three of them before it was killed by the rest. Those three dogs died with foam at their lips, and they were only three of many. This was another evil because when the foxes went mad their pelts became worthless and so, even if the storms had allowed us to travel, it would have been no use visiting the traps.

After a long time the blizzards ended and the weather grew calm and cold. All the people had survived though some of the old ones could hardly stir from the sleeping ledges. We younger men took the few remaining dogs and went searching for meat we had cached on the Flat Country. We found only a little because most of the caches were buried under hard drifts that had mounted so high they had covered the markers.

The women and children helped to keep famine at bay by digging under the drifts near the igloos for fish bones and scraps of old hides with which to make soup. By such means we hoped to cling to our lives until the warm winds and the lengthening days might bring the deer back to our country from the forested lands in the south.

But long after the time when the ice should have started to rot, it still lay heavy and hard on the rivers and lakes, and the days seemed to grow colder again until we wondered if winter would ever come to an end. We ate all the food we had, and the deer did not come. We waited . . . for there was nothing else we could do. We ate the last of our dogs, and still the deer did not come.

One day the men gathered in Owliktuk's snowhouse. His wife, Kunee, sat on the ledge with her child in her arms, and the child was dead. We knew it could not be very long before many of the women were nursing such sorrow. My cousin, Ohoto, put some thoughts into words.

'Perhaps people should go away from this place now. Perhaps they might go south to the place where the white man has come to live. It might happen that he would have food he would give us.'

The white man had only recently come to live on the edge of our country, to trade with us for foxes. It was a long way to his place and only Ohoto had been there before. Since we had no dogs, we knew we would have to carry everything on our backs, and the children and old people would not be able to ride on the sleds as they should. We knew some of them would not see the white man's place . . . but the child of Owliktuk and Kunee was dead. We decided to go.

The women rolled up a few skins to use for tent shelters and sleeping robes; the children carried whatever they could, and we men slung our packs on our shoulders and we left our camp by the River and set out into the south.

Soon after we started, the sun turned warm and for five days we walked up to our knees in melting snow. My wife's mother had lost count of the years she had lived, yet she walked with the rest and still helped to pitch camp at the end of each day. But on the fifth night she did not offer to help. She sat by herself with her back to a rock and spoke to none except Ilupalee, my daughter. She called the child to her.

From a distance I watched and listened as the old woman put her bony hands on my daughter's head. I heard her softly singing her spirit song to the child, the secret song she had received from her mother's mother and with which she could summon her helping spirit. Then I knew she had made up her mind what she must do.

It was her choice, and my wife and I could say nothing about it, not even to tell her of the sorrow we felt. During the night, she went from the camp. None saw her go. We did not speak her name after that for one may not use the name of a person who has gone out on the land to seek the Snow Walker until the name and the spirit it bears can be given again to a newly born child.

The next day we reached the Little Stick country which borders the forests. Here there was plenty of wood so we could at least have fires where we could warm ourselves. Toward evening we overtook Ohoto's family squatted beside a fire, melting water to drink since there was no food. Ohoto told me his daughter had fallen and could not rise again so they had to make camp. When the rest of the people came up, it was clear that many, both young and old, could not go on; and Ohoto thought we were still two or three days distant from the home of the white man.

I had been carrying Ilupalee on my shoulders most of the day and was so tired I could not think. I lay down by the fire and shut my eyes. Ilupalee lay beside me and whispered in my ear:

'A white hare is sitting behind the little trees over there.'

I thought this was only a dream born out of hunger so I did not open my eyes. But she whispered again:

'It is a big, fat hare. She Who Walked said it was there.'

This time I opened my eyes and got to my knees. I looked where she pointed and could see nothing except a patch of dwarf spruce. All the same I unslung the rifle from my pack and walked toward the trees.

Indeed it was there!

But one hare does not provide more than a mouthful of food for twenty-five people so we had to think carefully what should be done. It was decided that the three strongest men—Alekahaw, Ohoto and I—would eat the hare and thereby gain strength to go on to the white man's place. My wife built a fire apart from the camp so the others would not have to endure the smell of meat cooking. She boiled the hare and we three men shared it; but we left the guts, bones, skin and the head to make soup for the children.

We walked away from the camp along a frozen stream so we would not have to wade through the soft snow. My skin boots were thin and torn and my feet were soon numb because at each step we broke through the thin crust above the thaw water. I did not mind because my stomach was warm.

It was growing dark on the second day when we came to a clearing in a spruce woods on the shore of a lake where the white man had his house. His dogs heard us and howled and when we came near he opened the door and waited with the bright light of a lamp shining behind him. We stopped and stood where we were because he was a stranger, and a white man, and we had met very few white men. He spoke to us, but not in our language, so we could not reply. When he spoke again, very loudly, and still we did not reply, he went back into his house.

It grew cold as the darkness settled around us, and our wet boots became stiff as they froze. I thought of Ilupalee and wanted very much to do something, but did not know what we should do.

After a long time the door opened again and the white man came out. He was wiping his beard. We smelled hot fat from his house but he shut the door behind him and motioned us to follow him to another small cabin.

He unlocked the door and we went in. He lit a lamp and hung it on a rafter so we could see that the walls were piled high with boxes, but we looked hardest at the many bags of flour stacked in front of a table. We start to smile for we believed the white man understood our needs and would help us. We stood under the lamp watching the flame reflect light from the beads of cold fat still clinging to the white man's beard, and we gave ourselves up to the joy growing within us.

The white man opened a drawer in the table and took out a handful of small sticks of the kind used to show how much a trapper can have in exchange for the fox pelts he brings. Holding these sticks in his hand he spoke sharply in his own tongue. When we did not reply he went to a wall of the cabin, took down a fox pelt and laid it before us: then he pointed to the carrying bags which were slung on our shoulders.

The joy went out of us then. I made signs to show we had no fox pelts to trade, and Alekahaw opened his bag to show how empty it was. The white man's eyes were of a strange green colour and I could not look into them. I looked at his forehead instead while I waited for whatever must happen. Slowly his face grew red with anger, then he threw the sticks back in the drawer and began to shout at us.

Anger is something we fear since an angry man may do foolish and dangerous things. When I saw the anger in this man's face, I backed to the door. I wanted to go from that place but Alekahaw was braver than me. He stood where he was and tried to explain to the white man how it was at the camp where the rest of the people were starving. He pulled up his *holiktu* so the man could see for himself how Alekahaw's ribs stuck out from his body. Alekahaw touched his own face to show how tightly the skin was stretched over the bones.

The white man shrugged his shoulders. Perhaps he did not understand. He began turning down the flame in the lamp and we knew he would soon go back to his house, then the door would be shut against the needs of the people. Quickly Ohoto pulled two boxes of shells out of his bag. These were the last bullets he had and he had been saving them against the time when the deer would return. Now he put them on the table and pointed to the flour.

The white man shook his head. He was still angry. He picked up the lamp and started to go to the door. Alekahaw and Ohoto stepped out of his way, but something happened inside me and although I was frightened I would not let him pass.

He kept his eyes on me but he stretched out one hand behind him until it came to rest on a rifle hung on the wall. I could not make way for him then because I was afraid to move while he had his hand on that gun.

So we all stood still for a while. At last he picked up a small sack of flour and threw it over the table to fall at Ohoto's feet. Then he took the rifle, shoved me aside with the barrel, pushed the door open and told us to leave. We went outside and watched as he locked the door. We watched as he went back into his house.

A little while later we saw him looking out of his window. He still had the rifle in his hand so we knew there was no use remaining. We walked away into the darkness.

Day was breaking when we got back to the camp. Those who were still able to stand gathered in front of Owliktuk's tent and we told what we had to tell. We showed them the sack of flour which was so small a child could easily lift it.

Owliktuk spoke against us, blaming us because we had not taken the food that was needed. He said we could have repaid the white man next winter when the foxes were again good. But if we had tried to take food from the white man there would have been killing. Perhaps Owliktuk only spoke as he did because his second child was now going from him. The rest of the people said nothing but returned to their families with the small portions of flour which were their shares.

I carried my father's share to his tent. Although he had once been the best hunter among us and only the previous year had fathered a child on his third wife, he had aged very much during the winter and his legs had weakened until he could barely walk. When I told him what had happened and gave him the flour for himself, my step-mother and the small child, he smiled and said, 'One has a son who knows what may be done and what may not be done. One is glad no blood was shed. It may be that things will get better.'

It did not seem he was right about that. We had made the journey to the white man's place and it had come to so little. Now we were too weak to go back to our own land. And on the second day after we three men returned to the camp, the Snow Walker came to the children Aljut and Uktilohik. There was no mourning for them because those who still lived had no sorrow to spend on the dead.

Each day thereafter the sun shone more brightly. Spring was upon us and still the deer had not returned. One day I tried to visit my father to see how it was with him but I was unable to walk the short distance. I crawled back into my own tent where my wife sat rocking herself with her eyes closed and her mouth wide and gasping. Beside her my daughter sometimes wailed in the thin, dry voice of an old woman. I lay down on some brush inside the flap and together we waited.

Perhaps it was the next day when I awakened to hear someone shout. The shout came again and the voice seemed familiar and the words set my heart racing.

'*Here is a deer!*'

I caught my rifle by the muzzle and crawled into the morning sunlight. At first I was blinded but after a moment I saw a fine buck standing a little way off with his head high, watching the camp.

I raised my rifle with hands that could not seem to hold it. The sights wavered and the deer seemed to slide up and down the barrel. Clutching it tight, I took aim and fired. The buck flung up his forefeet and leapt toward the sheltering trees. I fired again and again until the rifle was empty but the shots all went wide. I could see them kicking up little spouts of snow but I could not hear the hard thud that tells a hunter when he has hit.

The deer ran away . . . but just when it was about to disappear in the trees it stumbled and fell. With all my strength I willed it not to get up. The deer's spirit struggled with mine until slowly the buck sank on his side.

Some of the people had come out into the sunlight and with weak voices were asking each other who had been shooting. 'Get out your knives!' I cried as loud as I could. 'One has killed a fat deer!'

At my words even those who could not walk found enough strength. People wept as they stumbled and staggered toward the deer carcass. The first ones to reach it clung to it like flies, sucking the blood that still bubbled out of its wound. They moved away after a while to make room for others, sobbing with pain and holding their hands to their bellies.

The women sliced into the carcass with their round knives and tore out the entrails, snatching at the little scraps of white fat that clung to the guts. The men cut off the legs at the lower joints and cracked the bones to get at the marrow. In only a short time the buck was changed into a pile of bones, steaming meat and red snow.

It grew warm under the sun and some people began returning to the shelters with meat for those who were too weak to move. Then I remembered that I had seen no one from the tent of my father, so I made my way there dragging part of a forequarter. The flap was down over the door but I pushed it aside and crawled in. My stepmother was lying under a piece of hairless old hide and she was holding her child against her dry dugs. Although they scarcely breathed they were both still alive. But of my father there was no sign.

I cut off a piece of meat, chewed it soft then pushed it into my stepmother's mouth and rubbed her neck till she swallowed. Then I took my little stepbrother to Ohoto's shelter, which was not far away, and Ohoto's wife made blood soup and fed the child with it while I went back to my father's place and chewed more meat for my stepmother. Before I left her, she was able to eat by herself but she could not yet talk so I did not know where my father had gone.

When I returned to my own place, I found my wife had roasted some ribs and boiled the deer's tongue. Ilupalee lay wrapped in a fresh piece of deerskin and it was good to hear her whimper with the pain of a full belly. That whole night we passed in eating and by the next day nothing of the buck remained for the ravens and foxes. The bones had been crushed and boiled for their fat, the skull had been opened and cleaned, and even the hooves had been made into soup. The strength of the buck had passed into the people and we were ready to return to our country.

Next day when I went to my father's tent my stepmother was able to stand. I told her that she and the child would now come and live in my tent, then I said, 'One looks about but does not see one's father.'

'*Eeee*,' she replied. 'He would not eat the flour you brought. He gave it to me and the child. Afterwards he went on the land to meet the Snow Walker.'

A little while later I told Ohoto about the voice I had heard. No one else had heard it and none of the people in the camp except me had known there was a deer nearby. Together Ohoto and I followed the marks where my father had stumbled down to the river, then crawled north on the ice. His tracks disappeared at a bend where the current had opened a hole, but close by we found the tracks of a deer. We followed the tracks until they circled back to the camp and came to an end at the place where I had killed the big buck. Neither Ohoto nor I said anything but we both knew whose voice I had heard.

In the autumn my wife will give birth to another child, and then the name of him who went to meet the Snow Walker that we might continue to live will surely be spoken again by the River of Men.

MAVIS GALLANT · b. 1922

From the Fifteenth District

Although an epidemic of haunting, widely reported, spread through the Fifteenth District of our city last summer, only three acceptable complaints were lodged with the police.

Major Emery Travella, 31st Infantry, 1914-18, Order of the Leopard, Military Beech Leaf, Cross of St Lambert First Class, killed while defusing a bomb in a civilian area 9 June, 1941, Medal of Danzig (posthumous), claims he is haunted by the entire congregation of St Michael and All Angels on Bartholomew Street. Every year on the Sunday falling nearest the anniversary of his death, Major Travella attends Holy Communion service at St Michael's, the church from which he was buried. He stands at the back, close to the doors, waiting until all the communicants have returned to their places, before he approaches the altar rail. His intention is to avoid a mixed queue of dead and living, the thought of which is disgusting to him. The congregation sits, hushed and expectant, straining to hear the Major's footsteps (he drags one foot a little). After receiving the Host, the Major leaves at once, without waiting for the Blessing. For the past several years, the Major has noticed that the congregation doubles in size as 9 June approaches. Some of these strangers bring cameras and tape recorders with them; others burn incense under the pews and wave amulets and trinkets in what they imagine to be his direction, muttering pagan gibberish all the while. References he is sure must be meant for him are worked into the sermons: 'And he that was dead sat up, and began to speak' (Luke 7:15), or 'So Job died, being old and full of days' (Job 42:17). The Major points out that he never speaks and never opens his mouth except to receive Holy Communion. He lived about sixteen thousand and sixty days, many of which he does not remember. On 23 September, 1914, as a young private, he was crucified to a cart wheel for five hours for having failed to salute an equally young lieutenant. One ankle was left permanently impaired.

The Major wishes the congregation to leave him in peace. The opacity of the living, their heaviness and dullness, the moisture of their skin, and the dustiness of their hair are repellent to a man of feeling. It was always his habit to avoid civilian crowds. He lived for six years on the fourth floor in Block E, Stoneflower Gardens, without saying a word to his neighbours or even attempting to learn their names. An affidavit can easily be obtained from the former porter at the Gardens, now residing at the Institute for Victims of Senile Trauma, Fifteenth District.

Mrs Ibrahim, aged thirty-seven, mother of twelve children, complains about being haunted by Dr L. Chalmeton of Regius Hospital, Seventh District, and by Miss Alicia Fohrenbach, social investigator from the Welfare Bureau, Fifteenth District. These two haunt Mrs Ibrahim without respite, presenting for her ratification and approval conflicting and unpleasant versions of her own death.

According to Dr Chalmeton's account, soon after Mrs Ibrahim was discharged as incurable from Regius Hospital he paid his patient a professional call. He arrived at a quarter past four on the first Tuesday of April, expecting to find the social investigator, with whom he had a firm appointment. Mrs Ibrahim was discovered alone, in a windowless room, the walls of which were coated with whitish fungus a quarter of an inch thick, which rose to a height of about forty inches from the floor. Dr Chalmeton inquired, 'Where is the social investigator?' Mrs Ibrahim pointed to her throat, reminding him that she could not reply. Several dark-eyed children peeped into the room and ran away. 'How many are yours?' the Doctor asked. Mrs Ibrahim indicated six twice with her fingers. 'Where do they sleep?' said the Doctor. Mrs Ibrahim indicated the floor. Dr Chalmeton said, 'What does your husband do for a living?' Mrs Ibrahim pointed to a workbench on which the Doctor saw several pieces of finely wrought jewellery; he thought it a waste that skilled work had been lavished on what seemed to be plastics and base metals. Dr Chalmeton made the patient as comfortable as he could, explaining that he could not administer drugs for the relief of pain until the social investigator had signed a receipt for them. Miss Fohrenbach arrived at five o'clock. It had taken her forty minutes to find a suitable parking space: the street appeared to be poor, but everyone living on it owned one or two cars. Dr Chalmeton, who was angry at having been kept waiting, declared he would not be responsible for the safety of his patient in a room filled with mould. Miss Fohrenbach retorted that the District could not resettle a family of fourteen persons who were foreign-born when there was a long list of native citizens waiting for accommodation. Mrs Ibrahim had in any case relinquished her right to a domicile in the Fifteenth District the day she lost consciousness in the road and allowed an ambulance to transport her to a hospital in the Seventh. It was up to the hospital to look after her now. Dr Chalmeton pointed out that housing of patients is not the business of hospitals. It was well known that the foreign poor preferred to crowd together in the fifteenth, where they could sing and dance in the streets and attend one another's weddings. Miss Fohrenbach declared that Mrs Ibrahim could easily have moved her bed into the kitchen, which was somewhat warmer and which boasted a window. When Mrs Ibrahim died, the children would be placed in foster homes, eliminating the need for a larger apartment. Dr Chalmeton remembers Miss Fohrenbach's then crying, 'Oh, why do all these people come here, where nobody wants them?' While he was trying to think of an answer, Mrs Ibrahim died.

In her testimony, Miss Fohrenbach recalls that she had to beg and plead with Dr Chalmeton to visit Mrs Ibrahim, who had been discharged from Regius Hospital without medicines or prescriptions or advice or instructions. Miss Fohrenbach had returned several times that April day to see if the Doctor had arrived. The first thing Dr Chalmeton said on entering the room was 'There is no way of helping these people. Even the simplest rules of hygiene are too complicated for them to follow. Wherever they settle, they spread disease and vermin. They have been responsible for outbreaks of aphthous stomatitis, hereditary hypoxia, coccidioidomycosis, gonorrheal arthritis, and scleroderma. Their eating habits are filthy. They never wash their hands. The virus that attacks them breeds in dirt. We took in the patient against all rules, after the ambulance drivers left her lying in the courtyard and drove off without asking for a receipt. Regius Hospital was built and endowed for ailing Greek scholars. Now it is crammed with unteachable persons who cannot read or write.' His cheeks and forehead were flushed, his speech incoherent and blurred. According to the social investigator, he was the epitome of the broken-down, irresponsible old rascals the Seventh District employs in its public services. Wondering at the effect this ranting of his might have on the patient, Miss Fohrenbach glanced at Mrs Ibrahim and noticed she had died.

Mrs Ibrahim's version of her death has the social investigator arriving first, bringing Mrs Ibrahim a present of a wine-coloured dressing gown made of soft, quilted silk. Miss Fohrenbach explained that the gown was part of a donation of garments to the needy. Large plastic bags, decorated with a moss rose, the emblem of the Fifteenth District, and bearing the words 'Clean Clothes for the Foreign-Born', had been distributed by volunteer workers in the more prosperous streets of the District. A few citizens kept the bags as souvenirs, but most had turned them in to the Welfare Bureau filled with attractive clothing, washed, ironed, and mended, and with missing buttons replaced. Mrs Ibrahim sat up and put on the dressing gown, and the social investigator helped her button it. Then Miss Fohrenbach changed the bed linen and pulled the bed away from the wall. She sat down and took Mrs Ibrahim's hand in hers and spoke about a new, sunny flat containing five warm rooms which would soon be available. Miss Fohrenbach said that arrangements had been made to send the twelve Ibrahim children to the mountains for special winter classes. They would be taught history and languages and would learn to ski.

The Doctor arrived soon after. He stopped and spoke to Mr Ibrahim, who was sitting at his workbench making an emerald patch box. The Doctor said to him, 'If you give me your social-security papers, I can attend to the medical insurance. It will save you a great deal of trouble.' Mr Ibrahim answered, 'What is social security?' The Doctor examined the patch box and asked Mr Ibrahim what he earned. Mr Ibrahim told him, and the Doctor said, 'But that is less than the minimum wage.' Mr Ibrahim said, 'What is a minimum wage?' The Doctor turned to Miss Fohrenbach, saying, 'We really must try and help them.' Mrs Ibrahim died. Mr Ibrahim, when he understood that nothing could be done, lay face down on the floor, weeping loudly. Then he remembered the rules of hospitality and got up and gave each of the guests a present—for Miss Fohrenbach a belt made of Syriac coins, a copy of which is in the Cairo Museum, and for the Doctor a bracelet of precious metal engraved with pomegranates, about sixteen pomegranates in all, that has lifesaving properties.

Mrs Ibrahim asks that her account of the afternoon be registered with the police as the true version and that copies be sent to the Doctor and the social investigator, with a courteous request for peace and silence.

Mrs Carlotte Essling, née Holmquist, complains of being haunted by her husband, Professor Augustus Essling, the philosopher and historian. When they were married, the former Miss Holmquist was seventeen. Professor Essling, a widower, had four small children. He explained to Miss Holmquist why he wanted to marry again. He said, 'I must have one person, preferably female, on whom I can depend absolutely, who will never betray me even in her thoughts. A disloyal thought revealed, a betrayal even in fantasy, would be enough to destroy me. Knowing that I may rely upon some one person will leave me free to continue my work without anxiety or distraction.' The work was the Professor's lifelong examination of the philosopher Nicolas de Malebranche, for whom he had named his eldest child. 'If I cannot have the unfailing loyalty I have described, I would as soon not marry at all,' the Professor added. He had just begun work on *Malebranche and Materialism.*

Mrs Essling recalls that at seventeen this seemed entirely within her possibilities, and she replied something like 'Yes, I see,' or 'I quite understand,' or 'You needn't mention it again.'

Mrs Essling brought up her husband's four children and had two more of her own, and died after thirty-six years of marriage at the age of fifty-three. Her husband haunts her with proof of her goodness. He tells people that Mrs Essling was born an angel, lived like an angel, and is an angel in eternity. Mrs Essling would like relief from this charge. 'Angel' is a loose way of speaking. She is astonished that the Professor cannot be more precise. Angels are created, not born. Nowhere in any written testimony will you find a scrap of proof that angels are 'good'. Some are merely messengers; others have a paramilitary function. All are stupid.

After her death, Mrs Essling remained in the Fifteenth District. She says she can go nowhere without being accosted by the Professor, who, having completed the last phase of his work *Malebranche and Mysticism,* roams the streets, looking in shop windows, eating lunch twice, in two different restaurants, telling his life story to waiters and bus drivers. When he sees Mrs Essling, he calls out, 'There you are!' and 'What have you been sent to tell me?' and 'Is there a message?' In July, catching sight of her at the open-air fruit market on Dulac Street, the Professor jumped off a bus, upsetting barrows of plums and apricots, waving an umbrella as he ran. Mrs Essling had to take refuge in the cold-storage room of the central market, where, years ago, after she had ordered twenty pounds of raspberries and currants for making jelly, she was invited by the wholesale fruit dealer, Mr Lobrano, aged twenty-nine to spend a holiday with him in a charming southern city whose Mediterranean Baroque churches he described with much delicacy of feeling. Mrs Essling was too startled to reply. Mistaking her silence, Mr Lobrano then mentioned a northern city containing a Gothic cathedral. Mrs Essling said that such a holiday was impossible. Mr Lobrano asked for one good reason. Mrs Essling was at that moment four months pregnant with her second child. Three stepchildren waited for her out in the street. A fourth stepchild was at home looking after the baby. Professor Essling, working on his *Malebranche and Money*, was at home, too, expecting his lunch. Mrs Essling realized she could not give Mr Lobrano one good reason. She left the cold-storage room without another word and did not return to it in her lifetime.

Mrs Essling would like to be relieved of the Professor's gratitude. Having lived an exemplary life is one thing; to have it thrown up at one is another. She would like the police to send for Professor Essling and tell him so. She suggests that the police find some method of keeping him off the streets. The police ought to threaten him; frighten him; put the fear of the Devil into him. Philosophy has made him afraid of dying. Remind him about how he avoided writing his *Malebranche and Mortality*. He is an old man. It should be easy.

VIRGIL BURNETT · b. 1928

Fallowfields

On a Saturday afternoon late in November a bus drew up at a crossroads in Southern Ontario where it rarely made a stop. Despite the raw wind that was blowing the vehicle stood there with its door open without anyone getting off.

'Who was it wanted Langenau?' the driver shouted over his shoulder. He pronounced the word as if its last syllable were 'gnaw'. Since he had already called the name of the place twice, there was impatience in his voice.

A man, whose name was Etheredge, suddenly started up in the back of the bus.

'Langenau?' he said. 'Did you say Langenau?'

He hauled his bag off the rack overhead and hurried forward.

'Are you sure this is Langenau?' he asked suspiciously.

The driver sighed. 'I've been on this run seventeen years, mister. This is it all right.'

Etheredge got down. The tails of his coat had hardly cleared the door when it closed. Before he could turn around the bus was on its way again. He looked bleakly about. There was nothing at the crossing to suggest that it deserved a name, nothing at all but a ramshackle frame building, once a store perhaps but now deserted, its windows boarded up. Nevertheless at each of the four approaches to the carrefour governmental signposts had been erected. On the two that Etheredge could read from where he stood, the same word was inscribed: Langenau.

He looked again at the shack. This time he noticed the black snout of an automobile protruding from the far side of the tumbled porch. Uncertainly he moved toward it. The car proved to be an old Citröen DS, an oddity in this part of Canada. Rummaging in its trunk was a young man wearing dark glasses, a suede jacket, and jeans.

Etheredge cleared his throat. The young man in the suede jacket straightened up.

'Mr Etheredge?'

The voice was soprano and the jacket full of bosom. The young man was in fact a young woman.

'Yes, I'm Etheredge.'

'Hedwig sent me,' the girl said. 'I'm supposed to drive you to Fallowfields.'

'Fallowfields?' Etheredge echoed in a mildly scornful tone that was characteristic of him. 'Is that what she calls her place?'

The girl looked at him as if he had said something stupid.

'That's what everybody round here calls it. That's its name.'

She got into the car and started its engine. Etheredge was about to join her when he saw that the seat next to her was already occupied. A large brindle cur sat there, or crouched there, as if preparing to launch itself at his throat. The animal appeared to be a cross between a Border Collie and a hyena. Its ears lay flat against its head; its fangs were ominously exposed; its eyes blazed with loathing.

'You'd better get in the back,' the girl said. 'Janis doesn't allow anyone to get very close to me.'

Warily Etheredge opened the rear door and climbed into the back seat. The watchful bitch shifted her position so that she could keep him in view. The tension in her ears and jaws relaxed, but her eyes never left his face.

The DS rolled forward, then turned onto the crossroad. At a rate far surpassing what Etheredge would have thought it capable of, the car accelerated and quickly left Langenau behind.

After a mile or so the girl took her right hand off the steering wheel, smoothed her short fair hair into a dovetail at the nape of her neck, then reached forward and snapped on the dashboard radio. It responded immediately in the voice of a country baritone.

'*There's women, there's girls, and there's ladies,*' it crooned.

'*There's yeses, there's noes, and there's maybes . . .*'

Etheredge groaned.

'How far is it to . . . to Fallowfields?' he called above the blare of the music.

'Not far,' the girl shouted back, 'not really far.'

As inadequate as this reply seemed to Etheredge, it proved to be true enough, for after a few minutes of hurtling along the empty, arrow-straight road, the car began to slow. It passed an abandoned schoolhouse, slowed even more, then stopped at the entrance to a tree-lined lane.

Etheredge glanced uneasily this way and that. Except for the schoolhouse behind and a silo a mile or so ahead, he could see no buildings.

'Well?' he demanded.

The girl looked at him in the rear-view mirror.

'This is as far as I go.'

'You were supposed to take me to Hedwig's house.'

'There's a tree down,' the girl said, nodding her head in the direction of the lane. 'Storm last night.'

Etheredge peered up the dark alley. A short distance from the mouth of it he could see a blasted sugar maple. It completely blocked the avenue.

'Late in the year for lightning,' the girl said laconically.

Etheredge knew better than to ask his next question, but he asked it anyway.

'How far will I have to walk?'

'Not far,' the girl said, 'not really far.'

It was already late in the day when Etheredge began his trek up to the house called Fallowfields. Once he got round the fallen maple, the going was easy enough for the slope was gentle. On either side of him grainfields rolled away toward the horizon. Up ahead there was only a patch of grey sky framed by the arching maple branches. At this season the fields were stripped of their fruit. The stubble in them was untidy, tatty-looking. The vistas across them were neither pleasant nor interesting to Etheredge, who would have preferred something less austere and more picturesque. Even so, he had to admit that there was something awesome about this landscape, or at least about its massive undulation, which reminded him oddly of the surge of the open sea.

A few paces short of the hill Etheredge was stopped in his tracks by a shrill monosyllabic cry, human, but as raucous as the cry of a gull. A moment later this distressing sound was made even more distressing by a succession of sharp explosions.

Gun shots, Etheredge thought nervously. Someone is firing a gun.

Uncertain what to do, he clutched his suitcase to his belly, as if he believed the shirts and socks and underwear inside could protect him from bullets. At first he could see nothing disturbing, then a horse's head appeared above the furrowed ground, and another, and another, until finally a team of five great draught animals, matched sorrels with flaxen manes, rose into view from a trough beyond a knoll. On a harrow behind the team a woman rode. She was stern, weathered, of indeterminate age. Even though she laboured in the fields, she wore a long black dress and a white coif, the anachronistic costume of Mennonite women. In her hand was a long ploughman's whip, the source, Etheredge reckoned, of the sounds he had taken to be gunshots.

Etheredge lowered his bag but didn't move. In fact he stood very, very still. For some reason that he didn't try to understand, he preferred not to attract the attention of the woman with the harrow.

The team passed very close to where he stood, so close that the woman could have cut him with her whip had she chosen to do so. Whether or not she was aware of his presence, he could not tell. If she saw him, she gave no sign of it. Her eyes were unswervingly on her horses, on their great iron-shod feet and their mighty rumps, and on the earth that stretched out before her waiting to be stirred by her massive tool.

Not until the team had descended once more into the trough beyond the knoll did Etheredge continue on his way. Another few moments brought him to the top of the hill. It was quite flat and at the centre of it, framed by pines, black cedars and more maples, stood Fallowfields.

The main body of the old mansion was cubical in form, two storeys high, built of ochre brick. It had tall windows, now tightly shuttered against the storm, broad cornices, and a classical portico to protect the front entrance. It was orderly, harmonious, Palladian in inspiration.

Orderly, that is, up to the level of the eaves. The higher reaches of the building seemed to have been conceived by a different architect, or if by the same one, by a different aspect of his nature. The attics were a dark and sinister jumble of slated mansards, oddly set dormers, widows' walks, towers, chimneys, wrought-iron finials. This part of the house was not merely Victorian, it was a phantasmagoria, the architecture of bad dreams.

'Looniness,' Etheredge decided, 'sheer looniness.'

He spoke aloud, as men so often do who find themselves alone is desolate places.

The words were hardly out of his mouth when the door beneath the portico opened and Hedwig appeared, or her face did at least. The rest of her was lost in darkness. She was wearing black and the entrance hall was unlighted.

Etheredge frowned. Why black? he asked himself, as if the colour could only signify mourning or some condition equally dire. For an instant the figure of the Mennonite ploughwoman loomed ominously in his mind.

As Hedwig came outdoors and down the stairs to meet him, he saw that there was nothing about her costume but its blackness to link her to the Mennonites. On the contrary everything about her mode of dress spoke of the Old Order's anathema: worldliness. The jabot of her silk shirt was Byronically loosened to expose her throat and the swell of her breast. A chain that might have served as a training collar for a largish dog cinched her waist. Velvet trousers narrowly encased her slender legs. Worldliness unquestionably, and to Etheredge's way of thinking, it was worldliness of a very comforting sort, the sort that might very soon provide him with a drink.

'I'm sorry you had to walk,' Hedwig said. 'We've had a storm.'

She looks different, Etheredge thought. Something about her is very different.

'I enjoyed it,' he lied. 'Have you cut your hair?'

Instead of answering she put out her hand to take his valise. Involuntarily his grip tightened. Her assumption, so familiar to him from their time together, that he was physically inept, annoyed him. It had always annoyed him. He wasn't an athlete, as she was, but he wasn't exactly a weakling either.

'I can manage,' he said, moving the bag away from Hedwig's reaching hand. Their fingers met briefly on the handle.

'I just thought . . .' she began, but whatever it was she meant to say, she thought better of it.

Instead she turned and led the way into the house. Although there was still a bit of daylight outside, the bare and lofty hall in which they now stood was stygian. A candle burned on the newel post of the spiral staircase at the far end of it.

'The hydro lines are down,' Hedwig explained, 'as well as my maple tree. We've no electricity, I'm afraid.'

No hot water, Etheredge thought, as he followed Hedwig along the hall. After his stroll in the brisk autumn air he had been hoping for a bath almost as fervently as he hoped for a drink.

'I'd like to wash up a bit,' he said rather grimly, 'even with cold water.'

'There's a lavatory under the stairs—that little door.'

She indicated another, taller door as well. 'I'll wait for you in here.'

Etheredge went to the foot of the stairs and put down his bag at last. Taking the candle with him, he entered the washroom. It was low and cramped, but he managed to attend to his needs. He was relieved to discover that the plumbing still functioned properly, although he didn't understand how since there was no electricity to drive a pump. Could there be a windmill, he asked himself, or a reservoir in the crazy attics of the house? By whatever means it worked, despite the very odd sounds that it made in the process— wheezing, choking sounds, and something like a giggle.

Hedwig was in the living-room, a space that was as long and high-ceilinged as the hall, but much broader and only a bit less dismal. A camper's kerosene lamp gave light to one end of the room; a wood fire in a black marble fireplace to the other. Above the mantlepiece was a shadowy portrait of a thoroughbred horse. Here and there about the other walls faded photographs were hung. There was very little furniture and what there was looked old and shabby. The only well-cared-for object in the room was a dressage saddle. It sat astride a sawhorse and fairly gleamed in the faint light. On the floor near it was strewn the litter necessary to the cleaning of tack: a pail half-filled with water, tins of saddle soap, jars of mink oil, bottles of neatsfoot, rags, both clean and dirty. A pair of mucky boots stood against the wall beside a slender whip.

It had always been one of Etheredge's chief grievances that Hedwig turned every room in which she lived into an antechamber to a stable. He said nothing of this now. It was no longer any of his business what Hedwig did with her rooms or anything else. Instead he asked about the painting.

'Is that Damaris?'

Hedwig smiled. 'No, but she looks like Damaris, doesn't she? The painting was in the house when I bought it, along with most of the furniture. It seemed a good omen.'

It would be like Hedwig, Etheredge thought, to buy a property because it had a picture of a horse some place about.

'The carpet didn't come with the house,' he said.

'Are you still cross about the carpet?'

'I was never cross, as you put it. The carpet was yours after all.'

'Yes, but the flat looked so empty without it.'

'I found another one,' Etheredge said evenly. 'A Bokkhara.'

Hedwig took his coat and put in on a chair near the door, then went to a sideboard and sorted through some bottles.

'Scotch or rye?' she asked.

'Still Scotch.' Who, he wondered, had been drinking her rye.

'Of course,' she said. 'There's no ice. The storm . . .'

Drink in hand Etheredge settled into an old armchair near the fire. Hedwig drew up a Windsor chair opposite him. She had no drink, which surprised Etheredge. When she was with him, she had cared too much for alcohol, or so he had believed.

'I brought the papers,' he said.

'Do you want me to sign them now? Shall I get my pen?'

Etheredge bristled. 'Don't be like that. I just thought I would mention . . .'

'That *is* why you're here, isn't it? To see that the papers get signed?'

'I suppose so.'

'They're the very last ones, aren't they?'

Etheredge took a deep drink. 'Yes, the last ones.'

'You might have saved yourself the trip by mailing them.'

'I don't trust the postal service in the city,' he replied, 'let alone out here.'

As he was saying this, he remembered Hedwig's indifference to all matters except those touching on horses and horsemanship. If the papers had been mailed, he had no guarantee that she would sign them, or even open the envelopes in which they came. And there was a lot of money involved.

Hedwig made a face that was not quite a smile.

'You don't trust them with anything so important as the last trans-action between us, you mean.'

'Not with anything at all,' Etheredge said sulkily.

She looked at her hands for a moment, then up at the painting of the horse.

'Damaris is coming along very well,' she said brightly. 'I should be able to show her Medium I this summer.'

Etheredge did not precisely remember what competition at the Medium I level entailed, but he knew that it was rigorous and well-advanced along the ladder of perfection that dressage riders and their horses together climb.

'You must let me know,' he said not very truthfully, 'if you bring her to town. I would like to see what the two of you can do.'

'Of course,' she promised.

Both of them knew, however, that she would not.

She offered him another drink, which he readily accepted. Staying sober, it seemed to him, would hardly make the time pass more rapidly.

'Tell me about your house,' he said for the want of anything else of say.

Again she looked down at her hands. They were folded neatly in her lap, the hands of a working woman, shapely, but hard and brown. There was no jewellery on them, not even a wrist watch. Nor was there any mark on her ring finger, nothing to suggest that she had once worn a wedding band.

'I don't know anything about it really, except it used to be an orphanage.'

Etheredge looked unconvinced. 'It wasn't built to be an orphanage. It's too grand.'

Hedwig got up, crossed the room, and took one of the photographs off the wall. She brought it back to Etheredge. The image was old and brown, a hundred years old, he judged from the quality of it, perhaps more. It was a view of Hedwig's house. A woman was standing in front of it with a group of children, little girls, a dozen of them, six on either side of her. They were dressed identically in black. One of them held the woman's hand.

Etheredge made no comment on this evidence.

'It's a lot of house for one person,' he said.

Hedwig glanced about the big, shadowy room.

'I bought it because of the arena. The house was just part of the deal. It's a fine arena, two-thirds regulation size—just right for my work. It's almost new, too. The man who was here before me bred hunters.'

'I suppose he went broke,' Etheredge said sourly, 'like all the other breeders we've known.'

'I'll see about some dinner,' Hedwig murmured, getting to her feet.

'He didn't go broke?'

She shook her head. 'No. He had a fall. He doesn't ride any more.'

'Does he walk?'

'No, he doesn't do that either.'

Hedwig withdrew to the kitchen, wherever that was. Musing, Etheredge finished his drink. When she returned, it was with a heavily laden tea cart. Because of the power failure the meal she had prepared was more like a picnic than a proper dinner. There were good things to eat, however, local products mostly, summer sausage and head-cheese, several chutneys, a green tomato relish, a salad of beets and red cabbage, old cheddar, black bread, a clutch of small firm apples.

'Ida Reds from my own orchard,' Hedwig said proudly.

There was also a bottle of wine. It had a Niagara label, but Etheredge found it very good, despite his prejudice for foreign vintages.

During the meal they spoke little. Travelling always made Etheredge hungry and today's trip was no exception. Hedwig ate with a grave sort of concentration that was peculiar to her. It was most evident when she was riding, but, Etheredge remembered, she was also like that when she made love. By nature she was earnest, profoundly earnest. When he first met her, Etheredge found this quality in her both touching and erotically exciting. Later, he found it intimidating.

'I saw the most extraordinary woman on my way up here,' Etheredge said, as he was finishing his cheese. 'She was ploughing or something with a lot of very big horses.'

Hedwig nodded. 'Suzannah Weber. She's my nearest neighbour.'

'A Mennonite?'

'That's right.'

'Do Mennonite women usually plough? It looks very much like men's work to me.'

Hedwig reach out for the wine bottle, deliberately filled Etheredge's glass, then her own.

'Suzannah lost her husband a couple of years ago,' she said.

About when you lost yours, Etheredge thought. He took an apple, cut it carefully, put a bite in his mouth.

'He hanged himself,' Hedwig continued.

Etheredge had some trouble swallowing the apple.

'I'm sorry,' he murmured, when his throat was clear.

Hedwig shrugged. 'Why should you be? It's nothing to do with you. Besides, he was horrible, dirty man.'

She got up and cleared away everything but the wine and a single glass.

'I'm going to check on Damaris,' she said. 'Would you like to see her?'

Etheredge looked at the wine bottle instead. 'I'll appreciate her more tomorrow, when I've had a good night's rest.'

'All right. I may be out there quite a while, so I'd better show you to your room. Why don't you bring the wine?'

Etheredge considered taking the bottle with him, but settled for finishing the glassful that he had instead. Hedwig had proceeded him into the hall. When he got out there, she was already climbing the circular stair. She had his valise in her hand, his coat over her arm.

'Bring the candle,' she called back to him as she disappeared in the darkness overhead.

Even with the candle Etheredge could see very little when he reached the second floor.

'Hedwig?' he muttered uncertainly. 'Hedwig?'

'Over here.'

He looked toward the sound of her voice. Somewhere down the inky corridor he made out a movement. Holding the candle higher he moved in that direction. His faint light revealed Hedwig's form. Framed in darkness, silvered by the candle's tentative beams, she seemed suddenly very lovely to him, as desirable as he remembered her in the days before the trouble between them began, in the days when he could perceive her with eyes unclouded by rancour.

Without really thinking about what he was doing, he put out his hand to her, seeking to touch her, on the shoulder perhaps, or the cheek, or the breast. Before his questing fingers reached her, however, she spun away and disappeared again in the gloom.

Her voice drifted back to him.

'In here,' she said. 'I've put you in here.'

It was a corner room, but after all the wandering about in the dark, Etheredge could not be sure at which corner of the house it was situated. Tightly closed interior shutters kept him from seeing outside, not that he was likely to be able to take his bearing on a night as dark and disagreeable as he imagined this one to be. The only pieces of furniture were a wash stand and a bed, both built of sombre oak in a country carpenter's version of a neogothic style. The bed was covered by a quilt, white on black, rigorously geometric. Etheredge's valise stood in the middle of the floor with his coat draped over it.

Hedwig's straight figure emerged from the shadows beyond the bed. Her arms were folded, protectively perhaps, across her bosom as she crossed to the door.

'Goodnight, then,' she said in a colourless voice.

'Hedwig . . .' he began again.

'I must look after Damaris,' She stepped into the corridor.

'Wait! You'll need a light.'

'I know the house,' she said. 'Sleep well.'

The room was cold and uncompromising, so Etheredge stripped and went directly to bed, neglecting to wash in what he knew must be icy water, neglecting even to search in his bag for his pajamas. He did not sleep immediately, or even soon. Naked beneath the heavy quilts he squirmed about trying to find some ease on the hard and alien mattress. Hedwig of course was the true cause of his discomfort. She was gone but her essence lingered after her, and her desirability, reborn now in Etheredge after the years of bitterness and the apathy they had engendered.

Without meaning to, certainly without wanting to, he drifted into a vague and disjointed meditation on the woman who once had been his wife. These speculations might have been intellectual in nature, or even spiritual. They were in fact almost exclusively physical. Quite against his will he found himself exploring in memory all the eccentricities of Hedwig's person, all the fleshy precincts that formerly were so familiar to him, so necessary, so much cherished. As this exploration continued it became increasingly intimate, almost morbidly specific. Inevitably it became lustful. As soon as he recognized the symptoms of his rut, which he considered to be both embarrassing and humiliating under the present circumstances, he struggled to suppress them. It was, however, too late. Already the inexorable mechanism had begun to turn. A tremor had developed in his lower viscera. His heartbeat had quickened. Weights had begun to shift in the organ between his thighs as hot blood surged here and there. He groaned aloud, thrashed about, struggled with the bedclothes—a helpless victim of those twin torments, diabolical in their sophistication, frustration and regret.

Finally he rested, or fell at least into a kind of stupor. He was very close to sleep but still awake enough to ask himself for what must have been the ten-thousandth time the question that had always been at the centre of his association with Hedwig.

'What is it that she wants?' he mumbled into the goosedown pillow. 'What?'

Once more he rolled over and dragged the quilt up about his ears. The last sound that he heard was the giggle of the plumbing beneath the stairs.

He did not sleep long—an hour perhaps, hardly more—and when he woke it was not because of the bed, or the quilt, or the bedroom's chill. What woke him was a sound, a thin, unmelodious song, the sort of ditty that some women croon over their babies, and most little girls over their dolls.

Disgruntled, and very drowsy still, Etheredge lay there listening. At first he could not make out the words; then, bit by bit, some of them became clear to him, if not exactly meaningful.

Now we dance,

Now we dance,

he heard, or thought he heard, and after that something witless and fading:

Looby, looby, loo . . . .

He sat up. Was it Hedwig's voice? It had to be, he supposed, and yet it didn't sound like her. Nor, so far as he knew, did she still play with dolls.

Rock a cradle empty,

the voice sang tonelessly,

Rock a cradle by . . . .

It wasn't Hedwig, Etheredge decided. It was a child.

Looby, looby, loo . . . .

'What the hell is going on?' he growled.

He tossed back the covers and got out of bed. The floor was like polar ice beneath his bare feet. He found the candle easily, but only after some stumbling about and a couple of sharp raps on the shins did he locate his coat and the matches he remembered were in its pocket. Shivering violently he put on the coat and lit the candle.

He went to the door and listened. A floor board creaked and the wind sighed, but no one was singing. He waited a moment, then abruptly opened the door. So far as he could see, the hall was empty. After another brief, listening pause he stepped into the corridor. As soon as he crossed the door sill, he felt a strange rush of wind, as if something had passed close to his face, a bird or a bat or an object thrown. Instinctively he put up a hand to shield his feeble light. Again a draught swept over him, sucking the flame sharply toward the stairwell.

'Damn!' Etheredge jerked his singed fingers away from the candle and shook his hand to cool it. The flame steadied, grew tall again, and even.

'Something's been left open.' he muttered. He could not resist the peevish reflection that it was very like Hedwig to forget to close the house properly.

Again the draught pulled at the flame, almost extinguishing it this time.

Looby, looby, looby light, someone sang. The voice, like the draught, seemed to come from the stairwell.

He moved in the direction, stealthily, determined to catch red-handed whoever was behaving so absurdly.

Roundabout, roundabout

Magotty pie . . . .

'At the foot of the stairs,' Etheredge said under his breath. 'There's a kid down there.'

Roundabout, roundabout . . . .

He reached the curving bannister. Holding the candle high, he leaned far out and peered into the depths below. Something, he thought, darted away from the light, or several somethings. Children, he told himself, pranksters from a neighbouring farm taking advantage of the blackout to tease a lonely woman.

Looby, looby, loo . . . .

'Hey, there,' Etheredge called, making his voice as gruff and authoritarian as possible, 'you kids bugger off.'

Without waiting for a response, he started down the steps to make sure that the intruders did as they were told. His approach, or the appearance of his naked white legs beneath the skirts of his overcoat, or something else perhaps, set off a peal of laughter in the downstairs hall. It bubbled and chirped, then rose to a high-pitched squeal and was finally lost in the sound of the wind outside.

'All right, damn it,' Etheredge snarled. 'You kids are asking for it.'

Fully prepared to lay on with a vengeance as soon as he found someone to punish, he reached the foot of the stairs. Again he raised the candle and peered out. There was no one, nothing. He strode the length of the hall and tried the front door. It was not only closed and locked, but barred by a heavy bolt as well. Turning aside he checked the living-room. It was warm still from the embers of the fire. It was also empty. In rapid succession he investigated the other rooms on the ground floor. He even looked in the lavatory beneath the stairs. There was no one anywhere. During this search he discovered two more exit doors—one to the cellar and another to the buildings outside in the back, which connected with the stables and the arena. Both of these were securely closed and locked. After all Hedwig had not shirked her custodial responsibilities.

Baffled, he returned to the stairwell. Could he have missed a door? Might there—he felt ridiculous even considering it—might there be a secret entrance to the house?

As if in reply to this unspoken question another sing-song chant began. This time it came from some place high above his head at the top of the spiralling stairs, from the dark irrational region of the attics.

Blind man . . . blind man . . .

The voice that did the singing was so thin and infantile, so painfully faint, that Etheredge could hardly make out the words.

Sure you cannot . . . see . . .?

Like a wind-up toy that was running down, the voice became weaker, slower, more indistinct with each syllable.

Turn . . . around . . . three times . . .

Try . . . to catch . . . me . . . eee . . .

And then it died away entirely.

Something about the quality of this voice, about its poignancy, its sweet melancholy, reached into Etheredge's tripes, gripped hard, and twisted. At last it dawned on him that he was involved in something more bizarre than the practical jokes of a band of farm children. This realization made him feel very cold. Like all northerners he had been cold before, but never as cold as this, and never with a cold of this kind.

Despite the chill, or perhaps because of it, for he was not a cowardly man, he started slowly up the steps again. Once more antic gusts of air played about him, threatening at any moment to steal his light. As a precaution against this eventuality, he transferred the candle to his left hand and put his right on the bannister. If his light happened to be blown out, he would not be entirely without guidance in the stairwell's uncompromising darkness.

There was no singing now, nor any other sound, except the soft tread of Etheredge's bare feet and the occasional groan of a hardwood step as he put his weight upon it. Even the wind, so persistent earlier, had died away to nothingness.

He reached the second floor landing and paused to listen. All was silence. He felt suddenly quite foolish. Could he have been mistaken about the songs? Surely he had heard something, but might not his groggy state—the wine, his bad dreams—have caused him to exaggerate perfectly ordinary phenomena? Was it possible that the sounds he had heard were nothing more than effects of the wind distorted somehow by this perverse old house and his own weary mind?

For a while longer he listened—listened to nothing. With each moment that he stood there he suspected more strongly that he had made the whole thing up. He felt very stupid. He also felt very cold, but naturally cold now, as anyone might who was wandering about a big old house in the middle of a November night. The two feelings conspired to convince him that he should go back to bed and forget that he had ever left it, or try to forget anyway.

He was about to do just that when, without any warning or reason, the flame of his candle began to shrink. Very slowly it diminished until it was only a tiny point of fire, the least gleam. Then it winked out completely.

Etheredge stiffened. All his rationalizations disappeared with the last of the light. He now knew, as certainly as he knew anything, that he was not alone in the stairwell. Something was close to him in the darkness, horribly close. Like a bird before an asp, he froze and waited for whatever it was to act.

When the song began again, it was sung by the same voice that had called him 'blind man' from the shadows at the head of the stairs. He had no difficulty hearing it now, for although it sang *pianissimo*, it did so firmly and defiantly, with perfect diction and in regular, even stately measure.

> *Blind man, blind man*
> *You only think you see.*
> *Turn around, turn around,*
> *Try to catch me.*
> *Turn east, turn west,*
> *Catch me if you can.*
> *You'll never, never catch me,*
> *Blind, blind man.*

The next morning Hedwig got up shortly after seven. She was pleased to find that during the night the electricity had been restored. There was light and plenty of hot water. After doing some stretching exercises, she took a shower, cleaned her teeth, brushed her hair lengthily. Before dressing she opened the shutters to observe the quality of the day.

It was calmer than the day before had been, but still overcast. The empty fields were dreary, funereal; the trees, flayed by recent gales, skeletal. To a person with a metaphysical turn of mind, this would almost certainly seem a day signifying death, the death of the year at any rate. To Hedwig it was a fine day for a hack.

Inspired by the idea of an outing, she dressed quickly and went in search of her breakfast. Not until she was out in the hall and found him blocking her way did she remember her houseguest. He was standing in the stairwell. His left hand was clutching a stump of candle; his right, the curving bannister. Except for an overcoat, loosely draped from his shoulders and indecently agape, he was naked. His lips were blue with cold.

'What are you doing out here, Charles?' Hedwig demanded. 'It's chilly in this hall. You'll catch your death dressed like that.'

He made no reply, nor did he move, not even to look at her.

'What is it, Charles?'

Still he said nothing. Hedwig stepped closer, then put out her hand, took his jaw between her fingers, and turned his face toward her. Their eyes met.

'What is it?' she repeated.

'*Looby, looby,*' he whispered through trembling lips, '*looby, looby, loo . . .*'

It took all Hedwig's considerable horsewoman's strength to pry Etheredge away from the bannister and get him back to his bed. It took both time and brandy, administered in liberal and frequent doses, to return him to something like his normal self. As soon as he achieved this state, he looked wildly about the austere little chamber, then leapt out of bed and began to put on his clothes.

'Call me a taxi,' he said.

'I'm going to call a doctor.'

'No time for that. I've got to get back to town.'

'But there's no bus for hours. . .'

Etheredge stopped her with a look. The appalling expression had come back into his eyes.

'Call me a taxi,' he rasped through clenched teeth.

Hedwig did as she was told. While she was telephoning, she heard Etheredge descending the staircase. He was moving rapidly, too rapidly for safety, it seemed to her.

She hung up and stared after him, then hesitated and crossed the hall to the bedroom he had used. It was stuffy and reeked of brandy. As she was opening the shutters, she noticed that Etheredge had forgotten his valise. She took it with her when she went downstairs.

Etheredge was at the front door fumbling with its locking mechanism.

'I'll get down to the road,' he said as Hedwig came up to him, 'so the driver won't have to wait.'

'No need for that. She'll pick you up here.'

Etheredge stopped fumbling, but continued to stare at the lock.

'The tree,' he said desperately. 'Wasn't there a tree?'

'Suzannah moved it.'

'Suzannah?'

'My neighbour.'

'She *moved* it!' The alarm in his voice amounted almost to terror.

'With her team,' Hedwig explained. 'You saw her horses, didn't you? She cleared the lane before she went in last night.'

He fumbled again, even more urgently. Hedwig reached forward and released the lock. The door swung open.

They went outside. Together they stood on the steps waiting for the taxi. Neither of them spoke. They heard the vehicle long before they saw it. It was the same DS as the day before. The same girl drove it. Janis was sitting beside her.

Hedwig opened the car door for Etheredge and held it as he climbed stiffly inside.

'The papers are in your bag,' she said, as she pushed the valise in after him.

He looked up vacantly: 'What papers?'

'The ones you brought all the way out here for me to sign.'

'Oh,' he said, as if he were only dimly aware of what she meant, 'those papers.'

Hedwig spoke softly to the cabdriver.

'But there won't be a bus through Langenau for hours,' Etheredge heard the blond girl say.

Hedwig shrugged, murmured something else.

'OK, Hedwig,' the girl said. 'You're the boss.'

She rolled up the window, put the DS in gear. It swung heavily about, then pulled away from the house.

I should have said something, Etheredge told himself as the DS gathered speed. I should at least have said goodbye.

At the entrance to the lane it occurred to him that he might still save face by waving. He twisted about and looked through the rear window. He did not, however, wave. He didn't even lift his hand. All he did was look.

Hedwig was standing where he had left her before the steps of the house. Her stance had not changed, nor had the expression on her face. Even so, she was very different for she had been joined by a group of children, little girls, a dozen of them, six on each side of her. They were dressed identically in black. One of them held Hedwig's hand.

Then they were gone. The DS had crested the hall, was gliding down the slope beyond. There was nothing now for Etheredge to see through the glass of the rear window but a black interlace of sugar maple branches.

The car reached the main road, paused, turned into it. The blond girl briefly fixed an eye on Etheredge through her mirror, then she looked back at the road and began to hum a tune. She put no words to it, but Etheredge recognized it as the same one he had heard on the radio the evening before, the one about the women, the girls, and the ladies—the yeses, the noes, and the maybes.

ANTONINE MAILLET · b. 1929

The Ghost of Lovers' Lane

If anyone feels a shock of recognition when reading this tale, he will be absolutely right: my story is about him. The rest are conceited fools of no interest whatsoever to the storyteller.

This story comes to me from Arthur, who got it from Pierre à Tom, who heard it from Thaddée à Louis, who had it told to him exactly as I'm telling it to you by none other than Johnny Picoté. All those lips and ears are the most respectable ones in La Pointe à Jérôme and, excepting mine, are very well thought of back behind my father's place. So I'll refrain from interfering and give you this story in its original form, just granting myself the right to introduce a little Acadian grammar and local syntax here and there.

But if the storytellers of La Pointe are to receive the credit for the merits of my tale, I suppose they'll also accept the blame, should one of those fools I mentioned earlier decide to take offence at not being in my story.

There were several people involved. Arthur made that much quite clear. Some say fifteen, others forty, a few would include the entire parish. Now that, if I may be allowed to venture an opinion, seems a bit steep. It's not that the parish wouldn't have been capable—it's the sprightliest, cheekiest little lady of a parish ever created by the archdiocese—but because in a story like this one, there simply isn't enough room for everybody.

After all, it's a question of priorities. You have to start by excluding the women and children, at least for the main roles. I repeat, the main roles, because as lookouts, and in certain roles as tale-bearers and gossips, you'd find all kinds. And to say that Calixte's widow did not have a hand in the affair ... But we'll talk about Calixte's widow later, at the right time and place.

At first no one seemed to take the matter seriously. A few fishermen from Fond de la Baie had reported that a drivelling old fool in Lovers' Lane was having visions of some sort, and that people were talking about it at La Pirogue. An apparition had appeared in front of him, they said, without believing in that apparition any more than they believed in the appearance of the Halley's Comet. But when, three days later, the same apparition showed itself to a couple of men from La Baie who were peacefully lugging their lobster traps, the drama entered its second phase.

The news followed the coast, turned the point, climbed the cliffs, and flooded the village in less than twenty-four hours. People repeated what they knew: that two of the most honest men in the Baie, carrying their traps and causing no one any harm, had come face to face with . . . That's where things turned awkward; no one knew what to call whatever it was. It was white, it moved along, and its shape might have been human if it had wriggled less; but it didn't stop; it looked like a scarecrow without really looking like one.

'Wouldn't it be a ghost?' asked a little girl from the Cap, without meaning any harm.

From then on, the thing was called by its name, and matters progressed very quickly. The entire parish took an interest in the ghost's comings and goings. In the end, they determined the exact time and place of its apparitions and grew accustomed, little by little, to its ways. Some daring young men from La Butte à Tim even made so bold as to touch it. But this particular spirit was not one to compromise with his ghostly duties, and disappeared. The show-offs of La Butte à Tim got off with a shake of the parochial head that left them with no wish to try again.

But the ghost proved to be a good sport, and three days later resumed its apparitions. And the parish became more and more familiar with its tricks.

Now here Johnny Picoté, the first teller of this tale, would surely had condescended to provide his public with the necessary geographical explanations, had he recognized among his listeners any strangers to La Pointe à Jérôme. I therefore take it upon myself to plump up the story a little, just to make things clearer, because I love you all. I swear that if that storyteller were alive—may his ashes rest in peace!—I'd leave it to him; but I must take this liberty because he's dead and buried, the poor departed soul.

The parish I'm talking about, the stage of this drama, lies in the most beautiful and blossoming region of the entire country. At the time, it was quite a plump little parish, decent and dauntless, but also as cunning and crafty as they come. Under its meek, well-mannered exterior was a town that would have been capable of declaring itself a republic, had it been pushed to do so. Fortunately, the entire country respected its whims and independent spirit, and there was peace.

But this did not stop certain little villages too close to it from envying this parish so nicely snuggled between the sea and the hills. A broad King's Highway crossed it from one end, to the other, and numerous trails and cow paths linked it to its neighbours. But above all, alone of its kind, it dominated the bay. You will say that other parishes have their bays, that water is certainly not lacking in the area, and that the sea belongs to everyone. I know, I know. But what concerns us here is this particular bay: the Baie. A bay seven miles long, formed by a dune of pure, flourlike sand, like no other in the world . . . more or less. And at the end of the dune, a bottleneck large enough to allow the schooners to pass, at night, without the neighbouring villages' knowing. By now you must be starting to grasp all the advantages of such a topography on the very edge of the ocean, during the golden days of commerce with the islands.

One moonless night, a little before midnight, the prow of a small schooner was making its way between the sandbanks and the rocks of the bottleneck, as far as possible from either side, and sailing up the bay in complete silence. Lamps and torches were extinguished before reaching the coast; but a lantern was lit and set to swing from port to starboard in the shrouds. On the rock in front, a farmer's lantern answered the one on the sea. Then the night became pitch black.

And the same business took place again on the following night.

As Pierre à Tom was to say later, the curious crowd that would collect to watch the apparition, at the end of Lovers' Lane, would have been able to discover a far greater mystery on the coast, had they but taken the trouble to go and look. But the curious crowd followed the ghost, and the sea was quiet.

It seems that sea would still be quiet to this day, Arthur told me, if the village of La Pirogue had not intervened. But Arthur was talking several years ago. Since then, the role played by Saint-Hilaire in this ghost business has been revealed, and especially the role played by those wicked creatures—the women of the village of Collette!

Saint-Hilaire and the village of Collette, as well as that of La Pirogue, were the closest neighbours of La Pointe à Jérôme. Belligerent, jealous, bloodthirsty neighbours. They always had their mouths open, ready to gobble up a pasture or a field that had belonged to my parish since the time of the very first pioneers. In vain we would put up the fences every spring—the very next winter would pull them down; and the villages of Collette and Saint-Hilaire would somehow manage to put back the pickets and posts at least another twenty feet. So I leave you to guess the frame of mind of those quarrelsome neighbours when they learned about the ghost!

They started by spitting in the face of anything that could be taken for a ghost or a spectre. They could not be made to believe, those people! They had lived long enough . . . But seeing that the ghost of Lovers' Lane went on with his apparitions all the same, they ended up by declaring the ghost the common property of all the villages on the coast.

At this, La Pointe à Jérôme leapt up in protest, and had a few wise old churchgoing folk not intervened, the whole matter would have ended pretty badly for all three parishes.

But the only one to suffer the consequences was the ghost.

All the storytellers agree that La Pointe à Jérôme was wrong in giving its neighbours the cold shoulder. Because even if they weren't the strongest, they were by far the worst spoilsports. And that's the most dangerous sort of village in a case as delicate and mysterious as that of Lovers' Lane. That's why so many will-o'the-wisps and pirate treasures have disappeared without a trace. The way to handle this matter correctly would have been to deal with the ghost on his own terms, and without getting hot around the collar. But tempers flared and the sacred nature of the adventure was soon forgotten.

The angry neighbours, realizing that they would not be allowed their share of the ghost, decided to use brute force. And that was the craziest, most foolhardy enterprise ever attempted in this part of the country. The contestants themselves, had they been able to foresee the consequences of their actions . . . But, as Thaddée would say, no one ever thinks of the consequences. As the outcome was to prove.

The storytellers have never agreed on the events that took place that celebrated night in Lovers' Lane. Some say they attacked from the coast; others say from the woods. According to Thaddée à Louis, they came directly down the King's Highway. All that is known for certain is that they battled all night, fighting over the ghost piece by piece, and that next morning both parishes found themselves red-faced and empty-handed, except for a few shreds of ghostly skin, as white as a sheet.

Each man returned to his cart or his boat, puzzled and ashamed, not daring to question too carefully either his neighbour's heart or his own. But this uneasy feeling was not to last very long, because it proved too much for the widow of Calixte.

'Don't you think we know bloody well what's going on?' she cried from door to door, from gate to gate.

No, she didn't know. No one knew just yet. But everyone suspected something, and Calixte's widow was going to get to the bottom of it before too long. Time was hanging heavy since the death of the ghost, and everybody felt the devil of an itch.

It has been said that Calixte's widow herself took charge of the matter, but there's no proof of that. Whoever led the enquiry, it was led straight to the coast, there where the dune and the solid ground meet, there where the little ship from the islands, unseen by the customs' men, was unloading its cargo of barrels and bottles.

The people of La Pointe à Jérôme and the neighbouring parishes had more than one reason to miss their ghost. For these mysterious beings who take the trouble of coming from so far away to disturb the living usually leave, along the way, a certain taste for this life.

And just to repeat the very words of Johnny Picoté, the first teller of the story, who told it to Thaddée à Louis, who reported it to Pierre à Tom, who passed it on to Arthur, who told me, the case of the ghost of Lovers' Lane was the greatest and last event of the Prohibition era in the entire eastern part of the country.

Translated by Alberto Manguel

TIMOTHY FINDLEY · b. 1930

Dreams

Doctor Menlo was having a problem: he could not sleep and his wife—the other Doctor Menlo—was secretly staying awake in order to keep an eye on him. The trouble was that, in spite of her concern and in spite of all her efforts, Doctor Menlo—whose name was Mimi—was always nodding off because of her exhaustion.

She had tried drinking coffee, but this had no effect. She detested coffee and her system had a built-in rejection mechanism. She also prescribed herself a week's worth of Dexedrine to see if that would do the trick. *Five mg at bedtime*—all to no avail. And even though she put the plastic bottle of small orange hearts beneath her pillow and kept augmenting her intake, she would wake half an hour later with a dreadful start to discover the night was moving on to morning.

Everett Menlo had not yet declared the source of his problem. His restless condition had begun about ten days ago and had barely raised his interest. Soon, however, the time spent lying awake had increased from one to several hours and then, on Monday last, to all-night sessions. Now he lay in a state of rigid apprehension—eyes wide open, arms above his head, his hands in fists—like a man in pain unable to shut it out. His neck, his back and his shoulders constantly harried him with cramps and spasms. Everett Menlo had become a full-blown insomniac.

Clearly, Mimi Menlo concluded, her husband was refusing to sleep because he believed something dreadful was going to happen the moment he closed his eyes. She had encountered this sort of fear in one or two of her patients. Everett, on the other hand, would not discuss the subject. If the problem had been hers, he would have said *such things cannot occur if you have gained control of yourself.*

Mimi began to watch for the dawn. She would calculate its approach by listening for the increase of traffic down below the bedroom window. The Menlos' home was across the road from The Manulife Centre—corner of Bloor and Bay Streets. Mimi's first sight of daylight always revealed the high, white shape of its terraced storeys. Their own apartment building was of a modest height and colour—twenty floors of smoky glass and polished brick. The shadow of the Manulife would crawl across the bedroom floor and climb the wall behind her, grey with fatigue and cold.

The Menlo beds were an arm's length apart, and lying like a rug between them was the shape of a large, black dog of unknown breed. All night long, in the dark of his well, the dog would dream and he would tell the content of his dreams the way that victims in a trance will tell of being pursued by posses of their nameless fears. He whimpered, he cried and sometimes he howled. His legs and his paws would jerk and flail and his claws would scrabble desperately against the parquet floor. Mimi—who loved this dog—would lay her hand against his side and let her fingers dabble in his coat in vain attempts to soothe him. Sometimes, she had to call his name in order to rouse him from his dreams because his heart would be racing. Other time, she smiled and thought: *at least there's one of us getting some sleep.* The dog's name was Thurber and he dreamed in beige and white.

Everett and Mimi Menlo were both psychiatrists. His field was schizophrenia; hers was autistic children. Mimi's venue was the Parkin Institute at the University of Toronto; Everett's was the Queen Street Mental Health Centre. Early in their marriage they had decided never to work as a team and not—unless it was a matter of financial life and death—to accept employment in the same institution. Both had always worked with the kind of physical intensity that kills, and yet they gave the impression this was the only tolerable way in which to function. It meant there was always a sense of peril in what they did, but the peril—according to Everett—made their lives worth living. This, at least, had been his theory twenty years ago when they were young.

Now, for whatever unnamed reason, peril had become his enemy and Everett Menlo had begun to look and behave and lose his sleep like a haunted man. But he refused to comment when Mimi asked him what was wrong. Instead, he gave the worst of all possible answers a psychiatrist can hear who seeks an explanation of a patient's silence: he said there was *absolutely nothing wrong.*

'You're sure you're not coming down with something?'

'Yes.'

'And you wouldn't like a massage?'

'I've already told you: no.'

'Can I get you anything?'

'No.'

'And you don't want to talk?'

'That's right.'

'Okay, Everett . . .'

'Okay, what?'

'Okay, nothing. I only hope you get some sleep tonight.'

Everett stood up. 'Have you been spying on me, Mimi?'

'What do you mean by *spying*?'

'Watching me all night long.'

'Well, Everett, I don't see how I can fail to be aware you aren't asleep when we share this bedroom. I mean—I can hear you grinding your teeth. I can see you lying there wide awake.'

'When?'

'All the time. You're staring at the ceiling.'

'I've never stared at the ceiling in my whole life. I sleep on my stomach.'

'You sleep on your stomach *if* you sleep. But you have not been sleeping. Period. No argument.'

Everett Menlo went to his dresser and got out a pair of clean pyjamas. Turning his back on Mimi, he put them on.

Somewhat amused at the coyness of this gesture, Mimi asked what he was hiding.

'Nothing!' he shouted at her.

Mimi's mouth fell open. Everett never yelled. His anger wasn't like that: it manifested itself in other ways, in silence and withdrawal, never shouts.

Everett was staring at her defiantly. He had slammed the bottom drawer of his dresser. Now he was fumbling with the wrapper of a pack of cigarettes.

Mimi's stomach tied a knot.

Everett hadn't touched a cigarette for weeks.

'Please don't smoke those,' she said. 'You'll only be sorry if you do.'

'And you,' he said, 'will be sorry if I don't.'

'But, dear . . .' said Mimi.

'Leave me for Christ's sake alone!' Everett yelled.

Mimi gave up and sighed and then she said: 'all right. Thurber and I will go and sleep in the living-room. Goodnight.'

Everett sat on the edge of his bed. His hands were shaking.

'Please,' he said—apparently addressing the floor. 'Don't leave me here alone. I couldn't bear that.'

This was perhaps the most chilling thing he could have said to her. Mimi was alarmed; her husband was genuinely terrified of something and he would not say what it was. If she had not been who she was—if she had not known what she knew—if her years of training had not prepared her to watch for signs like this, she might have been better off. As it was, she had to face the possibility the strongest, most sensible man on earth was having a nervous breakdown of major proportions. Lots of people have breakdowns, of course; but not, she had thought, the gods of reason.

'All right,' she said—her voice maintaining the kind of calm she knew a child afraid of the dark would appreciate. 'In a minute I'll get us something to drink. But first, I'll go and change . . . '

Mimi went into the sanctum of the bathroom, where her nightgown waited for her—a portable hiding-place hanging on the back of the door. 'You stay there,' she said to Thurber, who had padded after her. 'Mama will be out in just a moment.'

Even in the dark, she could gauge Everett's tension. His shadow—all she could see of him—twitched from time to time and the twitching took on a kind of lurching rhythm, something like the broken clock in their living-room.

Mimi lay on her side and tried to close her eyes. But her eyes were tied to a will of their own and would not obey her. Now she, too, was caught in the same irreversible tide of sleeplessness that bore her husband backward through the night. Four or five times she watched him lighting cigarettes—blowing out the matches, courting disaster in the bedclothes—conjuring the worst of deaths for the three of them: a flaming pyre on the twentieth floor.

All this behaviour was utterly unlike him; foreign to his code of disciplines and ethics; alien to everything he said and believed. *Openness, directness, sharing of ideas, encouraging imaginative response to every problem. Never hide troubles. Never allow despair* . . . These were his directives in everything he did. Now, he had thrown them over.

One thing was certain. She was not the cause of his sleeplessness. She didn't have affairs and neither did he. He might be ill—but whenever he'd been ill before, there had been no trauma; never a trauma like this one, at any rate. Perhaps it was something about a patient—one of his tougher cases; a wall in the patient's condition they could not break through; some circumstance of someone's lack of progress—a sudden veering towards a catatonic state, for instance—something that Everett had not foreseen that had stymied him and was slowly . . . what? Destroying his sense of professional control? His self-esteem? His scientific certainty? If only he would speak.

Mimi thought about her own worst case: a child whose obstinate refusal to communicate was currently breaking her heart and, thus, her ability to help. If ever she had needed Everett to talk to, it was now. All her fellow doctors were locked in a battle over this child; they wanted to take him away from her. Mimi refused to give him up; he might as well have been her own flesh and blood. Everything had been done—from gentle holding sessions to violent bouts of manufactured anger—in her attempt to make the child react. She was staying with him every day from the moment he was roused to the moment he was induced to sleep with drugs.

His name was Brian Bassett and he was eight years old. He sat on the floor in the furthest corner he could achieve in one of the observation-isolation rooms where all the autistic children were placed when nothing else in their treatment—nothing of love or expertise—had managed to break their silence. Mostly, this was a signal they were coming to the end of life.

There in his four-square, glass-box room, surrounded by all that can tempt a child if a child can be tempted—toys and food and story-book companions—Brian Bassett was in the process, now, of fading away. His eyes were never closed and his arms were restrained. He was attached to three machines that nurtured him with all that science can offer. But of course, the spirit and the will to live cannot be fed by force to those who do not want to feed.

Now, in the light of Brian Bassett's utter lack of willing contact with the world around him—his utter refusal to communicate—Mimi watched her husband through the night. Everett stared at the ceiling, lit by the Manulife building's distant lamps, borne on his back further and further out to sea. She had lost him, she was certain.

When, at last, he saw that Mimi had drifted into her own and welcome sleep, Everett rose from his bed and went out into the hall, past the simulated jungle of the solarium, until he reached the dining-room. There, all the way till dawn, he amused himself with two decks of cards and endless games of Dead Man's Solitaire.

Thurber rose and shuffled after him. The dining-room was one of Thurber's favourite places in all his confined but privileged world, for it was here—as in the kitchen—that from time to time a hand descended filled with the miracle of food. But whatever it was that his master was doing up there above him on the table-top, it wasn't anything to do with feeding or with being fed. The playing cards had an old and dusty dryness to their scent and they held no appeal for the dog. So he once again lay down and he took up his dreams, which at least gave his paws some exercise. This way, he failed to hear the advent of a new dimension to his master's problem. This occurred precisely at 5:45 A.M. when the telephone rang and Everett Menlo, having rushed to answer it, waited breathless for a minute while he listened and then said: 'yes' in a curious, strangulated fashion. Thurber—had he been awake—would have recognized in his master's voice the signal for disaster.

For weeks now, Everett had been working with a patient who was severely and uniquely schizophrenic. This patient's name was Kenneth Albright, and while he was deeply suspicious, he was also oddly caring. Kenneth Albright loved the detritus of life, such as bits of woolly dust and wads of discarded paper. He loved all dried-up leaves that had drifted from their parent trees and he loved the dead bees that had curled up to die along the window-sills of his ward. He also loved the spiderwebs seen high up in the corners of the rooms where he sat on plastic chairs and ate with plastic spoons.

Kenneth Albright talked a lot about his dreams. But his dreams had become, of late, a major stumbling block in the process of his recovery. Back in the days when Kenneth had first become Doctor Menlo's patient, the dreams had been overburdened with detail: 'over-cast,' as he would say, 'with characters' and over-produced, again in Kenneth's phrase, 'as if I were dreaming the dreams of Cecil B. de Mille'.

Then he had said: 'but a person can't really dream someone else's dreams. Or can they, Doctor Menlo?'

'No' had been Everett's answer—definite and certain.

Everett Menlo had been delighted, at first, with Kenneth Albright's dreams. They had been immensely entertaining—complex and filled with intriguing detail. Kenneth himself was at a loss to explain the meaning of these dreams, but as Everett had said, it wasn't Kenneth's job to explain. That was Everett's job. His job and his pleasure. For quite a long while, during these early sessions, Everett had written out the dreams, taken them home and recounted them to Mimi.

Kenneth Albright was a paranoid schizophrenic. Four times now, he had attempted suicide. He was a fiercely angry man at times—and at other times as gentle and as pleasant as a docile child. He had suffered so greatly, in the very worst moments of his disease, that he could no longer work. His job—it was almost an incidental detail in his life and had no importance for him, so it seemed—was returning reference books, in the Metro Library, to their places in the stacks. Sometimes—mostly late of an afternoon—he might begin a psychotic episode of such profound dimensions that he would attempt his suicide right behind the counter and even once, in the full view of everyone, while riding in the glass-walled elevator. It was after this last occasion that he was brought, in restraints, to be a resident patient at the Queen Street Mental Health Centre. He had slashed his wrists with a razor—but not before he had also slashed and destroyed an antique copy of *Don Quixote*, the pages of which he pasted to the walls with blood.

For a week thereafter, Kenneth Albright—just like Brian Bassett— had refused to speak or to move. Everett had him kept in an isolation cell, force-fed and drugged. Slowly, by dint of patience, encouragement and caring even Kenneth could recognize as genuine, Everett Menlo had broken through the barrier. Kenneth was removed from isolation, pampered with food and cigarettes, and he began relating his dreams.

At first there seemed to be only the dreams and nothing else in Kenneth's memory. Broken pencils, discarded toys and the telephone directory all had roles to play in these dreams but there were never any people. All the weather was bleak and all the landscapes were empty. Houses, motor cars and office buildings never made an appearance. Sounds and smells had some importance, the wind would blow, the scent of unseen fires was often described. Stairwells were plentiful, leading nowhere, all of them rising from a subterranean world that Kenneth either did not dare to visit or would not describe.

The dreams had little variation, one from another. The themes had mostly to do with loss and with being lost. The broken pencils were all given names and the discarded toys were given to one another as companions. The telephone books were the sources of recitations— hours and hours of repeated names and numbers, some of which— Everett had noted with surprise—were absolutely accurate.

All of this held fast until an incident occurred one morning that changed the face of Kenneth Albright's schizophrenia forever; an incident that stemmed—so it seemed—from something he had dreamed the night before.

Bearing in mind his previous attempts at suicide, it will be obvious that Kenneth Albright was never far from sight at the Queen Street Mental Health Centre. He was, in fact, under constant observation; constant, that is, as human beings and modern technology can manage. In the ward to which he was ultimately consigned, for instance, the toilet cabinets had no doors and the shower-rooms had no locks. Therefore, a person could not ever be alone with water, glass or shaving utensils. (All the razors were cordless automatics.) Scissors and knives were banned, as were pieces of string and rubber bands. A person could not even kill his feet and hands by binding up his wrists or ankles. Nothing poisonous was anywhere available. All the windows were barred. All the double doors between this ward and the corridors beyond were doors with triple locks and a guard was always near at hand.

Still, if people want to die, they will find a way. Mimi Menlo would discover this to her everlasting sorrow with Brian Bassett. Everett Menlo would discover this to his everlasting horror with Kenneth Albright.

On the morning of April 19th, a Tuesday, Everett Menlo, in the best of health, had welcomed a brand-new patient into his office. This was Anne Marie Wilson, a young and brilliant pianist whose promising career had been halted mid-flight by a schizophrenic incident involving her ambition. She was, it seemed, no longer able to play and all her dreams were shattered. The cause was simple, to all appearances: Anne Marie had a sense of how, precisely, the music should be and she had not been able to master it accordingly. 'Everything I attempt is terrible,' she had said—in spite of all her critical accolades and all her professional success. Other doctors had tried and failed to break the barriers in Anne Marie, whose hands had taken on a life of their own, refusing altogether to work for her. Now it was Menlo's turn and hope was high.

Everett had been looking forward to his session with this prodigy. He loved all music and had thought to find some means within its discipline to reach her. She seemed so fragile, sitting there in the sunlight, and he had just begun to take his first notes when the door flew open and Louise, his secretary, had said: 'I'm sorry, Doctor Menlo. There's a problem. Can you come with me at once?'

Everett excused himself.

Anne Marie was left in the sunlight to bide her time. Her fingers were moving around in her lap and she put them in her mouth to make them quiet.

Even as he'd heard his secretary speak, Everett had known the problem would be Kenneth Albright. Something in Kenneth's eyes had warned him there was trouble on the way: a certain wariness that indicated all was not as placid as it should have been, given his regimen of drugs. He had stayed long hours in one position, moving his fingers over his thighs as if to dry them on his trousers; watching his fellow patients come and go with abnormal interest—never, however, rising from his chair. An incident was on the horizon and Everett had been waiting for it, hoping it would not come.

Louise had said that Doctor Menlo was to go at once to Kenneth Albright's ward. Everett had run the whole way. Only after the attendant had let him in past the double doors, did he slow his pace to a hurried walk and wipe his brow. He didn't want Kenneth to know how alarmed he had been.

Coming to the appointed place, he paused before he entered, closing his eyes, preparing himself for whatever he might have to see. *Other people have killed themselves: I've seen it often enough*, he was thinking. *I simply won't let it affect me.* Then he went in.

The room was small and white—a dining-room—and Kenneth was sitting down in a corner, his back pressed out against the walls on either side of him. His head was bowed and his legs drawn up and he was obviously trying to hide without much success. An intern was standing above him and a nurse was kneeling down beside him. Several pieces of bandaging with blood on them were scattered near Kenneth's feet and there was a white enamel basin filled with pinkish water on the floor beside the nurse.

'Morowetz,' Everett said to the intern. 'Tell me what has happened here.' He said this just the way he posed such questions when he took interns through the wards at examination time, quizzing them on symptoms and prognoses.

But Morowetz the intern had no answer. He was puzzled. What had happened had no sane explanation.

Everett turned to Charterhouse, the nurse.

'On the morning of April 19th, at roughly ten-fifteen, I found Kenneth Albright covered with blood,' Ms Charterhouse was to write in her report. 'His hands, his arms, his face and his neck were stained. I would say the blood was fresh and the patient's clothing—mostly his shirt—was wet with it. Some—a very small amount of it—had dried on his forehead. The rest was uniformly the kind of blood you expect to find free-flowing from a wound. I called for assistance and meanwhile attempted to ascertain where Mister Albright might have been injured. I performed this examination without success. I could find no source of bleeding anywhere on Mister Albright's body.'

Morowetz concurred.

The blood was someone else's.

'Was there a weapon of any kind?' Doctor Menlo had wanted to know.

'No, sir. Nothing.' said Charterhouse.

'And was he alone when you found him?'

'Yes, sir. Just like this in the corner.'

'And the others?'

'All the patients in the ward were examined,' Morowetz told him.

'And?'

'Not one of them was bleeding.'

Everett said: 'I see.'

He looked down at Kenneth.

'This is Doctor Menlo, Kenneth. Have you anything to tell me?'

Kenneth did not reply.

Everett said: 'When you've got him back in his room and tranquillized, will you call me, please?'

Morowetz nodded.

The call never came. Kenneth had fallen asleep. Either the drugs he was given had knocked him out cold, or he had opted for silence. Either way, he was incommunicado.

No one was discovered bleeding. Nothing was found to indicate an accident, a violent attack, an epileptic seizure. A weapon was not located. Kenneth Albright had not a single scratch on his flesh from stem, as Everett put it, to gudgeon. The blood, it seemed, had fallen like the rain from heaven: unexplained and inexplicable.

Later, as the day was ending, Everett Menlo left the Queen Street Mental Health Centre. He made his way home on the Queen streetcar and the Bay bus. When he reached the apartment, Thurber was waiting for him. Mimi was at a goddamned meeting.

That was the night Everett Menlo suffered the first of his failures to sleep. It was occasioned by the fact that, when he wakened sometime after three, he had just been dreaming. This, of course, was not unusual—but the dream itself was perturbing. There was someone lying there, in the bright white landscape of a hospital dining-room. Whether it was a man or woman could not be told, it was just a human body, lying down in a pool of blood.

Kenneth Albright was kneeling beside this body, pulling it open the way a child will pull a Christmas present open—yanking at its strings and ribbons, wanting only to see the contents. Everett saw this scene from several angles, never speaking, never being spoken to. In all the time he watched—the usual dream eternity—the silence was broken only by the sound of water dripping from an unseen tap. Then, Kenneth Albright rose and was covered with blood, the way he had been that morning. He stared at Doctor Menlo, looked right through him and departed. Nothing remained in the dining-room but plastic tables and plastic chairs and the bright red thing on the floor that once had been a person. Everett Menlo did not know and could not guess who this person might have been. He only knew that Kenneth Albright had left this person's body in Everett Menlo's dream.

Three nights running, the corpse remained in its place and every time that Everett entered the dining-room in the nightmare he was certain he would find out who it was. On the fourth night, fully expecting to discover he himself was the victim, he beheld the face and saw it was a stranger.

But there are no strangers in dreams, he knew that now after twenty years of practice. *There are no strangers; there are only people in disguise.*

Mimi made one final attempt in Brian Bassett's behalf to turn away the fate to which his other doctors—both medical and psychiatric— had consigned him. Not that, as a group, they had failed to expend the full weight of all they knew and all they could do to save him. One of his medical doctors—a woman whose name was Juliet Bateman—had moved a cot into his isolation room and stayed with him twenty-four hours a day for over a week. But her health had been undermined by this and when she succumbed to the Shanghai flu she removed herself for fear of infecting Brian Bassett.

The parents had come and gone on a daily basis for months in a killing routine of visits. But parents, their presence and their loving, are not the answer when a child has fallen into an autistic state. They might as well have been strangers. And so they had been advised to stay away.

Brian Bassett was eight years old—*unlucky eight*, as one of his therapists had said—and in every other way, in terms of physical development and mental capability, he had always been a perfectly normal child. Now, in the final moments of his life, he weighed a scant thirty pounds, when he should have weighed twice that much.

Brian had not been heard to speak a single word in over a year of constant observation. Earlier—long ago as seven months—a few expressions would visit his face from time to time. Never a smile—but often a kind of sneer, a passing of judgement, terrifying in its intensity. Other times, a pinched expression would appear—a signal of the shyness peculiar to autistic children, who think of light as being unfriendly.

Mimi's militant efforts in behalf of Brian had been exemplary. Her fellow doctors thought of her as *Bassett's crazy guardian angel*. They begged her to remove herself in order to preserve her health. Being wise, being practical, they saw that all her efforts would not save him. But Mimi's version of being a guardian angel was more like being a surrogate warrior: a hired gun or a samurai. Her cool determination to thwart the enemies of silence, stillness and starvation gave her strengths that even she had been unaware were hers to command.

Brian Bassett, seated in his corner on the floor, maintained a solemn composure that lent his features a kind of unearthly beauty. His back was straight, his hands were poised, his hair was so fine he looked the very picture of a spirit waiting to enter a newborn creature. Sometimes Mimi wondered if this creature Brian Bassett waited to inhabit could be human. She thought of all the animals she had ever seen in all her travels and she fell upon the image of a newborn fawn as being the most tranquil and the most in need of stillness in order to survive. If only all the natural energy and curiosity of a newborn beast could have entered into Brian Bassett, surely, they would have transformed the boy in the corner into a vibrant, joyous human being. But it was not to be.

On the 29th of April—one week and three days after Everett had entered into his crisis of insomnia—Mimi sat on the floor in Brian Bassett's isolation room, gently massaging his arms and legs as she held him in her lap.

His weight, by now was shocking—and his skin had become

translucent. His eyes had not been closed for days—for weeks—and their expression might have been carved in stone.

'Speak to me. Speak,' she whispered to him as she cradled his head beneath her chin. 'Please at least speak before you die.'

Nothing happened. Only silence.

Juliet Bateman—wrapped in a blanket—was watching through the observation glass as Mimi lifted up Brian Bassett and placed him in his cot. The cot had metal sides—and the sides were raised. Juliet Bateman could see Brian Bassett's eyes and his hands as Mimi stepped away.

Mimi looked at Juliet and shook her head. Juliet closed her eyes and pulled her blanket tighter like a skin that might protect her for the next five minutes.

Mimi went around the cot to the other side and dragged the IV stand in closer to the head. She fumbled for a moment with the long plastic lifelines—anti-dehydrants, nutrients—and she adjusted the needles and brought them down inside the nest of the cot where Brian Bassett lay and she lifted up his arm in order to insert the tubes and bind them into place with tape.

This was when it happened—just as Mimi Menlo was preparing to insert the second tube.

Brian Bassett looked at her and spoke.

'No,' he said. 'Don't.'

Don't meant death.

Mimi paused—considered—and set the tube aside. Then she withdrew the tube already in place and she hung them both on the IV stand.

All right, she said to Brian Bassett in her mind, *you win.*

She looked down then with her arm along the side of the cot—and one hand trailing down so Brian Bassett could touch it if he wanted to. She smiled at him and said to him: 'not to worry. Not to worry. None of us is ever going to trouble you again.' He watched her carefully. 'Goodbye, Brian,' she said. 'I love you.'

Juliet Bateman saw Mimi Menlo say all this and was fairly sure she had read the words on Mimi's lips just as they had been spoken.

Mimi started out of the room. She was determined now there was no turning back and that Brian Bassett was free to go his way. But just as she was turning the handle and pressing her weight against the door—she heard Brian Bassett speak again.

'Goodbye,' he said.

And died.

Mimi went back and Juliet Bateman, too, and they stayed with him another hour before they turned out his lights. 'Someone else can cover his face,' said Mimi. 'I'm not going to do it.' Juliet agreed and they came back out to tell the nurse on duty that their ward had died and their work with him was over.

On the 30th of April—a Saturday—Mimi stayed home and made her notes and she wondered if and when she would weep for Brian Bassett. Her hand, as she wrote, was steady and her throat was not constricted and her eyes had no sensation beyond the burning itch of fatigue. She wondered what she looked like in the mirror, but resisted that discovery. Some things could wait. Outside it rained. Thurber dreamed in the corner. Bay Street rumbled in the basement.

Everett, in the meantime, had reached his own crisis and because of his desperate straits a part of Mimi Menlo's mind was on her husband. Now he had not slept for almost ten days. *We really ought to consign ourselves to hospital beds,* she thought. Somehow, the idea held no persuasion. It occurred to her that laughter might do a better job, if only they could find it. The brain, when over-extended, gives us the most surprisingly simple propositions, she concluded. *Stop,* it says to us. *Lie down and sleep.*

Five minutes later, Mimi found herself still sitting at the desk, with her fountain pen capped and her fingers raised to her lips in an attitude of gentle prayer. It required some effort to re-adjust her gaze and re-establish her focus on the surface of the window glass beyond which her mind had wandered. Sitting up, she had been asleep.

Thurber muttered something and stretched his legs and yawned, still asleep. Mimi glanced in his direction. *We've both been dreaming,* she thought, *but his dream continues.*

Somewhere behind her, the broken clock was attempting to strike the hour of three. Its voice was dull and rusty, needing oil.

Looking down, she saw the words *BRIAN BASSETT* written on the page before her and it occurred to her that, without this person, the words were nothing more than extrapolations from the alphabet—something fanciful we call a 'name' in the hope that, one day, it will take on meaning.

She thought of Brian Bassett with his building blocks—pushing the letters around on the floor and coming up with more acceptable arrangements: *TINA STERABBS . . . IAN BRETT BASS . . . BEST STAB the RAIN*: a sentence. He had known all along, of course, that BRIAN BASSETT wasn't what he wanted because it wasn't what he was. He had come here against his will, was held here against his better judgement, fought against his captors and finally escaped.

But where was here to Ian Brett Bass? Where was here to Tina Sterabbs? Like Brian Bassett, they had all been here in someone else's dreams, and had to wait for someone else to wake before they could make their getaway.

Slowly, Mimi uncapped her fountain pen and drew a firm, black line through Brian Bassett's name. *We dreamed him*, she wrote, *that's all. And then we let him go.*

Seeing Everett standing in the doorway, knowing he had just returned from another Kenneth Albright crisis, she had no sense of apprehension. All this was only as it should be. Given the way that everything was going, it stood to reason Kenneth Albright's crisis had to come in this moment. If he managed, at last, to kill himself then at least her husband might begin to sleep again.

Far in the back of her mind a carping, critical voice remarked that any such thoughts were *deeply unfeeling and verging on the barbaric*. But Mimi dismissed this voice and another part of her brain stepped forward in her defence. *I will weep for Kenneth Albright*, she thought, *when I can weep for Brian Bassett. Now, all that matters is that Everett and I survive.*

Then she strode forward and put out her hand for Everett's briefcase, set the briefcase down and helped him out of his topcoat. She was playing wife. It seemed to be the thing to do.

For the next twenty minutes Everett had nothing to say, and after he had poured himself a drink and after Mimi had done the same, they sat in their chairs and waited for Everett to catch his breath.

The first thing he said when he finally spoke was: 'finish your notes?'

'Just about,' Mimi told him. 'I've written everything I can for now.' She did not elaborate. 'You're home early,' she said, hoping to goad him into saying something new about Kenneth Albright.

'Yes,' he said. 'I am.' But that was all.

Then he stood up—threw back the last of his drink and poured another. He lighted a cigarette and Mimi didn't even wince. He had been smoking now three days. The atmosphere between them had been, since then, enlivened with a magnetic kind of tension. But it was a moribund tension, slowly beginning to dissipate.

Mimi watched her husband's silent torment now with a kind of clinical detachment. This was the result, she liked to tell herself, of her training and her discipline. The lover in her could regard Everett warmly and with concern, but the psychiatrist in her could also watch him as someone suffering a nervous breakdown, someone who could not be helped until the symptoms had multiplied and declared themselves more openly.

Everett went into the darkest corner of the room and sat down hard in one of Mimi's straight-backed chairs: the ones inherited from her mother. He sat, prim, like a patient in a doctor's office, totally unrelaxed and nervy; expressionless. Either he had come to receive a deadly diagnosis, or he would get a clean bill of health.

Mimi glided over to the sofa in the window, plush and red and deeply comfortable; a place to recuperate. The view—if she chose to turn only slightly sideways—was one of the gentle rain that was falling onto Bay Street. Sopping-wet pigeons huddled on the window-sill; people across the street in the Manulife building were turning on their lights.

A renegade robin, nesting in their eaves, began to sing.

Everett Menlo began to talk.

'Please don't interrupt,' he said first.

'You know I won't,' said Mimi. It was a rule that neither one should interrupt the telling of a case until they had been invited to do so.

Mimi put her fingers into her glass so the ice-cubes wouldn't click. She waited.

Everett spoke—but he spoke as if in someone else's voice, perhaps the voice of Kenneth Albright. This was not entirely unusual. Often, both Mimi and Everett Menlo spoke in the voices of their patients. What was unusual, this time, was that, speaking in Kenneth's voice, Everett began to sweat profusely—so profusely that Mimi was able to watch his shirt front darkening with perspiration.

'As you know,' he said, 'I have not been sleeping.'

This was the understatement of the year. Mimi was silent.

'I have not been sleeping because—to put it in a nutshell—I have been afraid to dream.'

Mimi was somewhat startled by this. Not by the fact that Everett was afraid to dream, but only because she had just been thinking of dreams herself.

'I have been afraid to dream, because in all my dreams there have been bodies. Corpses. Murder victims.'

Mimi—not really listening—idly wondered if she had been one of them.

'In all my dreams, there have been corpses,' Everett repeated. 'But I am not the murderer. Kenneth Albright is the murderer, and, up to this moment, he has left behind him fifteen bodies: none of them people I recognize.'

Mimi nodded. The ice-cubes in her drink were beginning to freeze her fingers. Any minute now, she prayed, they would surely melt.

'I gave up dreaming almost a week ago,' said Everett, 'thinking that if I did, the killing pattern might be altered; broken.' Then he said tersely, 'it was not. The killings have continued. . . .'

'How do you know the killings have continued, Everett, if you've given up your dreaming? Wouldn't this mean he had no place to hide the bodies?'

In spite of the fact she had disobeyed their rule about not speaking, Everett answered her.

'I know they are being continued because I have seen the blood.'

'Ah, yes. I see.'

'No, Mimi. No. You do not see. The blood is not a figment of my imagination. The blood, in fact, is the only thing not dreamed.' He explained the stains on Kenneth Albright's hands and arms and clothes and he said: 'It happens every day. We have searched his person for signs of cuts and gashes—even for internal and rectal bleeding. Nothing. We have searched his quarters and all the other quarters in his ward. His ward is locked. His ward is isolated in the extreme. None of his fellow patients was ever found bleeding—never had cause to bleed. There were no injuries—no self-inflicted wounds. We thought of animals. Perhaps a mouse—a rat. But nothing. Nothing. Nothing . . . We also went so far as to strip-search all the members of the staff who entered that ward and I, too, offered myself for this experiment. Still nothing. Nothing. No one had bled.'

Everett was now beginning to perspire so heavily he removed his jacket and threw it on the floor. Thurber woke and stared at it, startled. At first, it appeared to be the beast that had just pursued him through the woods and down the road. But, then, it sighed and settled and was just a coat; a rumpled jacket lying down on the rug.

Everett said: 'we had taken samples of the blood on the patient's hands—on Kenneth Albright's hands and on his clothing and we had these samples analyzed. No. It was not his own blood. No, it was not the blood of an animal. No, it was not the blood of a fellow patient. No, it was not the blood of any members of the staff . . .'

Everett's voice had risen.

'Whose blood was it?' he almost cried. 'Whose the hell was it?'

Mimi waited.

Everett Menlo lighted another cigarette. He took a great gulp of his drink.

'Well . . .' He was calmer now; calmer of necessity. He had to marshall the evidence. He had to put it all in order—bring it into line with reason. 'Did this mean that—somehow—the patient had managed to leave the premises—do some bloody deed and return without our knowledge of it? That is, after all, the only possible explanation. Isn't it?'

Mimi waited.

'Isn't it?' he repeated.

'Yes,' she said. 'It's the only possible explanation.'

'Except there is no way out of that place. There is absolutely no way out.'

Now, there was a pause.

'But one,' he added—his voice, again, a whisper.

Mimi was silent. Fearful—watching his twisted face.

'Tell me,' Everett Menlo said—the perfect innocent, almost the perfect child in quest of forbidden knowledge. 'Answer me this—be honest: is there blood in dreams?'

Mimi could not respond. She felt herself go pale. Her husband—after all, the sanest man alive—had just suggested something so completely mad he might as well have handed over his reason in a paper bag and said to her, *burn this*.

'The only place that Kenneth Albright goes, I tell you, is into dreams,' Everett said. 'That is the only place beyond the ward into which the patient can or does escape.'

Another—briefer—pause.

'It is real blood, Mimi. Real. And he gets it all from dreams. *My dreams*.'

They waited for this to settle.

Everett said: 'I'm tired. I'm tired. I cannot bear this any more. I'm tired . . .'

Mimi thought, *good. No matter what else happens, he will sleep tonight.*

He did. And so, at last, did she.

Mimi's dreams were rarely of the kind that engender fear. She dreamt more gentle scenes with open spaces that did not intimidate. She would dream quite often of water and of animals. Always, she was nothing more than an observer; roles were not assigned her; often, this was sad. Somehow, she seemed at times locked out, unable to participate. These were the dreams she endured when Brian Bassett died: field trips to see him in some desert setting; underwater excursions to watch him floating amongst the seaweed. He never spoke, and, indeed, he never appeared to be aware of her presence.

That night, when Everett fell into his bed exhausted and she did likewise, Mimi's dream of Brian Bassett was the last she would ever have of him and somehow, in the dream, she knew this. What she saw was what, in magical terms, would be called a disappearing act. Brian Bassett vanished. Gone.

Sometime after midnight on May Day morning, Mimi Menlo awoke from her dream of Brian to the sound of Thurber thumping the floor in a dream of his own.

Everett was not in his bed and Mimi cursed. She put on her wrapper and her slippers and went beyond the bedroom into the hall.

No lights were shining but the street lamps far below and the windows gave no sign of stars.

Mimi made her way past the jungle, searching for Everett in the living-room. He was not there. She would dream of this one day; it was a certainty.

'Everett?'

He did not reply.

Mimi turned and went back through the bedroom.

'Everett?'

She heard him. He was in the bathroom and she went in through the door.

'Oh,' she said, when she saw him. 'Oh, my God.'

Everett Menlo was standing in the bathtub, removing his pyjamas. They were soaking wet, but not with perspiration. They were soaking wet with blood.

For a moment, holding his jacket, letting its arms hang down across his belly and his groin, Everett stared at Mimi, blank-eyed from his nightmare.

Mimi raised her hands to her mouth. She felt as one must feel, if helpless, watching someone burn alive.

Everett threw the jacket down and started to remove his trousers. His pyjamas, made of cotton, had been green. His eyes were blinded now with blood and his hands reached out to find the shower taps.

'Please don't look at me,' he said. 'I . . . Please go away.'

Mimi said: 'no.' She sat on the toilet seat. 'I'm waiting here,' she told him, 'until we both wake up.'

JANE RULE · b. 1931

If There Is No Gate

Once before, when I was twenty, I thought I was losing my mind. Then, too, I'd been working hard, and I suppose I'd caught a touch of paranoia as one does a cold in the early spring, when there's a sudden thaw and a temporary aggression of crocuses. One feels unprepared, put upon. I don't remember just what it was, an excess of defensive energy, ill temper, loneliness. I only remember the fear, like a blown fuse in the nervous system, a darkness in the heart. I was driving out to the mental hospital to deliver a load of clothes and books my mother had collected from the neighbourhood. She spent all her time, and a good deal of mine, collecting comfort for distant, public catastrophes. It was her way of protecting herself and her family from the fraud of any private terror. We had no time for such nonsense. It was a compliment that she had allowed me to go, the first of her children to reach the age of immunity. She was a marvellously insensitive woman.

My old school uniform, neatly folded just as it had been in the bottom drawer of my dresser, was at the top of the box, an afterthought smelling faintly of camphor. I lifted the carton out of the trunk of the car, and following the signs marked OFFICE, carried it through the archway into the inner court. I had not intended to look around. I had intended to keep my eyes fixed on that shroud of my innocence, my anonymity, like a charmed relic of another life, but all about and above me the racket of cries startled me into the world. There behind great expanses of steel mesh, level upon level storying up against the light, were trapped covies of women, shrieking and calling like surprised birds. It was a gigantic aviary of madness. Some wailed, high and fierce, unmated in the limited and crowded sky. Others chattered and scolded to guard some memory of a shabby nest, of frail and greedy young. A few hopped mournfully, silently about, picking at scraps. There were pairs, too, bold and impersonal as doves under the eaves. One woman, holding another, rocked and sang a vacant lullaby, as pure as any bird song, as inhuman. I walked across the court, went into the office, and delivered the box. I was glad to walk back through that court, empty-handed.

Sometimes since then, when I have been disturbed at dawn by the distant, violent wings of geese or at dusk by the pedestrian entrance of a robin, I have used that human aviary as a touchstone of sanity. It has been for me one of the unnatural wonders of the world, like a great cathedral, a sanctuary where one can take all the fears of one's inhumanity, leave them at the feet of saints, and come away at peace.

But that day now seems a long way back in my memory, in feeling vaguer than more recent prayers. It is hard to recall not the scene so much as the sense of it: the exact, unspectacular relief of being an intentional, inhibited, insensitive human being. Perhaps the experience no longer becomes me, fits too smugly over my middle-aged humility, like a confirmation dress or a wedding gown. But, if that is so, then sanity itself must be a convention one can outgrow. One can, but one mustn't. Surely recovery, not discovery, is the way back to health.

Here they do not want me to recall the particulars of my life, to retrace my steps until I find the place, the precise moment of error. I am to ignore my conscious memory and the ordering power of my brain, as if moral interpretation of experience were a disease to be cured of. Instead, I am to enter the world of dreams and visions, abandon myself to the freakish chaos of a night's sleep, awaking clinging to the absurdities and obscenities out of Spiritus Mundi and talk or dance or paint them all the unordinary day long.

If I were in a cage, dressed in someone else's clothes, absent-minded, it would be so much simpler to be mad, but this is not a mental hospital. It is a kind of rest home, settled against the gentle Devon hills within taste of the sea. I have my own small room under the eaves, sunny, vines friendly at the window, like a picture in a children's book of poetry. I am free to do what I like, to go where I please, even out into the little village to buy fruit or a bottle of sherry. I wash out my own underthings, sew buttons on blouses, send my clothes to the cleaner. And my mind, untouched by the sudden willess attacks of fear that my body suffers, is more decorous and lucid than ever. I make polite, intelligent conversation with the doctors at afternoon tea in the garden. My own doctor, a woman of huge frame with a face warm and remote as the sun, was once a 'guest' here. She had gone from psychiatry to a silent order only to find, after five years, that it was not her vocation. It is peculiarly easy to talk to one in whom silence has lived so deeply. But it is peculiarly easy to talk to everyone here, guests and doctors. One simply learns to be mannerly in the presence of visions. If I come upon a girl dancing naked by the little stream that crosses the southwest corner of the property, I simply turn my eyes away to watch the gardener clipping the hedge or the swans copulating fiercely, awkwardly in the late afternoon sun. If I sit on a bench next to a boy who is sticking pins into the clay image of his father, I go on with my mending. But I am still, even after all these weeks, appalled, I cannot and do not wish to dance naked in the sun. I loathe fine bits of clay which circle my nails and mute the lines of my palms. I haven't the skill to paint what I have seen awake or dreaming, and, if I can be taught to value nightmares, I cannot be taught to value my own crude approximations of them. I am still trapped in the hope of real articularity.

When I first came here, in a daze of sedatives, I could not dream at all. I fell into sleep like a stone into water, settling deep and undisturbed in the darkness. Only when I was awake was I victim to sudden, unreasoning fears, fits of trembling exhaustion. I was willing then to talk, afraid as I was to make the journey back through the years alone, no longer trusting my own memory. But I agreed that it could not be grief or shame that had driven me here. The first I suffered when the only child I could have was born dead. I was so brave, so dull, that my husband finally took his weight of sympathy and tenderness to someone else, someone who needed him. The shame I found bearable, too, first in anger, then in resignation. My husband is a nervous, high spirited, good looking man with a flare for misery. I have none. I agreed, too, that it is something vaguer, deeper than these very personal, very limited experiences that challenges stability . . . or maintains it. And so I went where the doctor took me, gradually allowing myself to be taught to dream, then more slowly to admit the dream into the waking world.

I did not find the new habit hard to form, and for a while dreams did seem to replace memory. The first were not difficult to understand, perhaps because I could relate them to what had actually happened. I stood on a great raft in a violent sea. All around me friends drank cocktails and chatted, unaware of danger for themselves or of the desperate struggle I was involved in. I saw my dying child in the sea, in its face my own, as if I looked from its eyes and yet felt my fear. I threw a rope, but suddenly my husband was drowning, and, each time I tried to pull him aboard the raft, I found myself dragged nearer the edge. That loved face, out of whose eyes I could now see my own life threatened. I was lying on an operating table, asking for a doctor. The psychiatrist, in the habit of a nun, looked down at me and said, 'You know your child is dead.' Yes, I know. I have always known that. Then I was much younger, pleading with my mother. I did not want to walk up to a strange house, ring the doorbell, and ask for donations of eyes, arms, teeth, genitals. Mother opened a suitcase to show me what she had already collected. The eyes were only painted eggs, the arms and legs the broken pieces of my old china dolls. Then I saw a row of decaying teeth, hooked loosely into bone. Rain fell, peacefully, on shells, on sand, and my child slept among starfish and seaweed, rocking in the receding tide.

I did not mind recording those dreams; I had some conscious knowledge of each image, and gradually I recovered that old skill of sifting the simple facts from the irrelevant desires. The unconscious once recognized, however, will not continue to accommodate the moral intellect with fables.

What was I to do with the dream of myself soaking my husband's raincoat in the car radiator, then cutting it into strips and frying it for his breakfast? What was I to do with rules like 'Change I to you and add es' which I seemed to be teaching to strange natives? One night I dreamt of a gangster standing in the road, having his portrait painted by a dozen middle-aged women while he made a speech about the evils of suicide. He carried and waved two old frontier pistols to illustrate his talk, then suddenly dropped dead, his hair changing from black to red as he lay in the dust.

What shape could I make, standing in the studio before the canvas? The woman next to me was painting a series of pictures in which a crab slowly crawls from the surface of the earth to the centre, curls and flowers into a mating couple. What power she was in touch with I do not know as the mindless accuracy of her hand traced each new meaning. No power prompted me to paint strips of frying raincoat, a comic gangster.

I left the studio this morning for an appointment with the doctor. As I turned into the walk, my way was blocked by a young boy. He stood, exposing himself to a bird, a flower, or me. I could not tell. As the bird rose up, I felt one violent shudder of wings in my own passive womb, then the familiar, terrible vacancy. I did not hurry past him. There was no need. I walked as quietly as I have always walked down the path to the house.

'I did not dream it,' I said to the doctor, 'I saw it. If only they were my own dreams: I have seen spastic children cover their distorted faces with Hallowe'en masks in order to frighten their mothers. I have seen African tribal dancers chase imaginary lions through Windsor Great Park. I have seen two women, dressed for a party, wrestling in a row boat in the middle of the Serpentine.'

She did not answer.

'I wish you could understand me.'

I waited in her silence, thinking in her silence. It is not the unconscious world of my own nightmares where I find visions. I have never neglected the beached treasures and horrors of my own life. I know they are there, not to be collected and studied and saved, but to be left where they are as part of the natural landscape of the soul. It is not the child washing in the tide, the husband gone, the hopes cut adrift that have wrecked me on my own shore.

'It's the world outside myself and my control, the public catastrophes I cannot be held responsible for. It's other people's nightmares that live in my back garden.'

Still she did not speak.

'I can't go mad. I've tried. I have no vocation.'

'Nothing keeps you here,' she finally answered. 'There are no walls. There is no gate.'

My suitcase is open on the bed, my clothes neatly packed. As I stand here, waiting for the taxi to come, I can look down, through any one of the dozen small panes of the window, into the garden. There they all are in the ritual of afternoon tea. In the coming and going from the table, in the passing of cups, in the gathering and separating, it is rather like a dance, patterned and yet casual. There is the boy I encountered this morning, sitting quietly in the sun over by the stream. There is my painting companion, talking with the doctor. Now people begin to drift away, free in the garden, free in the world, a huge sky overhead, disturbed only occasionally by a cloud or a line of jet vapour droppings. It is I who am closed away in this small room under the eaves. If there are no walls, if there is no gate, I should like to have asked that huge framed, silent woman not what kept me in but what kept me out, but I should think, like me, she does not know.

W.P. KINSELLA · b. 1935

Shoeless Joe Jackson Comes to Iowa

My father said he saw him years later playing in a tenth-rate commercial league in a textile town in Carolina, wearing shoes and an assumed name.

'He'd put on 50 pounds and the spring was gone from his step in the outfield, but he could still hit. Oh, how that man could hit. No one has ever been able to hit like Shoeless Joe.'

Two years ago at dusk on a spring evening, when the sky was a robin's-egg blue and the wind as soft as a day-old chick, as I was sitting on the verandah of my farm home in eastern Iowa, a voice very clearly said to me, 'If you build it, he will come.'

The voice was that of a ballpark announcer. As he spoke, I instantly envisioned the finished product I knew I was being asked to conceive. I could see the dark, squarish speakers, like ancient sailors' hats, attached to aluminum-painted light standards that glowed down into a baseball field, my present position being directly behind home plate.

In reality, all anyone else could see out there in front of me was a tattered lawn of mostly dandelions and quack grass that petered out at the edge of a cornfield perhaps 50 yards from the house.

Anyone else was my wife Annie, my daughter Karin, a corn-coloured collie named Carmeletia Pope, and a cinnamon and white guinea pig named Junior who ate spaghetti and sang each time the fridge door opened. Karin and the dog were not quite two years old.

'If you build it, he will come,' the announcer repeated in scratchy Middle American, as if his voice had been recorded on an old 78-rpm record.

A three-hour lecture or a 500-page guide book could not have given me clearer directions: dimensions of ballparks jumped over and around me like fleas, cost figures for light standards and floodlights whirled around my head like the moths that dusted against the porch light above me.

That was all the instruction I ever received: two announcements and a vision of a baseball field. I sat on the verandah until the satiny dark was complete. A few curdly clouds striped the moon and it became so silent I could hear my eyes blink.

Our house is one of those massive old farm homes, square as a biscuit box with a sagging verandah on three sides. The floor of the verandah slopes so that marbles, baseballs, tennis balls, and ball bearings all accumulate in a corner like a herd of cattle clustered with their backs to a storm. On the north verandah is a wooden porch swing where Annie and I sit on humid August nights, sip lemonade from teary glasses, and dream.

When I finally went to bed, and after Annie inched into my arms in that way she has, like a cat that you suddenly find sound asleep in your lap, I told her about the voice and I told her that I knew what it wanted me to do.

'Oh love,' she said, 'if it makes you happy you should do it,' and she found my lips with hers, and I shivered involuntarily as her tongue touched mine.

Annie: she has never once called my crazy. Just before I started the first landscape work, as I stood looking out at the lawn and the cornfield wondering how it could look so different in daylight, considering the notion of accepting it all as a dream and abandoning it, Annie appeared at my side and her arm circled my waist. She leaned against me and looked up, cocking her head like one of the red squirrels that scamper along the power lines from the highway to the house. 'Do it, love,' she said, as I looked down at her, that slip of a girl with hair the colour of cayenne pepper and at least a million freckles on her face and arms, that girl who lives in blue jeans and T-shirts and at 24 could still pass for sixteen.

I thought back to when I first knew her. I came to Iowa to study. She was the child of my landlady. I heard her one afternoon outside my window as she told her girlfriends, 'When I grow up I'm going to marry . . .' and she named me. The others were going to be nurses, teachers, pilots or movie stars, but Annie chose me as her occupation. She was ten. Eight years later we were married. I chose willingly, lovingly to stay in Iowa, eventually rented this farm, bought this farm, operating it one inch from bankruptcy. I don't seem meant to farm, but I want to be close to this precious land, for Annie and me to be able to say, 'This is ours.'

Now I stand ready to cut into the cornfield, to chisel away a piece of our livelihood to use as dream currency, and Annie says, 'Oh, love, if it makes you happy you should do it.' I carry her words in the back of my mind, stored the way a maiden aunt might wrap a brooch, a remembrance of a long-lost love. I understand how hard that was for her to say and how it got harder as the project advanced. How she must have told her family not to ask me about the baseball field I was building, because they stared at me dumb-eyed, a row of silent, thickset peasants with red faces. Not an imagination among them except to forecast the wrath of God that will fall on the heads of pagans such as I.

He, of course, was Shoeless Joe Jackson.

> *Joseph Jefferson (Shoeless Joe) Jackson*
> *Born: Brandon Mills, S.C., 16 July, 1887*
> *Died: Greenville, S.C., 5 December, 1951*

In April, 1945, Ty Cobb picked Shoeless Joe as the best left fielder of all time.

He never learned to read or write. He created legends with a bat and a glove. He wrote records with base hits, his pen a bat, his book History.

Was it really a voice I heard? Or was it perhaps something inside me making a statement that I did not hear with my ears but with my heart? Why should I want to follow this command? But as I ask, I already know the answer. I count the loves in my life: Annie, Karin, Iowa, Baseball. The great god Baseball.

My birthstone is a diamond. When asked, I say my astrological sign is 'hit and run', which draws a lot of blank stares here in Iowa where 30,000 people go to see the University of Iowa Hawkeyes football team while 30 regulars, including me, watch the baseball team perform.

My father, I've been told, talked baseball statistics to my mother's belly while waiting for me to be born.

My father: born, Glen Ullin, N.D., 14 April, 1896. Another diamond birthstone. Never saw a professional baseball game until 1919 when he came back from World War I where he was gassed at Passchendaele. He settled in Chicago where he inhabited a room above a bar across from Comiskey Park and quickly learned to live and die with the White Sox. Died a little when, as prohibitive favourites, they lost the 1919 World Series to Cincinnati, died a lot the next summer when eight members of the team were accused of throwing that World Series.

Before I knew what baseball was, I knew of Connie Mack, John McGraw, Grover Cleveland Alexander, Ty Cobb, Babe Ruth, Tris Speaker, Tinker-to-Evers-to-Chance, and, of course, Shoeless Joe Jackson. My father loved underdogs, cheered for the Brooklyn Dodgers and the hapless St Louis Browns, loathed the Yankees, which I believe was an inherited trait, and insisted that Shoeless Joe was innocent, a victim of big business and crooked gamblers.

That first night, immediately after the voice and the vision, I did nothing except sip my lemonade a little faster and rattle the ice cubes in my glass. The vision of the baseball park lingered—swimming, swaying—seeming to be made of red steam, though perhaps it was only the sunset. There was a vision within the vision: one of Shoeless Joe Jackson playing left field. Shoeless Joe Jackson who last played major league baseball in 1920 and was suspended for life, along with seven of his compatriots, by Commissioner Keneshaw Mountain Landis, for his part in throwing the 1919 World Series.

'He hit .375 against the Reds in the 1919 World Series and played errorless ball,' my father would say, scratching his head in wonder.

Instead of nursery rhymes, I was raised on the story of the Black Sox Scandal, and instead of Tom Thumb or Rumpelstiltskin, I grew up hearing of the eight disgraced ballplayers: Weaver, Cicotte, Risberg, Felsch, Gandil, Williams, McMullin, and always Shoeless Joe Jackson.

'Twelve hits in an eight-game series. And *they* suspended *him*,' father would cry, and Shoeless Joe Jackson became a symbol of the tyranny of the powerful over the powerless. The name Keneshaw Mountain Landis became synonymous with the Devil.

It is more work than you might imagine to build a baseball field. I laid out a whole field, but it was there in spirit only. It was really only left field that concerned me. Home plate was made from pieces of cracked two-by-four imbedded in the earth. The pitcher's mound rocked like a cradle with I stood on it. The bases were stray blocks of wood, unanchored. There was no backstop or grandstand, only one shaky bleacher beyond the left field wall. There was a left field wall, but only about 50 feet of it, twelve feet high, stained dark green and braced from the rear. And the left field grass. My intuition told me that it was the grass that was important. It took me three seasons to hone that grass to its proper texture, to its proper colour. I made trips to Minneapolis and one or two other cities where the stadiums still have natural grass infields and outfields. I would arrive hours before a game and watch the groundskeepers groom the field like a prize animal, then stay after the game when in the cool of the night the same groundsmen appeared with hoses, hoes, rakes, and patched the grasses like medics attending wounded soldiers.

I pretended to be building a little league ballfield and asked their secrets and sometimes was told. I took interest in their total operation; they wouldn't understand if I told them I was building only a left field.

Three seasons I've spent seeding, watering, fussing, praying, coddling that field like a sick child until it glows parrot-green, cool as mint, soft as moss, lying there like a cashmere blanket. I began watching it in the evenings, sitting on the rickety bleacher just beyond the fence. A bleacher I had constructed for an audience of one.

My father played some baseball, Class B teams in Florida and California. I found his statistics in a dusty minor league record book. In Florida, he played for a team called the Angels and, by his records, was a better-than-average catcher. He claimed to have visited all 48 states and every major-league ballpark before, at 40, he married and settled down a two-day drive from the nearest major league team. I tried to play, but ground balls bounced off my chest and fly balls dropped between my hands. I might have been a fair designated hitter, but the rule was too late in coming.

There is the story of the urchin who, tugging at Shoeless Joe Jackson's sleeve as he emerged from a Chicago courthouse, said, 'Say it ain't so, Joe.'

Jackson's reply reportedly was, 'I'm afraid it is, kid.'

When he comes, I won't put him on the spot by asking. The less said the better. It is likely that he did accept some money from gamblers. But throw the Series? Never! Shoeless Joe led both teams in hitting in that 1919 Series. It was the circumstances. The circumstances. The players were paid peasant salaries while the owners became rich. The infamous Ten Day Clause, which voided contracts, could end any player's career without compensation, pension, or even a ticket home.

The second spring, on a tooth-achy May evening, a covering of black clouds lumbered off westward like ghosts of buffalo and the sky became the cold colour of a silver coin. The forecast was for frost.

The left-field grass was like green angora, soft as a baby's cheek. In my mind I could see it dull and crisp, bleached by frost, and my chest tightened.

Then I used a trick a groundskeeper in Minneapolis taught me, saying it was taught to him by grape farmers in California. I carried out a hose and making the spray so fine it was scarcely more than fog, I sprayed the soft, shaggy, spring grass all that chilled night. My hands ached and my own face became wet and cold, but as I watched, the spray froze on the grass, enclosing each blade in a gossamer-crystal coating of ice. A covering that served like a coat of armour to dispel the real frost that was set like a weasel upon killing in the night. I seemed to stand taller than ever before as the sun rose, turning the ice to eye-dazzling droplets, each a prism, making the field an orgy of rainbows.

Annie and Karin were at breakfast when I came in, the bacon and coffee smells and their laughter pulled me like a magnet.

'Did it work, love?' Annie asked, and I knew she knew by the look on my face that it did. And Karin, clapped her hands and complaining of how cold my face was when she kissed me, loved every second of it.

'And how did he get a name like Shoeless Joe?' I would ask my father, knowing full well the story but wanting to hear it again. And no matter how many times I heard it, I would still picture a lithe ballplayer, his great bare feet, white as baseballs, sinking into the outfield grass as he sprinted for a line drive. Then, after the catch, his toes gripping the grass like claws, he would brace and throw to the infield.

'It wasn't the least bit romantic,' my dad would say. 'When he was still in the minor leagues he bought a new pair of spikes and they hurt his feet; about the sixth inning he took them off and played the outfield in just his socks. The other players kidded him, called him Shoeless Joe, and the name stuck for all time.'

It was hard for me to imagine that a sore-footed young outfielder taking off his shoes one afternoon not long after the turn of the century could generate a legend.

I came to Iowa to study, one of the thousands of faceless students who pass through large universities, but I fell in love with Iowa. Fell in love with the land, the people, with the sky, the cornfields and Annie. Couldn't find work in my field, took what I could get. For years, each morning I bathed and frosted my cheeks with Aqua Velva, donned a three-piece suit and snap-brim hat, and, feeling like Superman emerging from a telephone booth, set forth to save the world from a lack of life insurance. I loathed the job so much that I did it quickly, urgently, almost violently. It was Annie who got me to rent the farm. It was Annie who got me to buy it. I operate it the way a child fits together his first puzzle, awkwardly, slowly, but when a piece slips into the proper slot, with pride and relief and joy.

I built the field and waited, and waited, and waited.

'It will happen, honey,' Annie would say when I stood shaking my head at my folly. People look at me. I must have a nickname in town. But I could feel the magic building like a storm gathering. It felt as if small animals were scurrying through my veins. I knew it was going to happen soon.

'There's someone on your lawn,' Annie says to me, staring out into the orange-tinted dusk. 'I can't see him clearly, but I can tell someone is there.' She was quite right, at least about it being *my* lawn, although, it is not in the strictest sense of the word a lawn, it is a left field.

I watch Annie looking out. She is soft as a butterfly, Annie is, with an evil grin and a tongue that travels at the speed of light. Her jeans are painted to her body and her pointy little nipples poke at the front of a black T-shirt with the single word RAH! emblazoned in waspish yellow capitals. Her red hair is short and curly. She has the green eyes of a cat.

Annie understands, though it is me she understands, and not always what is happening. She attends ballgames with me and squeezes my arm when there's a hit, but her heart isn't in it and she would just as soon be at home. She loses interest if the score isn't close or the weather warm, or the pace fast enough. To me it is baseball and that is all that matters. It is the game that is important—the tension, the strategy, the ballet of the fielders, the angle of the bat.

I have been more restless than usual this night. I have sensed the magic drawing closer, hovering somewhere out in the night like a zeppelin, silky and silent, floating like the moon until the time is right.

Annie peeks through the drapes. 'There *is* a man out there; I can see his silhouette. He's wearing a baseball uniform, an old-fashioned one.'

'It's Shoeless Joe Jackson,' I say. My heart sounds like someone flicking a balloon with their index finger.

'Oh,' she says. Annie stays very calm in emergencies. She Band-aids bleeding fingers and toes, and patches the plumbing with gum and good wishes. Staying calm makes her able to live with me. The French have the right words for Annie—she has a good heart.

'Is he the Jackson on TV? The one you yell, "Drop it, Jackson," at?'

Annie's sense of baseball history is not highly developed.

'No, that's Reggie. This is Shoeless Joe Jackson. He hasn't played major league baseball since 1920.'

'Well, aren't you going to go out and chase him off your lawn, or something?'

Yes. What am I going to do? I wish someone else understood. My daughter has an evil grin and bewitching eyes. She climbs into my lap and watches television baseball with me. There is a magic about her.

'I think I'll go upstairs and read for a while,' Annie says. 'Why don't you invite Shoeless Jack in for coffee?' I feel the greatest tenderness toward her then, something akin to the rush of love I felt the first time I held my daughter in my arms. Annie senses that magic is about to happen. She knows that she is not part of it. My impulse is to pull her to me as she walks by, the denim of her thighs making a tiny music. But I don't. She will be waiting for me and she will twine her body about me and find my mouth with hers.

As I step out on the verandah, I can hear the steady drone of the crowd, like bees humming on a white afternoon, and the voices of the vendors, like crows cawing.

A little ground mist, like wisps of gauze, snakes in slow circular motions just above the grass.

'The grass is soft as a child's breath,' I say to the moonlight. On the porch wall I find the switch, and the single battery of floodlights I have erected behind the left-field fence sputters to life. 'I've shaved it like a golf green, tended it like I would my own baby. It has been powdered and lotioned and loved. It is ready.'

Moonlight butters the whole Iowa night. Clover and corn smells are thick as syrup. I experience a tingling like the tiniest of electric wires touching the back of my neck, sending warm sensations through me like the feeling of love. Then, as the lights flare, a scar against the blue-black sky, I see Shoeless Joe Jackson standing out in left field. His feet spread wide, body bent forward from the waist, hands on hips, he waits. There is the sharp crack of the bat and Shoeless Joe drifts effortlessly a few steps to his left, raises his right hand to signal for the ball, camps under it for a second or two, catches the ball, at the same time transferring it to his throwing hand, and fires it into the infield.

I make my way to the left field, walking in the darkness far outside the third-base line, behind where the third-base stands would be. I climb up on the wobbly bleacher behind the fence. I can look right

down on Shoeless Joe. He fields a single on one hop and pegs the
ball to third.

'How does it play?' I holler down.

'The ball bounces true,' he replies.

'I know.' I am smiling with pride and my heart thumps mightily
against my ribs. 'I've hit a thousand line drives and as many
grounders. It's true as a felt-top table.'

'It is,' says Shoeless Joe. 'It is true.'

I lean back and watch the game. From where I sit the scene is as
complete as in any of the major league baseball parks I have ever
attended: the two teams, the stands, the fans, the lights, the vendors,
the scoreboard. The only difference is that I sit alone in the left field
bleacher and the only player who seems to have substance is Shoeless
Joe Jackson. When Joe's team is at bat, the left fielder below me is
transparent as if he were made of vapour. He performs mechanically,
but seems not to have facial features. We do not converse.

A great amphitheatre of grandstand looms dark against the sky, the
park is surrounded by decks of floodlights making it brighter than
day, the crowd buzzes, the vendors hawk their wares, and I cannot
keep the promise I made to myself not to ask Shoeless Joe Jackson
about his suspension and what it means to him.

While the pitcher warms up for the third inning we talk.

'It must have been . . . It must have been like . . .' but I can't find
the words.

'Like having a part of me amputated, slick and smooth and painless,
like having an arm or a leg taken off with one swipe of a scalpel, big
and blue as a sword,' and Joe looks up at me and his dark eyes seem
about to burst with the pain of it. 'A friend of mind used to tell about
the war, how him and a buddy was running across the field when a
piece of shrapnel took his friend's head off, and how the friend ran,
headless, for several strides before he fell. I'm told that old men wake
in the night and scratch itchy legs that have been dust for fifty years.
That was me. Years and years later, I'd wake in the night with the
smell of the ballpark in my nostrils and the cool of the grass on my
feet. The thrill of the grass . . .'

How I wish my father could be here with me. He died before we
had television in our part of the country. The very next year he could
have watched in grainy black and white as Don Larsen pitched a
no-hitter in the World Series. He would have loved hating the
Yankees as they won that game. We were always going to go to a

major-league baseball game, he and I. But the time was never right, the money always needed for something else. One of the last days of his life, late in the night while I sat with him because the pain wouldn't let him sleep, the radio dragged in a staticky station broadcasting a White Sox game. We hunched over the radio and cheered them on, but they lost. Dad told the story of the Black Sox Scandal for the last time. Told of seeing two of those World Series games, told of the way Shoeless Joe Jackson hit, told the dimensions of Comiskey Park, and how during the series the mobsters in striped suits sat in the box seats with their colourful women, watching the game and perhaps making plans to go out later and kill a rival.

'You must go,' he said. 'I've been in all sixteen major league parks. I want you to do it too. The summers belong to somebody else now, have for a long time.' I nodded agreement.

'Hell, you know what I mean,' he said, shaking his head.

I did indeed.

'I loved the game,' Shoeless Joe went on. 'I'd have played for food money. I'd have played free and worked for food. It was the game, the parks, the smells, the sounds. Have you ever held a bat or a baseball to your face? The varnish, the leather. And it was the crowd, the excitement of them rising as one when the ball was hit deep. The sound was like a chorus. Then there was the chug-a-lug of the tin lizzies in the parking lots and the hotels with their brass spittoons in the lobbies and brass beds in the rooms. It makes me tingle all over like a kid on his way to his first double-header, just to talk about it.'

The year after Annie and I were married, the year we first rented this farm, I dug Annie's garden for her; dug it by hand, stepping a spade into the soft black soil, ruining my salesman's hands. After I finished it rained, an Iowa spring rain as soft as spray from a warm hose. The clods of earth I had dug seemed to melt until the garden levelled out, looking like a patch of black ocean. It was near noon on a gentle Sunday when I walked out to that garden. The soil was soft and my shoes disappeared as I plodded until I was near the centre. There I knelt, the soil cool on my knees. I looked up at the low grey sky; the rain had stopped and the only sound was the surrounding trees dripping fragrantly. Suddenly I thrust my hands wrist-deep into the snuffy-black earth. The air was pure. All around me the clean smell of earth and water. Keeping my hands buried I stirred the earth with my fingers and I knew I loved Iowa as much as a man could love a piece of earth.

When I came back to the house Annie stopped me at the door, made me wait on the verandah, then hosed me down as if I were a door with too many handprints on it, while I tried to explain my epiphany. It is very difficult to describe an experience of religious significance while you are being sprayed with a garden hose by a laughing, loving woman.

'What happened to the sun?' Shoeless Joe says to me, waving his hand toward the banks of floodlights that surround the park.

'Only stadium in the big leagues that doesn't have them is Wrigley Field,' I say. 'The owners found that more people could attend night games. They even play the World Series at night now.'

Joe purses his lips, considering.

'It's harder to see the ball, especially at the plate.'

'When there are breaks they usually go against the ballplayers, right? But I notice you're three for three so far,' I add, looking down at his uniform, the only identifying marks a large S with an O in the top crook, an X in the bottom, and an American flag with 48 stars on his left sleeve near the elbow.

Joe grins 'I'd play for the Devil's own team just for the touch of a baseball. Hell, I'd play in the dark if I had to.'

I want to ask about the day in December, 1951. If he'd lasted another few years things might have been different. There was a move afoot to have his record cleared, but it died with him. I wanted to ask, but my instinct told me not to. There are things it is better not to know.

It is one of those nights when the sky is close enough to touch, so close that looking up is like seeing my own eyes reflected in a rain barrel. I sit in the bleacher just outside the left field fence. I clutch in my hand a hot dog with mustard, onions, and green relish. The voice of the crowd roars in my ears like the sea. Chords of the 'Star-spangled Banner' and 'Take Me Out to the Ballgame' float across the field. A Coke bottle is propped against my thigh, squat, greenish, the ice-cream-haired elf grinning conspiratorially from the cap.

Below me in left field, Shoeless Joe Jackson glides over the plush velvet grass, silent as a jungle cat. He prowls and paces, crouches ready to spring as, nearly 300 feet away, the ball is pitched. At the sound of the bat he wafts in whatever direction is required as if he were on ball bearings.

Then the intrusive sound of a screen door slamming reaches me, and I blink and start. I recognize it as the sound of the door to my house and looking into the distance, I can see a shape that I know is my daughter toddling down the back steps. Perhaps the lights or the crowd has awakened her and she has somehow eluded Annie. I judge the distance to the steps. I am just to the inside of the foul pole which is exactly 330 feet from home plate. I tense. Karin will surely be drawn to the lights and the emerald dazzle of the infield. If she touches anything, I fear it will all disappear, perhaps forever. Then as if she senses my discomfort she stumbles away from the lights, walking in the ragged fringe of darkness well outside the third-base line. She trails a blanket behind her, one tiny fist rubbing a sleepy eye. She is barefoot and wears a white flannelette nightgown covered in an explosion of daisies.

She climbs up the bleacher, alternating a knee and a foot on each step, and crawls into my lap, silently, like a kitten. I hold her close and wrap the blanket around her feet. The play goes on; her innocence has not disturbed the balance.

'What is it?' she says shyly, her eyes indicating that she means all that she sees.

'Just watch the left fielder,' I say. 'He'll tell you all you ever need to know about a baseball game. Watch his feet as the pitcher accepts the sign and gets ready to pitch. A good left fielder knows what pitch is coming and he can tell from the angle of the bat where the ball is going to be hit and, if he's good, how hard.'

I look down at Karin. She cocks one sky-blue eye at me, wrinkling her nose, then snuggles into my chest the index finger of her right hand tracing tiny circles around her nose.

The crack of the bat is sharp as the yelp of a kicked cur. Shoeless Joe whirls, takes five loping strides directly toward us, turns again, reaches up, and the ball smacks into his glove. The final batter dawdles in the on-deck circle.

'Can I come back again?' Joe asks.

'I built this left field for you. It's yours any time you want to use it. They play 162 games a season now.'

'There are others,' he says. 'If you were to finish the infield, why, old Chick Gandil could play first base, and we'd have the Swede at shortstop and Buck Weaver at third.' I can feel his excitement rising. 'We could stick McMullin in at second, and Cicotte and Lefty Williams would like to pitch again. Do you think you could finish the centre field? It would mean a lot to Happy Felsch.'

'Consider it done,' I say, hardly thinking of the time, the money, the backbreaking labour it entails. 'Consider it done,' I say again, then stop suddenly as an idea creeps into my brain like a runner inching off first base.

'I know a catcher,' I say. 'He never made the majors, but in his prime he was good. Really good. Played Class B ball in Florida and California . . .'

'We could give him a try,' says Shoeless Joe. 'You give us a place to play and we'll look at your catcher.'

I swear the stars have moved in close enough to eavesdrop as I sit in this single rickety bleacher that I built with my unskilled hands, looking down at Shoeless Joe Jackson. A breath of clover travels on the summer wind. Behind me, just yards away, brook water splashes softly in the darkness, a frog shrills, fireflies dazzle the night like red pepper. A petal falls.

'God, what an outfield,' he says. 'What a left field.' He looks up at me and I look down at him. 'This must be heaven,' he says.

'No. It's Iowa,' I reply automatically. But then I feel the night rubbing softly against my face like cherry blossoms; look at the sleeping girl-child in my arms, her small hand curled around one of my fingers; think of the fierce warmth of the woman waiting for me in the house; inhale the fresh-cut grass smell that seems locked in the air like permanent incense, and listen to the drone of the crowd, as below me Shoeless Joe Jackson tenses, watching the angle of the distant bat for a clue as to where the ball will be hit.

'I think you're right, Joe,' I say, but softly enough not to disturb his concentration.

AUDREY THOMAS · b. 1935

Joseph and His Brother

Joseph was our cook-steward—a king of legacy to us from our friends
Tom and Sheila who had been out there for two years and had left a
few weeks before our arrival. As we bumped up the road from the
coast to the university where we were to live, I took his picture out
of my passport case again and again—'my' cook-steward. He grinned
at me, a handsome, gap-toothed man. 'Lucky you,' said my English
mother-in-law. 'Fancy having servants.' I looked at his picture again,
then out the window. Women in beautiful bright-coloured cloths
stepped off the road and stood staring at us as we passed. Ragged
children appeared at the edges of villages, shouting and jumping—
'Bronie, Bronie, Bronie.' Two men, barefoot, their cloths slung over
their left shoulder, stood talking seriously at a crossroad. Each had a
Singer sewing machine on his head. Joseph spoke English, could read
and write a little, was an excellent cook. In the photograph he wore
a white sports shirt, not a traditional cloth. He would have his own
quarters. I tried to imagine myself giving him orders. The huge trees
of the rain forest towered above us on either side. Our children, in
spite of warnings about bumps, stood up on the back seat, waving
out the window. Lorries honked merrily and sped past us on blind
curves, their sides bulging with people. Most had signs painted across
the back, 'God's Time is Best' 'Psalm 100' 'Mind Your Own . . . .' Rusty
wrecks nearly hidden by giant ferns littered the side of the road. 'Take
it slowly at first,' said a man on the boat, 'Africa can eat you.' If we
opened the windows the red dust flew in at us, covered our skin and
hair, even our eyelashes, like paprika. What were the children feeling?
What did they think of all these black people, the heat, the forest
through which we were passing? What would they think of a cook-
steward? Near the end of the journey, outside the big town where we
would do our shopping, I saw scrawled on a blackboard easel, in
front of the Agip gas station, these words:

REX 8.30 TONIGHT
PAY UP OR DIE

I clutched my husband's hand. We were surrounded by taxis, lorries, walking figures, noise. The strangeness caught at my throat. Rex. 8.30 tonight. Pay up or die. What if he didn't like us and put something in our food. It was only the next day, when I asked Joseph about the sign, that I found out that Rex was the name of the local cinema. I laughed but was ashamed of my original interpretation. There was a rich smell of baked bread and ground-nuts roasting in the oven.

The white man is ashamed to be afraid of Africa and yet the shame does not completely obliterate the fear. That first night, children asleep under musty-smelling mosquito netting, we lay awake holding hands and listening to the drums. They were faint but seemed to come at us from all directions—dadada/dadada/dadada. Only recently the University watchmen had carried lanterns and bows and arrows. Some strange creature screamed over and over again from a distant tree. We laughed and kissed each other and laughed again. We had arrived to find Joseph standing grinning shyly on the doorstep. The children ran to him at once. 'Hello Joseph. Hello. We've brought you presents.' He patted each blond head and laughed. Did a cook-steward protect you against the darkness and the drums? Rex. 8.30 tonight. Pay up or die.

Joseph was everything that Tom and Sheila had assured us he would be. At six in the morning he came in from his quarters next door, began peeling and chopping grapefruits and oranges and paw-paw for the morning salad. All the fruits were green here. There was no such thing as yellow lemons or yellow grapefruit or orange oranges. Only the bananas remained their familiar selves, but smaller. Joseph chopped while the kettle boiled, mixed the fruit with a little sugar, then put it in the fridge to chill. (Fridges had locks here—stewards were thieves, the other women told me. You couldn't be too careful.) At six o'clock he brought us up our morning tea. 'Cock Cock Cock Cock Cock.' He always announced himself instead of knocking. We sat up in bed and listened to the Overseas Service of the BBC. The children woke, rubbed their eyes, ran in for a quick kiss and downstairs to find their beloved Joseph. They sat on the kitchen table eating thick slices of bread and marge while Joseph fried eggs and made toast. 'Madame', he called me, my husband, 'Master', in spite of all our egalitarian speeches. After breakfast he waited at the side of the road with other stewards and nurse-girls, each with one or more charges, for the little school bus which made the rounds of the compound. The African children taught our children to cry out, as they did, when they spied the driver turning into our road,

MONKEY
BANANA

COCOYAM
DRIVER!

MONKEY
BANANA
COCOYAM
DRIVER!

Joseph handed the children carefully up the steps, stood talking and flirting with Veronica, the nurse-girl next door, then went to his quarters for a break. At eleven he would bring me a cup of coffee where I sat writing at the long dining table, would lean on his broom and accept an offered cigarette (or rush off to a neighbouring road, if we were both out, and buy two 'Job' or 'Tusker for Man' for a penny from a woman he knew). He wouldn't sit down but would stand there, barefoot, in the worn khaki shorts and an undershirt reduced almost to the consistency of gauze, and he would tell me things. Compound gossip. So and so's wife was a bad woman, she could not keep a servant. Veronica was a bad girl, or as he put it, 'no good at all'. He was negotiating for a new wife, the daughter of one of the market women; he brought gifts of chocolate and money, but still the mother scorned him. What did I want for dinner? He had had a wife, and a child as well, but the wife was carrying on with someone else in her village and when he went to challenge and accuse her she put something in the soup that poisoned him—he was sick for a long time, sick proper. His stomach burned and his mouth was covered with blisters. He was not lucky with women—in general he felt that they were no good at all. His wife kept the child as was the custom here. Now he wore a magic charm around his neck although he was a Christian. (And sometimes, on his day off, he would come home late, laughing and singing—we could hear him from our open bedroom windows, stumbling down the steep gravel driveway, another Joseph, a stranger. But always alone, never with a woman. If a Revolution came, would he protect us?) But most of all he told me about his brother. Joseph's brother was a lorry driver on the Cape

Coast–Accra road and a great hero to Joseph. The boss of the lorry park was a brother as well, but by a different mother, and much older. It was a good job, if a dangerous one, and the brother had nearly enough saved to buy a sheet-iron roof for his house.

'How is your brother, Joseph?' I would say if the conversation lagged.

'Hey! Madame!' and he would tell me of the latest near accident or adventure. Like Joseph, his brother could read and write and was a fairly regular correspondent. Travellers also arrived from time to time at the kitchen door, asked for Joseph, sat on the back steps eating kola nuts and gossiping before they picked up their loads and continued. To Joseph, his brother lived a life of adventure and thrills. As he told his new tale, our steward's hands would clench with excitement. He would grip an imaginary wheel or use the broom as a stick-shift. The name of the lorry was 'God is Backin' Me'. The Cape Coast road was the sweetest road in the country, paved proper and with a fine breeze blowing across from the sea. To drive such a run was a prize. Joseph imagined himself up front in the driver's seat, laughing with the mate, honking his horn, scattering women and children, goats, chickens, all manner of lesser creatures, passing inferior lorries on dangerous curves and at equally dangerous speeds. Then, tale ended, he would blink his eyes and laugh and go down into the kitchen to make a salad for lunch. How very unadventurous his life must have seemed compared to that of his younger brother. Chopping fruit, preparing salad, serving, serving, serving. Servants serve, by definition. For Christmas Joseph wanted a cook's hat, tall, stiffly starched, and a mess jacket. We tried to dissuade him. The children, worried, took his side. The market woman threw his gifts to her daughter in his face. He laughed painfully, leaning on his broom. He wrung chickens' necks on the back stoop after the children had gone to school. Some of the other women had had four, five, seven stewards. They could not cook, they stole, they imported their wives and ragged children. 'You don't know how lucky you are.' Always water dripping through the filter, more water (already filtered) chilling in the (unlocked) fridge. Beautiful bread, beautiful curries, ground-nut soup, and salads, the children swinging their legs against the kitchen table, saying their teacher was very hard-o, begging ground nuts and stories of Anansi the trickster spiderman who could change himself into a yam, a stick of wood, a sleeping mat. Somehow, with Joseph there, the drums, the poison snakes (Joseph averting his eyes and beating, beating, beating with a stick) the soldier ants, the tsetse flies, the dangers, real or imagined, were kept in check. Joseph would take care of everything from dishes to disasters. 'You don't know how lucky you are.'

One morning, in his eighth month with us, toward the end of the dry season, when the land is so parched for water you swear that green has gone away forever and tempers flare like matches, Joseph came to me in great distress.

'Please, Madame. I need to return to my village.' He held a letter in his hand. In spite of the three-bladed fan overhead, the sweat poured down the backs of my legs and down my arms, leaving wet marks on my paper. Joseph's eyes were bloodshot, as if he were coming down with fever. I was horrified. To leave us now! The temperature in the kitchen, with the gas cooker on, must be well over 100 degrees. I tried to sound sympathetic.

'Why, Joseph, why?'

'My brother, Madame. My younger brother.'

'The lorry driver?'

'Yes, Madame. They say he is sick proper.'

'Fever?' I said.

He hesitated. I wondered if he were fed up, if the letter was a hoax.

'Yes, Madame.'

'What can *you* do?' My voice came more sharply than I intended.

'Please, I must go.'

I fell back on the old feminine excuse that I would have to ask my husband. Joseph agreed. I knew, however, what the answer would be and felt as if I had encountered the reality of Joseph as someone temporary in my life, for the first time.

For lunch we had the usual avocado salad, a bowl of freshly roasted nuts, bread still warm from the oven, a bowl of fruit. Never, now that I might lose it all, had it tasted so good. When the children went up for their nap we sat under the fan, drinking tea, and discussed what it was best to do. Of course we would have to let him go, and as soon as possible.

'But will he come back?' I was half-way through the first draft of a novel. Visions of thieving, incompetent stewards danced in my head.

'I think so. Anyway, blood ties are very strong here—we can't keep him.'

Two weeks later he was back. (Two weeks of the gas cylinder

running out on me, the children whining for mashed banana 'the way Joseph makes it', of stumbling around a kitchen as hot as an inferno, of washing-up—how quickly I had managed to forget the tyranny of housework—of making my coffee break myself.)

'Well, Joseph.'

'Eh! Madame!' He went to put his things away and, to my surprise, did not return for a cigarette and a gossip.

'What's wrong with Joseph?' the children asked, worried.

'Why doesn't he laugh?'

On his day off he came back very drunk, singing and stumbling. The drums seemed closer now, and louder too. 'What do you think has happened?' We whispered to one another, lighting a candle against the darkness. 'Has the brother died?'

On Monday I could stand it no longer. After the school bus had left I walked next door to Joseph's quarters—something I had never done before—with a package of cigarettes in my hand. He was sitting outside under the paw-paw tree, just sitting and sitting.

'Joseph,' I said, 'I am your friend' (and yet wondering at the same time if that were so). 'Is you brother dead?' He opened his eyes. We were the same age, Joseph and I, and yet for a minute I saw him as an old, old man.

'Dead? No Madame, my brother is not dead.'

I sat down on the grass beside him—the tree shading us from the growing heat of the sun—and offered him a cigarette. Absently he took two and lighting one, stuck the other behind his ear.

'Eh Madame,' he said, expelling a great cloud of smoke, 'No one knows the story of tomorrow's dawn.'

'What is it, what has happened?'

That was ten years ago and yet I remember that moment, that morning, as clearly as if it were yesterday, this morning, half an hour ago. I remember the prickly grass on my bare legs and the heat, and the poinsettia hedge in the distance. I remember a butterfly as red as wine and the sound of somebody pounding fou-fou in the distance. I remember the dress I wore and Joseph's smooth brown skin and the unripe paw-paws hanging above our heads. Was I ever there or was it all a dream?

Joseph's brother was driving his lorry from Cape Coast to Techiman on a certain Monday night. He picked up, at an intermediate town, a woman passenger. She was attractive but dressed, rather oddly, in black velvet. Joseph's brother put her on the front seat between himself and his mate. It was very late and the lorry was nearly empty. He judged her to be a prostitute and told her that he loved her. He suggested taking her on to Techiman to sleep with him. The mate said that she declined but that he nevertheless sped through the town of her destination without stopping. He let the mate out at the junction to his village and went on to Techiman where he spent the night with her in a resthouse, even though he was supposed to return the lorry to the lorry-park. In the morning, instead of returning to his step-brother as usual, he took the lorry and the woman to Dixcove, right off his beat. She left him and he returned to Techiman, giving his step-brother boss only a vague and unsatisfactory account of his behaviour. A few days later, on a holiday, some fellow villagers, also working in Techiman, approached the lorry driver and said one of them had died and they would like him to carry the corpse home to his ancestral village, a distance of about 250 miles. At first he refused for a corpse is dangerous cargo—the spirit of the dead man, if uneasy, can wreck the lorry. They begged and begged, however, and finally he consented so the funeral party set off. But on the way he suddenly stopped the lorry and told his mate that he could see the woman in black velvet. He shouted to her—'Ho! If you are going, it is I who will go with you!' No one else could see her, yet he was restrained with great difficulty and persuaded to drive on and deliver the corpse to his village. The same thing happened the following Sunday on his usual run. He told the mate he saw the woman in black velvet; again he called out, 'If you are going, I will go with you!'

When an elder of the family was consulted (for the mate could not keep the story to himself and reported to the step-brother) the old man said that the spirit of the corpse was troubling Joseph's brother and that such a young driver should not have been made to drive such a heavy load. He made some medicine for the young man to bathe in.

The next morning he appeared quite well and set off on the regular run between Cape Coast and the capital. Past yellow taxis and rickety tro-tros, walking figures, enormous head loads like strange crowns upon their heads, the palm trees bowed down, the silver backsides of their leaves gleaming in the sun. Copra set out to dry. Billboards advertising Club beer, the Weekly Lotto, Queen Elizabeth gin, Agip gas, the Atomic-Paradise Nite Club. Past the town of Elmina with its castle-cum-fort where 200 years ago the Director General (Dutch) had drunk himself mad out of boredom and locked his chief merchant in a cage, like a wild beast, throwing bones through the bars, from time to time, for him to chew, while the civet cats prowled in the courtyard (Kaatplaz) down below. Yet just beyond the town he again saw the woman in black velvet, shouted, stopped the lorry and began to weep. The mate found another driver in the next town and by the time they reached Cape Coast Joseph's brother was talking 'basa-basa' or crazy, and the step-brother took him to the mission hospital. They could find nothing physically wrong with him and he was taken home to his village. That is when Joseph received the letter. He sighed.

'He did not know me, Madame. A tall.'

For the past week Joseph and his step-brother had taken the younger brother from shrine to shrine, to a succession of fetish priests and medicine men, but there seemed to be nothing that anyone could do. Sadly, Joseph had decided to return to us.

Things were never the same after that day. Although he was kind and attentive as before, some spark had gone out of Joseph. He laughed rarely and never with his old, high humour. Letters came saying that the brother was now completely mute, that another relative had taken over the driver's job on the lorry named 'God is Backin' Me'. On one occasion the step-brother and some other relations had taken him to Accra for a few days, in the hopes of seeing a doctor. While they were resting at their lodgings he disappeared. They eventually went to the police who had, in fact, taken him to the mental hospital. But there he made signs that he wanted a pen and paper, wrote his name and temporary address and a request to be taken home. He was pronounced not mad and sent home with his relatives. Within two months he had reverted to childhood and had to be led by the hand. Joseph, sweeping the lounge or listening to the children, brooded on the cruel fate of his brother. He stopped his search for a new wife and we did not dare to tease him.

When the Easter holidays came and I could leave the children with my husband, I offered to drive Joseph down to his village so he could see his brother for himself. I must confess that my motives were not entirely altruistic.

Early one morning we set off, a thermos of ice water in the glove compartment, a few presents for Joseph's relatives tucked in a straw basket. Down we went toward the Coast Road, reversing the route of that strange journey so many months before. At the edge of a town we passed a group of men in the orange-coloured mourning cloth of the region; I tried not to see it as a omen. Joseph hardly spoke the whole way down. When we arrived the brother was sitting composedly in the yard, and I did not notice, until I went to shake hands, that he was in handcuffs and chained to a tree. The relatives stood around us in a circle, hoping we had brought some magic cure that would make the young man well again. 'I hear you have been ill,' I said. 'How do you feel now?' Joseph translated for me, a nervous smile on his lips.

'I feel something knocking in my eyes,' said the brother. 'Somebody kicked my head. I have written Tamale, Accra, Takordi. One cedi is a hundred pesewas.'

'Basa-basa,' said the family, apologetically. 'Basa-basa.' They pointed to their heads.

As for the woman in black velvet, when I questioned him, he said he did not recall her.

I left Joseph there for a few days and returned alone, hurrying to get through the forest before dark and the drums began.

One other thing Joseph told me. His people believe that sexual intercourse with a ghost results in death.

ALISTAIR MACLEOD · b. 1936

As Birds Bring Forth the Sun

Once there was a family with a Highland name who lived beside the sea. And the man had a dog of which he was very fond. She was large and grey, a sort of staghound from another time. And if she jumped up to lick his face, which she loved to do, her paws would jolt against his shoulders with such force that she would come close to knocking him down and he would be forced to take two or three backward steps before he could regain his balance. And he himself was not a small man, being slightly over six feet and perhaps one hundred and eighty pounds.

She had been left, when a pup, at the family's gate in a small handmade box and no one knew where she had come from or that she would eventually grow to such a size. Once, while still a small pup, she had been run over by the steel wheel of a horse-drawn cart which was hauling kelp from the shore to be used as fertilizer. It was in October and the rain had been falling for some weeks and the ground was soft. When the wheel of the cart passed over her, it sunk her body into the wet earth as well as crushing some of her ribs; and apparently the silhouette of her small crushed body was visible in the earth after the man lifted her to his chest while she yelped and screamed. He ran his fingers along her broken bones, ignoring the blood and urine which fell upon his shirt, trying to soothe her bulging eyes and her scrabbling front paws and her desperately licking tongue.

The more practical members of his family, who had seen run-over dogs before, suggested that her neck be broken by his strong hands or that he grasp her by the hind legs and swing her head against a rock, thus putting an end to her misery. But he would not do it.

Instead, he fashioned a small box and lined it with woollen remnants from a sheep's fleece and one of his old and frayed shirts. He placed her within the box and placed the box behind the stove and then he warmed some milk in a small saucepan and sweetened it with sugar. And he held open her small and trembling jaws with his left hand while spooning in the sweetened milk with his right, ignoring the needle-like sharpness of her small teeth. She lay in the box most of the remaining fall and into the early winter, watching everything with her large brown eyes.

Although some members of the family complained about her presence and the odour from the box and the waste of time she involved, they gradually adjusted to her; and as the weeks passed by, it became evident that her ribs were knitting together in some form or other and that she was recovering with the resilience of the young. It also became evident that she would grow to a tremendous size, as she outgrew one box and then another and the grey hair began to feather from her huge front paws. In the spring she was outside almost all the time and followed the man everywhere; and when she came inside during the following months, she had grown so large that she would no longer fit into her accustomed place behind the stove and was forced to lie beside it. She was never given a name but was referred to in Gaelic as *cù mòr glas*, the big grey dog.

By the time she came into her first heat, she had grown to a tremendous height, and although her signs and her odour attracted many panting and highly aroused suitors, none was big enough to mount her and the frenzy of their disappointment and the longing of her unfulfillment were more than the man could stand. He went, so the story goes, to a place where he knew there was a big dog. A dog not as big as she was, but still a big dog, and he brought him home with him. And at the proper time he took the *cù mòr glas* and the big dog down to the sea where he knew there was a hollow in the rock which appeared only at low tide. He took some sacking to provide footing for the male dog and he placed the *cù mòr glas* in the hollow of the rock and knelt beside her and steadied her with his left arm under her throat and helped position the male dog above her and guided his blood-engorged penis. He was a man used to working with the breeding of animals, with the guiding of rams and bulls and stallions and often with the funky smell of animal semen heavy on his large and gentle hands.

The winter that followed was a cold one and ice formed on the sea and frequent squalls and blizzards obliterated the offshore islands and caused the people to stay near their fires much of the time, mending clothes and nets and harness and waiting for the change in season. The *cù mòr glas* grew heavier and even more large until there was hardly room for her around the stove or even under the table.

And then one morning, when it seemed that spring was about to break, she was gone.

The man and even his family, who had become more involved than they cared to admit, waited for her but she did not come. And as the frenzy of spring wore on, they busied themselves with readying their land and their fishing gear and all of the things that so desperately required their attention. And then they were into summer and fall and winter and another spring which saw the birth of the man and his wife's twelfth child. And this it was summer again.

That summer the man and two of his teenaged sons were pulling their herring nets about two miles offshore when the wind began to blow off the land and the water began to roughen. They became afraid that they could not make it safely back to shore, so they pulled in behind one of the offshore islands, knowing that they would be sheltered there and planning to outwait the storm. As the prow of their boat approached the gravelly shore, they heard a sound above them, and looking up they saw the *cù mòr glas* silhouetted on the brow of the hill which was the small island's highest point.

'*M'eudal cù mòr glas*' shouted the man in his happiness—*m'eudal* meaning something like dear or darling; and as he shouted, he jumped over the side of his boat into the waist-deep water, struggling for footing on the rolling gravel as he waded eagerly and awkwardly towards her and the shore. At the same time, the *cù mòr glas* came hurtling down towards him in a shower of small rocks dislodged by her feet; and just as he was emerging from the water, she met him as she used to, rearing up on her hind legs and placing her huge front paws on his shoulders while extending her eager tongue.

The weight and speed of her momentum met him as he tried to hold his balance on the sloping angle and the water rolling gravel beneath his feet, and he staggered backwards and lost his footing and fell beneath her force. And in that instant again, as the story goes, there appeared over the brow of the hill six more huge grey dogs hurtling down towards the gravelled stand. They had never seen him before; and seeing him stretched prone beneath their mother, they understood, like so many armies, the intention of their leader.

They fell upon him in a fury, slashing his face and tearing aside his lower jaw and ripping out his throat, crazed with blood-lust or duty or perhaps starvation. The *cù mòr glas* turned on them in her own savagery, slashing and snarling and, it seemed, crazed by their mistake; driving them bloodied and yelping before her, back over the brow of the hill where they vanished from sight but could still be heard screaming in the distance. It all took perhaps little more than a minute.

The man's two sons, who were still in the boat and had witnessed it all, ran sobbing through the salt water to where their mauled and mangled father lay; but there was little they could do other than hold his warm and bloodied hands for a few brief moments. Although his eyes 'lived' for a small fraction of time, he could not speak to them because his face and throat had been torn away, and of course there was nothing they could do except to hold and be held tightly until that too slipped away and his eyes glazed over and they could no longer feel his hands holding theirs. The storm increased and they could not get home and so they were forced to spend the night huddled beside their father's body. They were afraid to try to carry the body to the rocking boat because he was so heavy and they were afraid that they might lose even what little of him remained and they were afraid also, huddled on the rocks, that the dogs might return. But they did not return at all and there was no sound from them, no sound at all, only the moaning of the wind and the washing of the water on the rocks.

In the morning they debated whether they should try to take his body with them or whether they should leave it and return in the company of older and wiser men. But they were afraid to leave it unattended and felt that the time needed to cover it with protective rocks would be better spent in trying to get across to their home shore. For a while they debated as to whether one should go in the boat and the other remain on the island, but each was afraid to be alone and so in the end they managed to drag and carry almost float him towards the bobbing boat. They lay him facedown and covered him with what clothes there were and set off across the still-rolling sea. Those who waited on the shore missed the large presence of the man within the boat and some of them waded into the water and others rowed out in skiffs, attempting to hear the tearful message called out across the rolling waves.

The *cù mòr glas* and her six young dogs were never seen again, or perhaps I should say they were never seen again in the same way. After some weeks, a group of men circled the island tentatively in their boats but they saw no sign. They went again and then again but found nothing. A year later, and grown much braver, they beached their boats and walked the island carefully, looking into the small sea caves and the hollows at the base of the wind-ripped trees, thinking perhaps that if they did not find the dogs, they might at least find their whitened bones; but again they discovered nothing.

The *cù mòr glas*, though, was supposed to be sighted here and there for a number of years. Seen on a hill in one region or silhouetted on a ridge in another or loping across the valleys or glens in the early morning or the shadowy evening. Always in the area of the half perceived. For a while she became rather like the Loch Ness Monster or the Sasquatch on a smaller scale. Seen but not recorded. Seen where there were no cameras. Seen but never taken.

The mystery of where she went became entangled with the mystery of whence she came. There was increased speculation about the handmade box in which she had been found and much theorizing as to the individual or individuals who might have left it. People went to look for the box but could not find it. It was felt she might have been part of a *buidseachd* or evil spell cast on the man by some mysterious enemy. But no one could go much farther than that. All of his caring for her was recounted over and over again and nobody missed any of the ironies.

What seemed literally known was that she had crossed the winter ice to have her pups and had been unable to get back. No one could remember ever seeing her swim; and in the early months at least, she could not have taken her young pups with her.

The large and gentle man with the smell of animal semen often heavy on his hands was my great-great-great-grandfather, and it may be argued that he died because he was too good at breeding animals or that he cared too much about their fulfilment and well-being. He was no longer there for his own child of the spring who, in turn, became my great-great-grandfather, and he was perhaps too much there in the memory of his older sons who saw him fall beneath the ambiguous force of the *cù mòr glas*. The youngest boy in the boat was haunted and tormented by the awfulness of what he had seen. He would wake at night screaming that he had seen the *cù mòr glas a'bhàis*, the big grey dog of death, and his screams filled the house and the ears and minds of the listeners, bringing home again and again the consequences of their loss. One morning, after a night in which he saw the *cù mòr glas a'bhàis* so vividly that his sheets were drenched with sweat, he walked to the high cliff which faced the island and there he cut his throat with a fish knife and fell into the sea.

The other brother lived to be forty, but, again so the story goes, he found himself in a Glasgow pub one night, perhaps looking for answers, deep and sodden with the whiskey which had become his anaesthetic. In the half darkness he saw a large, grey-haired man sitting by himself against the wall and mumbled something to him. Some say he saw the *cù mòr glas a'bhàis* or uttered the name. And perhaps the man heard the phrase through ears equally affected by drink and felt he was being called a dog or a son of a bitch or something of that nature. They rose to meet one another and struggled outside into the cobblestoned passageway behind the pub where, most improbably, there were supposed to be six other large, grey-haired men who beat him to death on the cobblestones, smashing his bloodied head into the stone again and again before vanishing and leaving him to die with his face turned to the sky. The *cù mòr glas a'bhàis* had come again, said his family, as they tried to piece the tale together.

This is how the *cù mòr glas a'bhàis* came into our lives, and it is obvious that all of this happened a long, long time ago. Yet with succeeding generations it seemed the spectre had somehow come to stay and that it had become *ours*—not in the manner of an unwanted skeleton in the closet from a family's ancient past but more in the manner of something close to a genetic possibility. In the deaths of each generation, the grey dog was seen by some—by women who were to die in childbirth; by soldiers who went forth to the many wars but did not return; by those who went forth to feuds or dangerous love affairs; by those who answered mysterious midnight messages; by those who swerved on the highway to avoid the real or imagined grey dog and ended in masses of crumpled steel. And by one professional athlete who, in addition to his ritualized athletic superstitions, carried another fear or belief as well. Many of the man's descendants moved like careful hemophiliacs, fearing that they carried unwanted possibilities deep within them. And others, while they laughed, were like members of families in which there is a recurrence over the generations of repeated cancer or the diabetes which comes to those beyond middle age. The feeling of those who may say little to others but who may say often and quietly to themselves, 'It has not happened to me,' while adding always the cautionary '*yet.*'

I am thinking all of this now as the October rain falls on the city of Toronto and the pleasant, white-clad nurses pad confidently in and out of my father's room. He lies quietly amidst the whiteness, his head and shoulders elevated so that he is in that hospital position of being neither quite prone nor yet sitting. His hair is white upon his pillow and he breathes softly and sometimes unevenly, although it is difficult ever to be sure.

My five grey-haired brothers and I take turns beside his bedside, holding his heavy hands in ours and feeling their response, hoping ambiguously that he will speak to us, although we know that it may tire him. And trying to read his life and ours into his eyes when they are open. He has been with us for a long time, well into our middle age. Unlike those boys in that boat of so long ago, we did not see him taken from us in our youth. And unlike their youngest brother who, in turn, became our great-great-grandfather, we did not grow into a world in which there was no father's touch. We have been lucky to have this large and gentle man so deep into our lives.

No one in this hospital has mentioned the *cù mòr glas a'bhàis.* Yet as my mother said ten years ago, before slipping into her own death as quietly as a grownup child who leaves or enters her parents' house in the early hours, 'It is hard to *not* know what you do know.'

Even those who are most sceptical, like my oldest brother who has driven here from Montreal, betray themselves by their nervous actions. 'I avoided the Greyhound bus stations in both Montreal and Toronto,' he smiled upon his arrival, and then added, 'Just in case.'

He did not realize how ill our father was and has smiled little since then. I watch him turning the diamond ring upon his finger, knowing that he hopes he will not hear the Gaelic phrase he knows too well. Not having the luxury, as he once said, of some who live in Montreal and are able to pretend they do not understand the 'other' language. You cannot *not* know what you do know.

Sitting here, taking turns holding the hands of the man who gave us life, we are afraid for him and for ourselves. We are afraid of what he may see and we are afraid to hear the phrase born of the vision. We are aware that it may become confused with what the doctors call 'the will to live' and we are aware that some beliefs are what others would dismiss as 'garbage'. We are aware that there are men who believe the earth is flat and that the birds bring forth the sun.

Bound here in our own peculiar mortality, we do not wish to see or see others see that which signifies life's demise. We do not want to hear the voice of our father, as did those other sons, calling down his own particular death upon him.

We would shut our eyes and plug our ears, even as we know such actions to be of no avail. Open still and fearful to the grey hair rising on our necks if and when we hear the scrabble of the paws and the scratching at the door.

ERIC MCCORMACK · b. 1938

No Country for Old Men

It is a Christmas party. An old man conjures up for us the bitterness of an old war, his mind penetrating the years. He remembers the wisps of trees in the dawn haze of a dale of passion. He remembers dark, rain-filled craters, seducing the war-weary to death by drowning. He remembers the trenches joining together with intricate stitchery fabrics of opposing weft. He remembers the scattering of corpses in the half-light of no man's land, arms still protecting their dead faces. He remembers the emerging shapes of hillocks of shells, innocent-seeming as heaps of canned dog food. He remembers, his eyes hollow, the echoing snap of the fixing of bayonets at dawn: our soldiers, uniformed in grey mud, suck on a last cheap cigarette. They smell the heavy smell of tobacco wafting across from the other trenches, where German soldiers puff securely on huge carved pipes, weighty as Mausers.

'All dead now. All losers in the long run.'

He says this without a smile. We listen intently.

'My own life is a miracle. Feel here. Feel the shrapnel? It floats around in my flesh like bits of broken eggshell in the white of an egg. Notice how I stoop to draw breath? Mustard gas, inhaled sixty years ago.'

The old man speaks of one regret. We are all ears.

'Of those I killed, I remember clearly only one German soldier, a boy as young as myself. I was on sentry duty on Christmas day. I woke from a doze and found him leaning over me in his alien helmet. His hand was reaching into his kitbag. I stabbed upwards, as I had been taught, thrusting till I saw the blood appear on his lips. I pulled down. The blood drained along the bayonet's gutter neatly, as it should. As he fell, his kitbag spilled out a bottle of wine and a loaf of white bread. Too late, my comrades came running to tell me there was a Christmas truce amongst us, no war for the day. We hid the murdered soldier so that they would not stop bringing the wine and the bread.'

That is the old man's regret. Now he means to tell us of a dream. We listen urgently.

'For the last seven nights I have dreamt of that murder. I see myself back in the trenches, the German soldier leaning over me. I know what I must do. I jab the bayonet up into his stomach, holding it till I see the blood at his lips. I pull down, noticing how neatly the blood drains along the bayonet's gutter. Then I step back from the body, and I am in my study. I walk to my desk and open the right-hand drawer. I carefully place the bloody bayonet on top of a sheaf of notepaper, close the drawer, and go back to bed. I have dreamt this for seven nights. On six of the mornings when I awoke, I went to the desk drawer to check, just in case. Only the blank paper confronted me. But this morning, Christmas morning, something was not the same. Even after I awoke, I could still feel the chill of the trenches in my bones, I could remember the weight of the bayonet in my hand. I arose, aware of the beat of my heart. The light of the first snowfall reflected into my study. I walked towards the desk: this time I had no doubt I would find in it the bayonet, on a sheet of blood-stained paper. I gripped the handle of the drawer firmly and wrenched it open. I found nothing. Just a sheaf of clean white paper as before. No miracle had happened. I was the same as other men. I could not cheat a nightmare, steal a part of it, smuggle it into the waking world. Was I not foolish to think that I would find in my desk the bayonet from my dream?'

He appeals to us, his face tired, his eyes pleading. We are ready to forgive anything. Then a grave young man I do not know stands up from amongst the group of listeners. He speaks quietly, his voice compelling. We make a circle round him.

'Last night I dreamt about a Christmas party. In the dream, one of the guests, an old man whose face I cannot remember, tells a group of people (I am one of them) how he murdered a German soldier on a Christmas day long ago. He says he is haunted by a nightmare in which he commits the murder over again, and that he has tried to end it by bringing the weapon out of the nightmare, without success. He begs for pity. The party finishes, and in my dream I follow him to his home. It is snowing. He enters his house. I watch over his shoulder as he bends over the desk in his study. He slides open the right-hand drawer. There, on a sheaf of stained paper, lies a black-handled bayonet. The old man reaches in the drawer and slowly raises the blade, still red with the blood of the victim, to his own red lips. After that I awoke.'

Now his eyes are burning as he stares at the old man. The old man lowers his head before us all. He stands still, makes no appeal, for he knows there is no forgiveness in us.

MARGARET ATWOOD · b. 1939

Death by Landscape

Now that the boys are grown up and Rob is dead, Lois has moved to a condominium apartment in one of the newer waterfront developments. She is relieved not to have to worry about the lawn, or about the ivy pushing its muscular little suckers into the brickwork or the squirrels gnawing their way into the attic and eating the insulation off the wiring, or about strange noises. This building has a security system, and the only plant life is in pots in the solarium.

Lois is glad she's been able to find an apartment big enough for her pictures. They are more crowded together then they were in the house, but this arrangement gives the walls a European look: blocks of pictures, above and beside one another, rather than one over the chesterfield, one over the fireplace, one in the front hall, in the old acceptable manner of sprinkling art around so it does not get too intrusive. This way has more of an impact. You know it's not supposed to be furniture.

None of the pictures is very large, which doesn't mean they aren't valuable. They are paintings, or sketches and drawings, by artists who were not nearly as well known when Lois began to buy them as they are now. Their work later turned up on stamps, or as silk-screen reproductions hung in the principals' offices of high schools, or as jigsaw puzzles, or on beautifully printed calendars sent out by corporations as Christmas gifts, to their less important clients. These artists painted in the twenties and thirties and forties; they painted landscapes. Lois has two Tom Thomsons, three A.Y. Jacksons, a Lawren Harris. She has an Arthur Lismer, she has a J.E.H. MacDonald. She has a David Milne. They are pictures of convoluted tree trunks on an island of pink wave-smoothed stone, with more islands behind; of a lake with rough, bright, sparsely wooded cliffs; of a vivid river shore with a tangle of bush and two beached canoes, one red, one grey; of a yellow autumn woods with the ice-blue gleam of a pond half-seen through the interlaced branches.

It was Lois who'd chosen them. Rob had no interest in art, although he could see the necessity of having something on the walls. He left all the decorating decisions to her, while providing the money, of course. Because of this collection of hers, Lois's friends—especially the men—have given her the reputation of having a good nose for art investments.

But this is not why she bought the pictures, way back then. She bought them because she wanted them. She wanted something that was in them; although she could not have said at the time what it was. It was not peace: she does not find them peaceful in the least. Looking at them fills her with a wordless unease. Despite the fact that there are no people in them or even animals, it's as if there is something, or someone, looking back out.

When she was thirteen, Lois went on a canoe trip. She'd only been on overnights before. This was to be a long one, into the trackless wilderness, as Cappie put it. It was Lois's first canoe trip, and her last.

Cappie was the head of the summer camp to which Lois had been sent ever since she was nine. Camp Manitou, it was called; it was one of the better ones, for girls, though not the best. Girls of her age whose parents could afford it were routinely packed off to such camps, which bore a generic resemblance to one another. They favoured Indian names and had hearty, energetic leaders, who were called Cappie or Skip or Scottie. At these camps you learned to swim well and sail, and paddle a canoe, and perhaps ride a horse or play tennis. When you weren't doing these things you could do Arts and Crafts, and turn out dingy, lumpish clay ashtrays for your mother—mothers smoked more, then—or bracelets made of coloured braided string.

Cheerfulness was required at all times, even at breakfast. Loud shouting and the banging of spoons on the tables were allowed, and even encouraged, at ritual intervals. Chocolate bars were rationed, to control tooth decay and pimples. At night, after supper, in the dining hall or outside around a mosquito-infested campfire ring for special treats, there were singsongs. Lois can still remember all the words to 'My Darling Clementine', and to 'My Bonnie Lies Over the Ocean', with acting-out gestures: a rippling of the hands for 'the ocean', two hands together under the cheek for 'lies'. She will never be able to forget them; which is a sad thought.

Lois thinks she can recognize women who went to these camps, and were good at it. They have a hardness to their handshakes, even now; a way of standing, legs planted firmly and farther apart than usual; a way of sizing you up, to see if you'd be any good in a canoe; the front, not the back. They themselves would be in the back. They would call it the stern.

She knows that such camps still exist, although Camp Manitou does not. They are one of the few things that haven't changed much. They now offer copper enamelling, and functionless pieces of stained glass baked in electric ovens, though judging from the productions of her friend's grandchildren the artistic standards have not improved.

To Lois, encountering it in the first year after the war, Camp Manitou seemed ancient. Its log-sided buildings with the white cement in between the half-logs, its flagpole ringed with whitewashed stones, its weathered grey dock jutting out into Lake Prospect, with its woven rope bumpers and its rusty rings for tying up, its prim round flowerbed of petunias near the office door, must surely have been there always. In truth it dated only from the first decade of the century; it had been founded by Cappie's parents, who'd thought of camping as bracing to the character, like cold showers, and had been passed along to her as an inheritance, and an obligation.

Lois realized, later, that it must have been a struggle for Cappie to keep Camp Manitou going, during the Depression and then the war, when money did not flow freely. If it had been a camp for the very rich, instead of the merely well off, there would have been fewer problems. But there must have been enough Old Girls, ones with daughters, to keep the thing in operation, though not entirely ship-shape: furniture was battered, painted trim was peeling, roofs leaked. There were dim photographs of these Old Girls dotted around the dining hall, wearing ample woollen bathing suits and showing their fat, dimpled legs, or standing, arms twined, in odd tennis outfits with baggy skirts.

In the dining hall, over the stone fireplace that was never used, there was a huge moulting stuffed moose head, which looked some-how carnivorous. It was a sort of mascot; its name was Monty Manitou. The older campers spread the story that it was haunted, and came to life in the dark, when the feeble and undependable lights had been turned off or, due to yet another generator failure, had gone out. Lois was afraid of it at first, but not after she got used to it.

Cappie was the same: you had to get used to her. Possibly she was forty, or thirty-five, or fifty. She had fawn-coloured hair that looked as if it was cut with a bowl. Her head jutted forward, jigging like a chicken's as she strode around the camp, clutching notebooks and checking things off in them. She was like their minister in church: both of them smiled a lot and were anxious because they wanted things to go well; they both had the same overwashed skins and stringy necks. But all this disappeared when Cappie was leading a singsong, or otherwise leading. Then she was happy, sure of herself, her plan face almost luminous. She wanted to cause joy. At these times she was loved, at others merely trusted.

There were many things Lois didn't like about Camp Manitou, at first. She hated the noisy chaos and spoon-banging of the dining hall, the rowdy singsongs at which you were expected to yell in order to show that you were enjoying yourself. Hers was not a household that encouraged yelling. She hated the necessity of having to write dutiful letters to her parents claiming she was having fun. She could not complain, because camp cost so much money.

She didn't much like having to undress in a roomful of other girls, even in the dim light, although nobody paid any attention, or sleeping in a cabin with seven other girls, some of whom snored because they had adenoids or colds, some of whom had nightmares, or wet their beds and cried about it. Bottom bunks made her feel closed in, and she was afraid of falling out of top ones; she was afraid of heights. She got homesick, and suspected her parents of having a better time when she wasn't there than when she was, although her mother wrote to her every week saying how much they missed her. All this was when she was nine. By the time she was thirteen she liked it. She was an old hand by then.

Lucy was her best friend at camp. Lois had other friends in winter, when there was school and itchy woollen clothing and darkness in the afternoons, but Lucy was her summer friend.

She turned up the second year, when Lois was ten, and a Bluejay. (Chickadees, Bluejays, Ravens, and Kingfishers—these were the names Camp Manitou assigned to the different age groups, a sort of totemic clan system. In those days, thinks Lois, it was birds for girls, animals for boys: wolves, and so forth. Though some animals and birds were suitable and some were not. Never vultures, for instance; never skunks, or rats.)

Lois helped Lucy to unpack her tin trunk and place the folded clothes on the wooden shelves, and to make up her bed. She put her in the top bunk right above her, where she could keep an eye on her.

Already she knew that Lucy was an exception, to a good many rules; already she felt proprietorial.

Lucy was from the United States, where the comic books came from, and the movies. She wasn't from New York or Hollywood or Buffalo, the only American cities Lois knew the names of, but from Chicago. Her house was on the lake shore and had gates to it, and grounds. They had a maid, all of the time. Lois's family only had a cleaning lady twice a week.

The only reason Lucy was being sent to *this* camp (she cast a look of minor scorn around the cabin, diminishing it and also offending Lois, while at the same time daunting her) was that her mother had been a camper here. Her mother had been a Canadian once, but had married her father, who had a patch over one eye, like a pirate. She showed Lois the picture of him in her wallet. He got the patch in the war. 'Shrapnel,' said Lucy. Lois, who was unsure about shrapnel, was so impressed she could only grunt. Her own two-eyed, unwounded father was tame by comparison.

'My father plays golf,' she ventured at last.

'*Everyone* plays golf,' said Lucy. 'My *mother* plays golf.'

Lois's mother did not. Lois took Lucy to see the outhouses and the swimming dock and the dining hall with Monty Manitou's baleful head, knowing in advance they would not measure up.

This was a bad beginning; but Lucy was good-natured, and accepted Camp Manitou with the same casual shrug with which she seemed to accept everything. She would make the best of it, without letting Lois forget that this was what she was doing.

However, there were things Lois knew that Lucy did not. Lucy scratched the tops off all her mosquito bites and had to be taken to the infirmary to be daubed with Ozonol. She took her T-shirt off while sailing, and although the counsellor spotted her after a while and made her put it back on, she burnt spectacularly, bright red, with the X of her bathing-suit straps standing out in alarming white; she let Lois peel the sheets of whispery-thin burned skin off her shoulders. When they sang 'Alouette' around the campfire, she did not know any of the French words. The difference was that Lucy did not care about the things she didn't know, whereas Lois did.

During the next winter, and subsequent winters, Lucy and Lois wrote to each other. They were both only children, at a time when this was thought to be a disadvantage, so in their letters they pretended to be sisters, or even twins. Lois had to strain a little over this, because Lucy was so blonde, with translucent skin and large blue eyes like a doll's, and Lois was nothing out of the ordinary; just a tallish, thinnish, brownish person with freckles. They signed their letters LL, with the L's entwined together like the monograms on a towel. (Lois and Lucy, thinks Lois. How our names date us. Lois Lane, Superman's girlfriend, enterprising female reporter; 'I Love Lucy'. Now we are obsolete, and it's little Jennifers, little Emilys, little Alexandras and Carolines and Tiffanys.)

They were more effusive in their letters than they ever were in person. They bordered their pages with X's and O's, but when they met again in the summers it was always a shock. They had changed so much, or Lucy had. It was like watching someone grow up in jolts. At first it would be hard to think up things to say.

But Lucy always had a surprise or two, something to show, some marvel to reveal. The first year she had a picture of herself in a tutu, her hair in a ballerina's knot on the top of her head; she pirouetted around the swimming dock, to show Lois how it was done, and almost fell off. The next year she had given that up and was taking horseback riding. (Camp Manitou did not have horses.) The next year her mother and father had been divorced, and she had a new stepfather, one with both eyes, and a new house, although the maid was the same. The next year, when they had graduated from Bluejays and entered Ravens, she got her period, right in the first week of camp. The two of them snitched some matches from their counsellor, who smoked illegally, and made a small fire out behind the farthest outhouse, at dusk, using their flashlights. They could set all kinds of fires by now; they had learned how in Camp-craft. On this fire they burned one of Lucy's used sanitary napkins. Lois is not sure why they did this, or whose idea it was. But she can remember the feeling of deep satisfaction it gave her as the white fluff singed and the blood sizzled, as if some wordless ritual had been fulfilled.

They did not get caught, but then they rarely got caught at any of their camp transgressions. Lucy had such large eyes, and was such an accomplished liar.

This year Lucy is different again: slower, more languorous. She is no longer interested in sneaking around after dark, purloining cigarettes from the counsellor, dealing in black market candy bars. She is pensive, and hard to wake in the mornings. She doesn't like her stepfather, but she doesn't want to live with her real father either, who has a new wife. She thinks her mother may be having a love affair with a doctor; she doesn't know for sure, but she's seen them smooching in his car, out on the driveway, when her stepfather wasn't there. It serves him right. She hates her private school. She has a boyfriend, who is sixteen and works as a gardener's assistant. This is how she met him: in the garden. She describes to Lois what it is like when he kisses her: rubbery at first, but then your knees go limp. She has been forbidden to see him, and threatened with boarding school. She wants to run away from home.

Lois has little to offer in return. Her own life is placid and satisfactory, but there is nothing much that can be said about happiness. 'You're so lucky,' Lucy tells her, a little smugly. She might as well say *boring* because this is how it makes Lois feel.

Lucy is apathetic about the canoe trip, so Lois has to disguise her own excitement. The evening before they are to leave, she slouches into the campfire ring as if coerced and sits down with a sigh of endurance, just as Lucy does.

Every canoe trip that went out of camp was given a special sendoff by Cappie and the section leader and counsellors, with the whole section in attendance. Cappie painted three streaks of red across each of her cheeks with a lipstick. They looked like three-fingered claws marks. She put a blue circle on her forehead with fountain-pen ink, and tied a twisted bandanna around her head and stuck a row of frazzle-ended feathers around it, and wrapped herself in a red and black Hudson's Bay blanket. The counsellors, also in blankets but with only two streaks of red, beat on tom-toms made of round wooden cheese-boxes with leather stretched over the top and nailed in place. Cappie was Chief Cappeosota. They all had to say 'How!' when she walked into the circle and stood there with one hand raised.

Looking back on this, Lois finds it disquieting. She knows too much about Indians: this is why. She knows, for instance, that they should not even be called Indians, and that they have enough worries without other people taking their names and dressing up as them. It has all been a form of stealing.

But she remembers, too, that she was once ignorant of this. Once she loved the campfire, the flickering of light on the ring of faces, the sound of the fake tom-toms, heavy and fast like a scared heartbeat; she loved Cappie in a red blanket and feathers, solemn, as a chief should be, raising her hand and saying, 'Greetings, my Ravens.' It was not funny, it was not making fun. She wanted to be an Indian. She wanted to be adventurous and pure, and aboriginal.

'You go on big water,' says Cappie. This is her idea—all their ideas—of how Indians talk. 'You go where no man has ever trod. You go many moons.' This is not true. They are only going for a week, not many moons. The canoe route is clearly marked, they have gone over it on a map, and there are prepared campsites with names which are used year after year. But when Cappie says this—and despite the way Lucy rolls up her eyes—Lois can feel the water stretching out, with the shores twisting away on either side, immense and a little frightening.

'You bring back much wampum,' says Cappie. 'Do good in war, my braves, and capture many scalps.' This is another of her pretences: that they are boys, and blood-thirsty. But such a game cannot be played by substituting the word 'squaw'. It would not work at all.

Each of them has to stand up and step forward and have a red line drawn across her cheeks by Cappie. She tells them they must follow in the paths of their ancestors (who most certainly, thinks Lois, looking out the window of her apartment and remembering the family stash of daguerreotypes and sepia-coloured portraits on her mother's dressing table, the stiff-shirted, black-coated, grim-faced men and the beflounced women with their severe hair and their corseted respectability, would never have considered heading off onto an open lake, in a canoe, just for fun).

At the end of the ceremony they all stood and held hands around the circle, and sang taps. This did not sound very Indian, think Lois. It sounded like a bugle call at a military post, in a movie. But Cappie was never one to be much concerned with consistency, or with archaeology.

After breakfast the next morning they set out from the main dock, in four canoes, three in each. The lipstick stripes have not come off completely, and still show faintly pink, like healing burns. They wear their white denim sailing hats, because of the sun, and thin-striped T-shirts, and pale baggy shorts with the cuffs rolled up. The middle one kneels, propping her rear end against the rolled sleeping bags. The counsellors going with them are Pat and Kip. Kip is no-nonsense; Pat is easier to wheedle, or fool.

There are white puffy clouds and a small breeze. Glints come from the little waves. Lois is in the bow of Kip's canoe. She still can't do a J-stroke very well, and she will have to be in the bow or the middle for the whole trip. Lucy is behind her; her own J-stroke is even worse.

She splashes Lois with her paddle, quite a big splash.

'I'll get you back,' says Lois.

'There was a stable fly on your shoulder,' Lucy says.

Lois turns to look at her, to see if she's grinning. They're in the habit of splashing each other. Back there, the camp has vanished behind the first long point of rock and rough trees. Lois feels as if an invisible rope has broken. They're floating free, on their own, cut loose. Beneath the canoe the lake goes down, deeper and colder than it was a minute before.

'No horsing around in the canoe,' says Kip. She's rolled her T-shirt sleeves up to the shoulder; her arms are brown and sinewy, her jaw determined, her stroke perfect. She looks as if she knows exactly what she is doing.

The four canoes keep close together. They sing, raucously and with defiance; they sing 'The Quartermaster's Store', and 'Clementine', and 'Alouette'. It is more like bellowing than singing.

After that the wind grows stronger, blowing slantwise against the bows, and they have to put all their energy into shoving themselves through the water.

Was there anything important, anything that would provide some sort of reason or clue to what happened next? Lois can remember everything, every detail; but it does her no good.

They stopped at noon for a swim and lunch, and went on in the afternoon. At last they reached Little Birch, which was the first campsite for overnight. Lois and Lucy made the fire, while the others pitched the heavy canvas tents. The fireplace was already there, flat stones piled into a U. A burned tin can and a beer bottle had been left in it. Their fire went out, and they had to restart it. 'Hustle your bustle,' said Kip. 'We're starving.'

The sun went down, and in the pink sunset they brushed their teeth and spat the toothpaste froth into the lake. Kip and Pat put all the food that wasn't in cans into a packsack and slung it into a tree, in case of bears.

Lois and Lucy weren't sleeping in a tent. They'd begged to be allowed to sleep out; that way they could talk without the others hearing. If it rained, they told Kip, they promised not to crawl dripping into the tent over everyone's legs: they would get under the canoes. So they were out on the point.

Lois tried to get comfortable inside her sleeping bag, which smelled of musty storage and of earlier campers, a stale salty sweetness. She curled herself up, with her sweater rolled up under her head for a pillow and her flashlight inside her sleeping bag so it wouldn't roll away. The muscles of her sore arms were making small pings, like rubber bands breaking.

Beside her Lucy was rustling around. Lois could see the glimmering oval of her white face.

'I've got a rock poking into my back,' said Lucy.

'So do I,' said Lois. 'You want to go into the tent?' She herself didn't but it was right to ask.

'No,' said Lucy. She subsided into her sleeping bag. After a moment she said, 'It would be nice not to go back.'

'To camp?' said Lois.

'To Chicago,' said Lucy. 'I hate it there.'

'What about your boyfriend?' said Lois.

Lucy didn't answer. She was either asleep or pretending to be.

There was a moon, and a movement of the trees. In the sky there were stars, layers of stars that went down and down. Kip said that when the stars were bright like that instead of hazy it meant bad weather later on. Out on the lake there were two loons, calling to each other in their insane, mournful voices. At the time it did not sound like grief. It was just background.

The lake in the morning was flat calm. They skimmed along over the glassy surface, leaving V-shaped trails behind them; it felt like flying. As the sun rose higher it got hot, almost too hot. There were stable flies in the canoes, landing on a bare arm or leg for a quick sting. Lois hoped for wind.

They stopped for lunch at the next of the named campsites, Lookout Point. It was called this because, although the site itself was down near the water on a flat shelf of rock, there was a sheer cliff nearby and a trail that led up to the top. The top was the lookout, although what you were supposed to see from there was not clear. Kip said it was just a view.

Lois and Lucy decided to make the climb anyway. They didn't want to hang around waiting for lunch. It wasn't their turn to cook, though they hadn't avoided much by not doing it, because cooking lunch was no big deal, it was just unwrapping cheese and getting out the bread and peanut butter, though Pat and Kip always had to do their woodsy act and boil up a billy can for their own tea.

They told Kip where they were going. You had to tell Kip where you were going, even if it was only a little way into the woods to get dry twigs for kindling. You could never go anywhere without a buddy.

'Sure,' said Kip, who was crouching over the fire, feeding driftwood into it. 'Fifteen minutes to lunch.'

'Where are they off to?' said Pat. She was bringing their billy can of water from the lake.

'Lookout,' said Kip.

'Be careful,' said Pat. She said it as an afterthought, because it was what she always said.

'They're old hands,' Kip said.

Lois looks at her watch: it's ten to twelve. She is the watch-minder; Lucy is careless of time. They walk up the path, which is dry earth and rocks, big rounded pinky-grey boulders or split-open ones with jagged edges. Spindly balsam and spruce trees grow to either side, the lake is blue fragments to the left. The sun is right overhead; there are no shadows anywhere. The heat comes up at them as well as down. The forest is dry and crackly.

It isn't far, but it's a steep climb and they're sweating when they reach the top. They wipe their faces with their bare arms, sit gingerly down on a scorching-hot rock, five feet from the edge but too close for Lois. It's a lookout all right, a sheer drop to the lake and a long view over the water, back the way they've come. It's amazing to Lois that they've travelled so far, over all that water, with nothing to propel them but their own arms. It makes her feel strong. There are all kinds of things she is capable of doing.

'It would be quite a dive off here,' says Lucy.

'You'd have to be nuts,' says Lois.

'Why?' says Lucy. 'It's really deep. It goes straight down.' She stands up and takes a step nearer the edge. Lois gets a stab in her midriff, the kind she gets when a car goes too fast over a bump. 'Don't,' she says.

'Don't what?' says Lucy, glancing around at her mischievously. She knows how Lois feels about heights. But she turns back. 'I really have to pee,' she says.

'You have toilet paper?' says Lois, who is never without it. She digs in her shorts pocket.

'Thanks,' says Lucy.

They are both adept at peeing in the woods: doing it fast so the mosquitoes don't get you, the underwear pulled up between your knees, the squat with the feet apart so you don't wet your legs, facing downhill. The exposed feeling of your bum, as if someone is looking at you from behind. The etiquette when you're with someone else is not to look. Lois stands up and starts to walk back down the path, to be out of sight.

'Wait for me?' says Lucy.

Lois climbed down, over and around the boulders, until she could not see Lucy; she waited. She could hear the voices of the others, talking and laughing, down near the shore. One voice was yelling, 'Ants! Ants!' Someone must have sat on an ant hill. Off to the side, in the woods, a raven was croaking, a hoarse single note.

She looked at her watch: it was noon. This is when she heard the shout.

She has gone over and over it in her mind since, so many times that the first, real shout has been obliterated, like a footprint trampled by other footprints. But she is sure (she is almost positive, she is nearly certain) that it was not a shout of fear. Not a scream. More like a cry of surprise, cut off too soon. Short, like a dog's bark.

'Lucy?' Lois said. Then she called 'Lucy!' By now she was clambering back up, over the stones of the path. Lucy was not up there. Or she was not in sight.

'Stop fooling around,' Lois said. 'It's lunch time.' But Lucy did not rise from behind a rock or step out, smiling, from behind a tree. The sunlight was all around; the rocks looked white. 'This isn't funny!' Lois said, and it wasn't, panic was rising in her, the panic of a small child who does not know where the bigger ones are hidden. She could hear her own heart. She looked quickly around; she lay down on the ground and looked over the edge of the cliff. It made her feel cold. There was nothing.

She went back down the path, stumbling; she was breathing too quickly; she was too frightened to cry. She felt terrible, guilty and dismayed, as if she had done something very bad, by mistake; something that could never be repaired. 'Lucy's gone,' she told Kip.

Kip looked up from her fire, annoyed. The water in the billy can was boiling. 'What do you mean, gone?' she said. 'Where did she go?'

'I don't know,' said Lois. 'She's just gone.'

No one had heard the shout, but then, no one had heard Lois calling, either. They had been talking among themselves, by the water.

Kip and Pat went up to the lookout and searched and called, and blew their whistles. Nothing answered.

Then they came back down, and Lois had to tell exactly what had happened. The other girls all sat in a circle and listened to her. Nobody said anything. They all looked frightened, especially Pat and Kip. They were the leaders. You did not just lose a camper like this, for no reason at all.

'Why did you leave her alone?' said Kip.

'I was just down the path,' said Lois. 'I told you. She had to go to the bathroom.' She did not say *pee* in front of people older than herself.

Kip looked disgusted.

'Maybe she just walked off into the woods and got turned around,' said one of the girls.

'Maybe she's doing it on purpose,' said another.

Nobody believed either of these theories.

They took the canoes and searched around the base of the cliff, and peered down into the water. But there had been no sound of falling rock; there had been no splash. There was no clue, nothing at all. Lucy had simply vanished.

That was the end of the canoe trip. It took them the same two days to go back that it had taken coming in, even though they were short a paddler. They did not sing. After that the police went, in a motor-boat, with dogs; they were the Mounties and the dogs were German shepherds, trained to follow trails in the woods. But it had rained since, and they could find nothing.

Lois is sitting in Cappie's office. Her face is bloated with crying, she's seen that in the mirror. By now she feels numbed; she feels as if she has drowned. She can't stay here. It has been too much of a shock. Tomorrow her parents are coming to take her away. Several of the other girls who were on the canoe trip are being collected in the same way. The others will have to stay, because their parents are in Europe, or cannot be reached.

Cappie is grim. They've tried to hush it up, but of course everyone in camp knows. Soon the papers will know too. You can't keep it quiet, but what can be said? What can be said that makes any sense? 'Girl vanishes in broad daylight, without a trace.' It can't be believed; other things, worse things, will be suspected. Negligence, at the very least. But they have always taken such care. Bad luck will gather around Camp Manitou like a fog; parents will avoid it, in favour of other, luckier places. Lois can see Cappie thinking all this, even through her numbness. It's what anyone would think.

Lois sits on the hard wooden chair in Cappie's office, beside the old wooden desk, over which hangs the thumbtacked bulletin board of normal camp routine, and gazes at Cappie through her puffy eyelids. Cappie is now smiling what is supposed to be a reassuring smile. Her manner is too casual: she's after something. Lois has seen this look on Cappie's face when she's been sniffing out contraband chocolate bars, hunting down those rumoured to have snuck out of their cabins at night.

'Tell me again,' says Cappie, 'from the beginning.'

Lois has told her story so many times by now, to Pat and Kip, to Cappie, to the police, that she knows it word for word. She knows it, but she no longer believes it. It has become a story. 'I told you,' she said. 'She wanted to go to the bathroom. I gave her my toilet paper. I went down the path, I waited for her. I heard this kind of shout. . . .'

'Yes,' says Cappie, smiling confidingly, 'but before that. What did you say to one another?'

Lois thinks. Nobody has asked her this before. 'She said you could dive off there. She said it went straight down.'

'And what did you say?'

'I said you'd have to be nuts.'

'Were you mad at Lucy?' says Cappie, in an encouraging voice.

'No,' says Lois. 'Why would I be mad at Lucy? I wasn't ever mad at Lucy.' She feels like crying again. The times when she has in fact been mad at Lucy have been erased already. Lucy was always perfect.

'Sometimes we're angry when we don't know we're angry,' says Cappie, as if to herself. 'Sometimes we get really mad and we don't even know it. Sometimes we might do a thing without meaning to, or without knowing what will happen. We lose our tempers.'

Lois is only thirteen, but it doesn't take her long to figure out that Cappie is not including herself in any of this. By *we* she means Lois. She is accusing Lois of pushing Lucy off the cliff. The unfairness of this hits her like a slap. 'I didn't!' she says.

'Didn't what?' said Cappie softly. 'Didn't what, Lois?'

Lois does the worst thing, she begins to cry. Cappie gives her a look like a pounce. She's got what she wanted.

Later, when she was grown up, Lois was able to understand what this interview had been about. She could see Cappie's desperation, her need for a story, a real story with a reason in it; anything but the senseless vacancy Lucy had left for her to deal with. She wanted Lois to supply the reason, to be the reason. It wasn't even for the news-papers or the parents, because she could never make such an accusa-tion without proof. It was for herself: something to explain the loss of Camp Manitou and of all she had worked for, the years of enter-taining spoiled children and buttering up parents and making a fool of herself with feathers stuck in her hair. Camp Manitou was in fact lost. It did not survive.

Lois worked all this out, twenty years later. But it was far too late. It was too late even ten minutes afterwards, when she'd left Cappie's office and was walking slowly back to her cabin to pack. Lucy's clothes were still there, folded on the shelves, as if waiting. She felt the other girls in the cabin watching her with speculation in their eyes. *Could she have done it? She must have done it.* For the rest of her life, she has caught people watching her in this way.

Maybe they weren't thinking this. Maybe they were merely sorry for her. But she felt she had been tried and sentenced, and this is what has stayed with her: the knowledge that she had been singled out, condemned for something that was nor her fault.

Lois sits in the living room of her apartment, drinking a cup of tea. Through the knee-to-ceiling window she has a wide view of Lake Ontario, with its skin of wrinkled blue-grey light, and of the willows of Centre Island shaken by a wind which is silent at this distance, and on this side of the glass. When there isn't too much pollution she can see the far shore, the foreign shore; though today it is obscured.

Possibly she could go out, go downstairs, do some shopping; there isn't much in the refrigerator. The boys say she doesn't get out enough. But she isn't hungry; and moving, stirring from this space, is increasingly an effort.

She can hardly remember, now, having her two boys in the hospital, nursing them as babies; she can hardly remembering getting married, or what Rob looked like. Even at the time she never felt she was paying full attention. She was tired a lot, as if she was living not one life but two: her own, and another, shadowy life that hovered around her and would not let itself be realized: the life of what would have happened if Lucy had not stepped sideways, and disappeared from time.

She would never go up north, to Rob's family cottage or to any place with wild lakes and wild trees, and the calls of loons. She would never go anywhere near. Still, it was as if she was always listening for another voice, the voice of a person who should have been there but was not. An echo.

While Rob was alive, while the boys were growing up, she could pretend she didn't hear it, this empty space in sound. But now there is nothing much left to distract her.

She turns away from the window and looks at her pictures. There is the pinkish island, in the lake, with the intertwisted trees. It's the same landscape they paddled through, that distant summer. She's seen travelogues of this country, aerial photographs; it looks different from above, bigger, more hopeless: lake after lake, random blue puddles in dark green bush, the trees like bristles.

How could you ever find anything there, once it was lost? Maybe if they cut it all down, drained it all away, they might find Lucy's bones, sometime, wherever they are hidden. A few bones, some buttons, the buckle from her shorts.

But a dead person is a body; a body occupies space, it exists somewhere. You can see it; you put it in a box and bury it in the ground, and then it's in a box in the ground. But Lucy is not in a box, or in the ground. Because she is nowhere definite, she could be anywhere.

And these paintings are not landscape paintings. Because there aren't any landscapes up there, not in the old, tidy European sense, with a gentle hill, a curving river, a cottage, a mountain in the background, a golden evening sky. Instead there's a tangle, a receding maze, in which you can become lost almost as soon as you step off the path. There are no backgrounds in any of these paintings, no vistas; only a great deal of foreground that goes back and back, endlessly, involving you in its twists and turns of tree and branch and rock. No matter how far back in you go, there will be more. And the trees themselves are hardly trees; they are currents of energy, charged with violent colour.

Who knows how many trees there were on the cliff just before Lucy disappeared? Who counted? Maybe there was one more, afterwards.

Lois sits in her chair and does not move. Her hand with the cup is raised halfway to her mouth. She hears something, almost hears it: a shout of recognition, or of joy.

She looks at the paintings, she looks into them. Every one of them is a picture of Lucy. You can't see her exactly, but she's there, in behind the pink stone island or the one behind that. In the picture of the cliff she is hidden by the clutch of fallen rocks towards the bottom, in the one of the river shore she is crouching beneath the overturned canoe. In the yellow autumn woods she's behind the tree that cannot be seen because of the other trees, over beside the blue sliver of pond; but if you walked into the picture and found the tree, it would be the wrong one, because the right one would be farther on.

Everyone has to be somewhere, and this is where Lucy is. She is in Lois's apartment, in the holes that open inwards on the wall, not like windows but like doors. She is here. She is entirely alive.

SEAN VIRGO · b. 1940

Haunt

If my love were an earthly knight,
As he's an elfin grey,
I wad na gie my ain true-love
For nae Lord that ye hae.

I can see that it will become a Bison. Then if they don't redecorate
the room it will change again. But I can't see yet what it might become
next. After all, I don't suppose, on reflection, that anyone would even
see the bison forming. Would they see, with some misgivings perhaps
about the upkeep and hygiene of the room, anything but a patch
where the ceiling paint has flaked? When I arrived, however, there
was only a crack—suggesting, maybe, a twig of driftwood, a kris, an
electric spark. And what a bestiary has since squeezed through that
crack. Every morning there is paint dust on my blankets—though
would the orderly notice that? I doubt it. The old government-issue
paint has been falling, a powdered rain, constantly. And I have
anticipated every form (all but the starfish: that, I admit, surprised
me). They usually reach perfection about mid-afternoon and may live
for two days, never more than three. Not that I would mind if they
brought in the decorators—some of the terminal wards are in mag-
nolia now, I know. But there would be something, whatever the
colour—a brush mark, a bristle bedded in the paint, who knows?

But the Bison will be splendid—I can see where his great chest will
bulge, and where the flaking will slow down on the other side so that
the rump will fall, almost pathetically away. Thundering through the
halls of Lascaux, scattering bats and spirits. Spurning tiny lamps and
giant shadows. Letting in the ghosts.

Before the Bison dies, Dan will visit me again. I'll watch the ceiling
and he'll watch the japonica outside the window. And count the waxy
blossoms 'til he can go. When he comes the next time he will tell me
that he and Jane have a baby girl, but I can't see yet whether he will
come anymore. Dan has become a very dull ghost. He would not, I'm

sure, remember the Burmese Harp. 'Dan,' I cried, 'I am sad now.'

And he had smiled to a man leaving the seat behind us. I suppose they shared a consoling attitude about my sentimental self, weeping in the houselights' glare. Yes, he was a little proud of possessing someone who could feel so, but . . . 'Come on outside,' the usherette said as she banged the last seat up and coughed beneath the exit. 'Come on now.' For was I not keeping the usherette from her last bus home? So I passed her impatient rainshoes and: 'I'm sorry—good—night,' he told her. Shrugging probably. Smiling. Sharing. Then he was all mine again in the outside, fog-small night, which was my world if not ours.

After I said, 'Please let's walk,' he was stiff beside me and found me hard and angry. The fog in Nottingham is terrifying really, for every car and bus looms out of it, on the brink of lonely death. And the island people inside the bright, breath-steamed windows ought to shiver every other second. That was how I was thinking, and talking about the film was pointless. For beneath the Oriental melodrama I didn't see, no I didn't, the essential sentimentality of the whole thing.

Away from the streets, on the track across the reclaimed, desolate flats. Some night bird cried, twice and again from one of the marshy pools over towards the river. To follow the haunt of that call back would be to find some warm, feathered creature shifting on its webbed feet. Or incredibly in that low, cold wasteland, the burning brood-heat of a next. Lonely haunts. The mud path sucked at my shoes, drawing me to the pools—my university room seemed far off and senseless. I've sometimes driven a car at night in the country and come to a corner. Out in the field it's so black and velvet that to drive through the hedge seems irresistible. See the headlights leap through the long night, catching a tree perhaps, a mile away on the other side of the valley. And the crash would be sudden of course—the glide through the night gone as time suddenly speeds up—crack! 'Why, Dan, we don't need to talk,' I said.

'But we're not *close* in silence as we sometimes are,' he accused.

How many times did he ask me what I was thinking? A compulsion with him to know. But I couldn't, and didn't want to anyway. 'I have feelings, not thoughts.'

'Yes, but what sort . . .'

'No, Dan, I won't tear them down and give you the pieces. Leave me alone.'

'Alright then if you don't want me.' Oh the kid he was. But though that wasn't what I meant, why should I make the effort to apologize and set it right? His sulking demanded more than his questions.

So at a fence we had to cross he came close again and kissed me. Making tender motions—but how mechanical it seemed in my mood, and ugh! his tongue was cold. 'Not now Dan,' I said angrily. Unkind to deflate him, I know; to push his hand from my familiar thigh. But they demand so much when they intrude like that. They face mystery with habit—*it's always done the trick before* their dumb skulls echo. But it's never before. The bird was calling across the mud again.

Dan left me at the light by the university gates. I didn't run after him. I didn't call after him.

In my room, alone with the call, no light and naked. That was the only way that felt right. I think I felt like a novice at a shrine, or perhaps—but I don't remember that clearly so there's no point in talking about it. My home-reared self that I had so recently chipped through, probably said all mystery and revelation would be religious—Christ!—or poetic.

THE SOUND OF THAT BIRD! The empty, crying, flat cold call of the flats. That shabby yellow room echoes like a great cave. God! DESOLA-TION—the grey cry winging down every last cleft and channel, cursing the tunnels and retreats with the chill of marshes open under the wet sky. And stirring beside me, shivering in the darkness, he reached for the warmth of my skin.

The cry went out like a candle. I went rigid. Silly, stupid, student girl—leaping gracelessly for the light switch. As I leapt for the bedclothes in my empty room I heard him fade like a sigh.

I was there for half an hour, clinging to my blankets and common-sense. But it didn't go for company in one of the neighbouring rooms—I hardly even considered that. Because soon I was angry with myself. For panicking, but most of all for trying to explain away what was true. If impossible.

By the time I tried to call him back I was so self-conscious that it didn't deserve to work. I turned off the light. Pushed up the window sash. Fumbled inwardly for a ritual. Leant out and craned my head awkwardly round, trying to face the river, the sandstone sill cold and rough on my breasts. 'Come back please,' I called softly. 'I'm sorry I was frightened.'

'I am here,' he said quietly beside me.

I have it all mapped out. Every inch, every covert and defile of memory. I just don't read the map, that's all. Dr English says no—that I've pushed it down, or in or away, and won't look at it. He says that if I read the map I'd be better. If I let him read it he'd show me the way out. Ha!

He really is wrong. It's just like a fantastic intense love letter. You read it once (not even very closely, just gliding from peak to peak) then for some reason you don't look at it again. Perhaps it's near you always—in your purse, your coat pocket, or just a drawer, and maybe like an amulet. You know what's in it, and need what's in it, but you just keep it closed. Every so often you'll just touch the envelope with a love-prayer. But someday when it's almost forgotten you know you'll read it again and everything will come back—only clearer and fuller than the first time.

He was cold you see. And the cry of which he was a part had clutched onto me, and I hadn't shrugged it off. So he followed me back. Into my room. But the only warmth he could use would be mine, and in the close, suffocating air of the pipe-framed room, he shivered beside me.

But the map is blurred there, nowhere else but there. So I must invent for a few minutes, and the truth of my invention shall suffice. Perhaps I said:

'Who are you?'

'Where are you from?'

'How old are you?'

'What do you want?'

'Why did you choose me?'

'Am I going mad?'

'What shall I do?'

'Am I making this all up?'

and perhaps I said nothing.

And he may just have insisted (he would have). 'I am, I am,' telling me, insisting in his need, shivering.

Why don't I remember? I just had knowledge, that's all. The real knowledge that precludes proof, leaves no corner for doubt. The map swims towards focus again past the few tranced steps towards my bedside. My face turned self-consciously upward—like a blind girl trying to gauge exactly the position of her lover's eyes—to give some impression of normal contact.

'Oh I wish that—that the rest of this place, building, wasn't here.' Slipping seated as I spoke, bending and stretching for the extra warmth in the linen sheets, feeling him all along my body for the first time. At first he was almost without form . . . me beside a fenwaste pool clutching nothing but wet and cold, ripple and chill immersion to my breast. I was so squeamish: how dirty, stagnant, lost and rotten it seemed. Then sinking in, like a dreamer drowning, the clammy revulsion spread rippling and at its centre was the thin, pathetic, skeletal need that was my new lover. Sinking and coming into me on marshwaves of aloneness, till the pool was inside me, and the flats and the sky. My body arching into the fall of sleep to the thrilling cold call untuning my skinny womb.

Poor Dan—I think he's dead and dull and he really wants to be the way he is. He keeps coming to see me too, but the only time we've ever talked and *said* anything was a nostalgia thing. And then he got embarrassed suddenly when he was almost in the hospital sheets with me. Loyalty to Jane. The awful thing was that I was just playing a game somehow, showing my power. Nothing in that past could ever really excite me. I look back at it with a condescension that I can't avoid for its innocence. I love it but it's a pity-love.

Really it *is* poor Dan. Because the only Dan that was ever really alive is mine—locked up in my memory box, and he can't have it back. He's just vaguely aware of another person altogether that was him in a day. What he does remember embarrasses him anyway. It's not something you can give back to someone—his own earlier self—but sometimes I feel guilty about owning it: as tough I should painlessly, decently destroy it.

When he sits by my bed, watching the window, tracing his finger along the candlewick grooves of my bedspread, I think *Dan, is this thick-fingered clod anything to do with Dan and Jill?* We ought to be able to eye-touch and say, *I understand. A bond remains to be acknowledged. Thank you.* Instead he talks about Jane, clearing his throat every third word, and I'm perverse and shrewish and insensitive. But he still comes, or has so far. Oh he probably thinks he pities me.

Like the day after . . . . The phone rang. Dan. Every other time I had babysat for the Naismiths he had come in across the lawn from the residences when he saw the children's light go out. At least he had phoned and not just materialized tonight by the wisteria, tapping at the french windows. I felt I couldn't say no—almost anything not to

get hard and hot and angry—but it seemed such an intrusion on what
I had looked forward to: a solitude and silence to myself in that big
house, away from everything but the upstairs dreams of sleeping
children.

What you don't see inside yourself you can't read to anyone, and
rapt Jenny was soon a distracted girl fidgeting beside me. I got her to
bed soon. As I went downstairs she called through the door ajar, 'Was
she a nice witch, Jill?'

'I don't think she was good or bad, Jenny,' I said. 'She just had the
power to give the Fisherman what he wanted. Now off to sleep—
good girl.'

'Goodnight.'

'Goodnight, love.'

I had to feel carefully with my feet at the last turn of the stairs. The
light had suddenly faded out of the day. Darkness was creeping up
to the lower branches of the trees. The garden was flooded in
distance. I put no lights on except in the kitchen and raced through
the tidying, washing, cleaning. Then, with that light off and the
darkness outside up to the treetops, the house was mine for a precious
while. I stood on the hearthrug, slowly feeling naked, and moved
slowly across the room, wading in silence. Through the french
windows the evening star was blading the pine trees and above,
wherever I looked, I could will smaller stars into life. So gently, that
there was no metal sound, I turned the brass handle—that there was
no hinge noise or creak of wood, I let in the air. And lumpy Dan came
from the lawn. Crashing and trampling poor fool though he came
with famous stealth; and a sigh like a dying well slipped away round
the house as he came in.

I started talking, gaily, too loudly, quickly. I made brittle enthusiasm dance over the evening, the trivia of bedding the children.
Too quickly I intercepted every half-comment of Dan's, agreeing with
him and expanding his words and cooking up comparable feelings
in myself.

I was on my feet all the time, in a silly, nervous dance across the
hearthrug and round the end of the sofa. Dan followed me and I giggled
tauter and tauter as I played the distance between us like mismatched
magnets. Dan's face gradually turned to a frown of bewilderment. He
sat on the sofa's arm and I at the other end subsided into the tweed
cushions and the plundering tick of the mantelpiece clock. An inscribed
mahogany wedding present from Mrs Naismith's godmother.

Dr English is ashamed of his yellow dog teeth. He talks without moving his lips. Laughs at his own jokes like water in a plughole. He has kids who make model aeroplanes and a wife who came second in the county golf championships. Madness is reduced to four complexes and two formulas for being honest with yourself. He'd like to get layed by almost anyone. But he has locked up in little card boxes all the secrets you said when you didn't know what was happening, that are maybe secrets even from yourself. He's a very *knowing* little face. Is it all bluff? *I know something you don't know.*

If I spoke about that evening to him, he'd want to be told why it was important in my memory and what it implied about my real feelings for Dan. *Knowingly.* Well the reason it's important, Freudipus, is simply that I read a book from the library this morning—fairy stories—and I found the Fisherman and his Soul with little Jenny's voice from the stairs calling through the waves just when the witch cuts off the shadow-soul on the beach. And off it went. To wander in the cold.

So much of that evening's left off the map anyway. Only when Dan produced some flowers I suddenly felt very guilty and fickle and threw my arms around him with a lot of real tenderness, so that we were making love, next thing, on the sofa. A door banged open in the evening wind. He hadn't closed the french windows securely, but he was always so sensitive about me getting distracted that I didn't say anything. Besides it was nice, though cold, to have the wind browsing along the floor and over us as we closed together.

But the wind spun a web around us and water rose against our skin while the voices cried nearer and farther without and within our attention. Ducks' wings whistled through our air, there were soft-shelled eggs stirring and awakening within our groins, voices of silt and drift piling through centuries of experience reduced to slime. *Who are we? What are we?* they called to us. 'Who are you?' I cried, knowing my strange lover for the second time. *I am all that place and time* they chorused like frogs *my hands are webbed and my belly is feathered—my legs are roots and my limbs are pools and my bones are sunken stone—I am every bone and crime and love left by the river—I am the sum of things here when they die and they have been dying and piling up since the wind first blew—*

What *man* are you? Who were you, alive? I wept, as mounting surges of fullness crammed me and pushed me and pushed at me. *No man needs your life like I do—I am a time and a place—Jill is becoming one with me—Jill gave acceptance to the cry and shall become not—Jill—Jill out of time and place—Becoming—Becoming—*

Coming. I was a thin-slewed sky trapped in the roof of a cave with no way out ever: suffocating and shackled in all the space in the world. The shaking cave filled up with cries and echoes.

'JILL, for God's sake, JILL.' Dan was looking at me fearfully with a pull of new disgust at his lip. 'You're sweating. All cold and sticky. Are you all right? Are you all right, for Christ's sake? You've been having some kind of fit. Are you sick?'

I was very quiet and looked straight back into his face. I felt come all over. I was nothing (which is very quiet, you know, and calm: it comes after the echo when you hold your breath and close your eyes, willing the wary cave to be smaller and smaller till you can pretend it's all inside your head). Calmness is calming. His eyes relaxed, honest and blue, and he started to dismiss his revulsion and stroke my lank weeds of hair. Some joke about getting carried away, some pet name we used to use, some pet name for. . . yet in true Chatterley style our groins had been christened, and the idiot from miles away used it then. Fool!

Oh where's my tenderness gone; where's it gone? Poor Dan . . . but I lay doused in the sperm of time. No more than a tree or boulder could, could love his humanity, and I hadn't learned enough yet just to *include* it as my lover did. I still haven't learned enough. For, Doctor, Doctor, the map is still unfinished. Uncharted areas to the north. And what is scale when you huddle without breath in the high cave watching cracks take shape in the roof and walls but never, never lasting?

I had to renounce him of course. I stayed alive and so my ghost went back unsatisfied. The hill I climbed, high above the Trent, was clean and deserted but only half a mile from a farm and a crossroad, and dotted with sycamores, tamed and friendly trees. I chose early afternoon too, with the sun bright on the spring grass and daisies, and a small herd of full-uddered, soft-eyed Jersey cows swishing and feeding. I was high above the river and miles from the flats, and though the wind blew through my dress up there, it was without bite or backbone: an empty, child wind.

'I must live. I must have some fun,' I said to the river and marshes. 'You must leave me, so don't call to me anymore. I know I'm making it too simple but it's the only way I can be free of you and I can't even say I'm sorry or feel weak about it.' The wind played in my skirt and I held it down with my right hand, taming my hair with my left. 'You'll probably get me when the time comes, but let it wait like it does for other people. I want to be warm and here-and-now and be sometimes with people.' And he went. Down there he just gave up and did not try to reach me or appeal. It felt good. I lay down on the grass and did child things with the wind, singing to the sky, and peering into the tiny world of a sorrel leaf. Swallows were wing-legging over the grass while mare's tails softened the sky and a ring-dove talked coos in the woods. I didn't know then that we were one flesh and beyond divorce.

It seems strange that it was Dan and Jane who brought me in to Geoffrey English before I was sent here. Dan, who wrote to my father after the first week about my state of mind, so that I told him it was over and to leave me alone. Who hovered round a bit during classes but soon left me to my daemon lover. Of whom he knew nothing. And Jane. Soon Dan was putting me down to experience and holding her hand in the library. People talked to Dan and Jane as they had of Dan and Jill, and the Christmas vacations came and went. I only stayed at home for a week and then came back to the lover I had.

Any time I was alone he was around me and, on a deserted campus near a winter city, I was almost always alone. The university park seemed full of ghosts anyway: pale spectres of crowds and lovers, of dances and parties and lectures. Perhaps there was the ghost, too, of myself, as I had been the previous autumn. One night when I was walking beside the lake a figure crossed in front of me and disappeared into the rhododendrons. I recognized it to be a ghost (the only one I have never *seen*) and also myself—when I was about fifteen. I would not have been surprised at all if I had passed Dan and Jill absorbed in each other and loving—in this place but another time.

But most of the time I was taken up with him. I must have passed those days like a crazy girl, out in the wet, walking and talking with myself, but I chose not to pass near anyone who might have thought as much. More than once I lay down on a cold, clear night and had him come into me while I watched Orion strike and buckle under the Bull's great horns. I was a fit audience for the star pageantry which recurred again and again in the frozen, toppling attitudes of completion. They are beyond people. And so was I, with my love whispering around me always of slow, drawn-out things: of the death of rocks and riverbeds and the passing of forests and towns, of the perpetual fog whose liftings were only moments in time, and all these things moving in the easy rhythm that was my love's blood-flow, now drawing on mine. How could those weeks not have changed me? But I was in love with it—I seemed cold and old and immortal, an old and queenly witch with fossils in her fingerbones, seeing all even beyond pitying.

But one day I met Mrs Naismith with Jenny and the baby and when my lover drew off the left me to talk with them I had to run crying away. Back in my room I fought to keep him from returning to me. Term began in two days, friends and classes would regather, there *was* the real world and I was lost. *They are nothing* he told me over and over as he cried his need for me.

'Yes, they're nothing,' I said, 'but I am nothing too, like them. They are my kind.'

They will be gone from here in a moment, gone from life in a day, and you will still be here with me watching and knowing.

'No, I am not lost and dead. I am alive like them.'

Are you?

Are you? Are you? Lost, and dead. Lost. And. Dead. KNOWING. Dead. Lost.

Through the term I kept him off for days sometimes, making myself work in with the other world and half-succeeding at it, but always readmitting his cold, grey finality in the end and often going off with him away from everyone. But I wanted the warm world now, and once I laughed with some people at a party and liked them again and kissed someone goodnight after a happy walk home. It was on that day that I went up on the hill and waved him away from me under a spring windrise.

'It's a monstrous loving, this need,' I had grown accustomed to tell him.

Just your existence and your constant need for me—that's all there is.

Do you know what it's like to be possessed by someone who is so constant that there is never any change in the quality of his voice or touch or mood? Or in his asking. The monotony of the spirit that includes and isn't bound by time.

'There's no fun,' I had also said. 'I know we're out of all that, but I am lazy sometimes, or weak—can't there be any laughter?'

And he would let me know: *Laughter is to face death and defeat with . . . we include these things—Laughter signifies nothing.*

Dr English's laugh. He had seen me a few times in those days when my father insisted. He felt I should socialize more, study less. Even Daddy seemed to realize he wasn't doing me much good. A good doctor would have hung garlic flowers at my window. Or something.

I suppose I knew underneath that there wasn't much left of me through the rest of that year. Half of me was sucked into the grey mud flats. But there was the other kind of laughter to pretend with, and a play to paint the set for, exams, parties. The hollow, sucked out centre of me, gave way just before the summer break. Going down hop. I was with a boy from the theatre, full of gin and a bit manic. We met up with Dan and Jane, engagement ring and all, and still the warm laughter came—it was going to be all right. I waited on the staircase while Michael went for some more drinks, and watched in the huge front windows the reflections of the dancing, jostling, calling people. I know I was pleased with myself: drunken, happy crowds had for so long disgusted me more than any other kind, but tonight I could love them as a warm and frail animal I was part of. Then through the reflections a car light down on the boulevard flashed upon water.

Without having to search, my flying feet took me to Dan's old car, always open and the keys in it. Perhaps it was the drinks that shortened the drive to the river, but I just know about the headlights waving in the summer half-dark, picking out poles, trees, fences. Everything conspired quickly to get me to the destination. Which had been the starting place. One time. The little humped bridge on the back lane and then the flats. Onto the mud, losing shoes, running, calling, crying. I tore at my clothes, my skin, at any warmth in me, and through my breaths I heard the cry beginning harshly to summon me.

I would find the very pool, the heart of him all. The bird splashed away from me at its edge and the cry closed down upon us by a patch of water, smeared slightly with oil and brightened by the clouds which threw back down the lights of the power station across the river. In the pool was myself looking up through terrible hair. My shadow self had shoulders all bones, breasts swaying near the foul pool surface, and a pulled down mouth twisting and working in a puppet's labour. If I could cut loose the shadow he would come up to me through my eyes in the pool and I would be cold and patient forever. The cry was everywhere—it called, dreadfully, from my own throat.

Jane shivered in her white raincoat, scared and a little sick, with a few pieces of my muddy clothes hanging over her arm. The hem of her evening-dress was heavy with black water. Dan splashing across to take my shoulder and pull me up, saying and saying, 'Jill it's all right, love. It's going to be all right.'

TIM WYNNE-JONES · b. 1948

The Woman with the Lounge-Act Hair

I stayed at the motel from *Psycho* last night.

It's been moved to the Yellowhead Highway, just northwest of Langenburg, Saskatchewan. I couldn't drive any further that night, not the kind of nights they have around here.

The motel from *Psycho*, a lousy black-and-white print, on a gravel lot the size of a football field. They moved most of the desolate scenery, too. They couldn't afford the hill or the Gothic mansion, but there was a bog around back.

I circled the place in my car a couple of times, like a dog about to take a nap. No cars. No other unsuspecting travellers. I pulled up in front of the office with the chlorine-green vacancy sign in the window. I entered. No birds mounted in the office, unless you count the Black Hawks losing to the Oilers on the TV. Tony Perkins' kid sister waited for a commercial to serve me.

'You should get a No Vacancy sign,' I suggested, pleasantly enough. 'Save yourself some money.'

She slammed my Visa through the machine. I think she was sore the Hawks were losing. I asked for a wake-up call. She handed me a Big Ben alarm.

Room One. What else. I hit the bed a few times to scare away the lumps. I turned on the TV. I got a bright yellow attempted murder in Yorkton. The parking lot of a club, the RCMP looking stumped. The RCMP looking jaundiced. I didn't bother to adjust the set.

No soap in the bathroom. Just a few hairs someone left behind. I looked closer. I'd seen those hairs before, plenty of them. I remembered the first time. It was a Holiday Inn. Not the Holiday Inn, the one with no surprises. I'd stopped for a drink. She was under the table—my table. Her hair was something else: all soft lights and pale upholstery. A blonde baby grand, lots of luscious ferns in blonde pots, and intimate blonde tables each bathed in its own lamplight, each with its own telephone.

I looked at her for a long time. When my eyes calmed down a bit, I alerted the proprietor. 'There's a bombshell under my table,' I said. He told me not to be alarmed. He already knew she was there. I ordered a Gibson. I don't drink Gibsons. I don't know what came over me. I remember nudging the woman gently in the rump with my toe. She just lay there.

Seeing those hairs in my bathroom, I knew we were on the same road. I looked at the shower curtain. It was wet.

The woman with the lounge-act hair. I saw her again after the first time in the Holiday Inn. In other places, other bars along the road. Never more than a glimpse. I'm a salesman. I drive too much on a full stomach. For months on end I only talk to people I don't know. The only people I do know are other salesmen. It's gotten so I don't know anyone I know, any more. We salesmen are like the early Christian saints. We communicate surreptitiously in bars. Not wanting to arouse the locals. Not wanting to get stoned.

I couldn't stand Room One. I was too tired to sleep. I opened the door and stared out at the night. One thing about the prairies: the air is fresh and there's plenty of it. It was May. Cool. I stepped out. The lights in the office were out except for the futile Vacancy sign. I felt a disturbance in the wind. A train, probably. There are a lot of trains out here, or maybe just one really big train.

I walked around back to the bog. I stared down into the mud. There was probably a DeSoto in there with a body in the trunk. There sure weren't any DeSotos in the parking lot. Beyond the bog there was a forest. Poplars. Short trees that spend more time sleeping than growing. They were trembling noisily, winter still fresh in their memory. I walked the perimeter of the parking lot.

I imagined I heard an owl take off. Dive. I stopped and listened for the scream of a vole or some other night-crawling thing.

I climbed a fence and dropped down into the dry grass of the ditch which skirted the highway. I walked along, the Yellowhead on my left, the forest on my right. I walked for some time before I heard her. I heard high heels falter on gravel. I heard her swear, drunkenly, at no one. Then I saw her up ahead, though I have no idea what light illuminated her. There was no moon, no farmhouse, no cars. But there she was, as slim as a wraith, just a little more substantial than the night.

I closed in on her. She prepared herself: re-established a shoulder strap, corrected the fall of her dress. She didn't turn around. She seemed intent on her forward progress, slow and uncertain as it was. She patted unsuccessfully at her plumage. She had been through something: the chairs and tables in her hair were overturned, some of the lamps were smashed.

'There isn't anywhere for fifty miles,' I said.

'You're telling me,' she replied, without turning. Somebody must have thrown a telephone through the mirror over the bar. I could hear the glass falling in your voice.

I was almost beside her now and almost beside myself with wanting to see her face.

'Believe me,' I said. 'I know the territory.'

'So do I,' she said, querulously. 'We're on the same circuit.'

I took her elbow, turned her to me.

'I've murdered someone,' she said.

'Maybe,' I said. I wondered if I had only imagined her response.

'You've got to help me, Winchy,' she said.

I looked into what I could see of her eyes. Perhaps there was some light. Something she'd picked up back at the motel, green and buzzing. No one had called me Winchy in thirty years.

'Get me outa here, Winchy.'

The headlights came out of nowhere, lighting half her face. She shrank from me towards the woods. I couldn't move. I watched her fade into the trees. At the last minute I dropped, spread eagle, into the grass. The headlights passed. There was a third light, a red one, revolving on the car's roof. When the dark was complete again I called out, scarcely believing the name I was saying.

'Maxine?'

I listened. Nothing but the wind, shaking the winter out of the poplars.

'Maxine!' I called out, more urgently.

'Sshhhhhhh,' said the poplars. I wished I were an owl.

Night and cold and tiredness overcame me. I headed back to the motel. I opened the door to Room One. I flipped on the light.

I heard the shower.

I flipped the light off. I pulled the chair out from the desk and sat down to wait, and watch the steam roll under the bathroom door. She was in there for about an hour. Finally she emerged, backlit, with a towel around her torso and another wound around her hair.

'It's a wonder there's anything left of you,' I said. She seemed not to notice me. She dropped her towel. Her body was angular, her breasts heavy. She found a terrycloth bathrobe in my suitcase and put it on.

'I was so cold,' she said.

She hugged herself, still cold. She pulled back the covers on the bed and slipped in. She switched on the bedside light. She pulled the bedclothes up around her and her knees up to her chest. Her lips were trembling. Red, full lips, cut from the prime. Skin, almost translucently pale. She looked at me plaintively. I stayed where I was.

'They suspect you came this way,' I said. 'It's only a matter of time.'

'You can hide me,' she said.

'Maybe,' I said, shifting uneasily under her level gaze. 'What'd this woman do to you, anyway?'

Her eyes narrowed. 'I didn't tell you it was a woman,' she said.

'I saw it on the news,' I replied.

Her eye flickered as if there were something caught in it. 'I don't know what came over me,' she said. She began to massage her head with the towel. Her eyes closed.

'She reminded me of someone. Someone from my past,' she said, at last. 'I found myself staring at her. The others at the bar made fun of me. I didn't care. She did. She got up to leave. I followed. When she saw me following her, she ran. I ran too, out into the parking lot. And then, then. . . .'

She looked at me plaintively again. 'Hasn't this ever happened to you?' her eyes seemed to say. I must have answered yes. She stopped shivering.

'Take off the towel,' I said.

Obediently she unwound her turban. Her hair fell wetly, around her shoulders, down to the bedclothes where it seemed to bleed mercury on the blue sheets.

'I've never cut it,' she said.

'How many victims have there been?' I asked.

She settled her head back on the pillow. She shrugged her shoulders. 'You'll always be number one, Winchy,' she said. I stared. Hard. Wanting her.

'You've got to remember what happened,' I said.

'Help me,' she said, and held out her arms to me.

I was doing my own remembering. A night in the woodshed on

the abandoned farm when we were still kids. 'Dammit!' I shouted, and brought my fist down hard on the arm of my chair. 'You don't try to kill someone because they look like someone from your past!'

Her lips drew tight and bloodless. I could see some of the old temper rise in her face. But then her eyebrow arched and her eyes lit up as she grasped what I had said. What I had goddamned said!

'The bitch didn't die!'

It was an advantage I had not meant to surrender.

'They want you for questioning,' I said hastily. 'They don't like the looks of this. There have been other cases.' I was grasping at straws. She knew it. 'You're in big trouble, Maxine.'

Feeble.

The band of muscle around her mouth softened. I'd lost my handicap.

'I knew I could count on you, Winchy,' she said. 'Come here!' She patted the bed beside her.

'Jesus!'

She pretended to sulk. 'Poor Winchy,' she said. 'Doesn't know whether to love or hate Maxine.'

She could still do it to me. Play out her line and I'd bite every time. 'I didn't mind the mischief,' I blurted. 'I didn't mind being blamed for what you did.'

'No,' she said. 'Winchy never minded a little punishment. After all, Maxine was just imaginary, wasn't she? That's what Winchy thought.'

I could feel the hook in my cheek. I went cold all over. Room One was suddenly filled with the sound of a six-inch-tall Big Ben. I didn't dare look at her. I didn't dare close my eyes. I'd see it all again. The woodshed. Maxine. The night I broke the news to her and she broke the news to me. But it was too late. With my eyes wide open, she had me and she was reeling me back, back. . . .

We were eight years old.

'Maxine! Maxine!' I called, all breathless, having run the whole way from the house. I pushed open the broken door of the shed. I knew she'd be there. I couldn't see her, but I was too full of the thrill of bad news to hold it in any longer. 'My parents won't put up with you any more. That's what they said. You're too naughty, Maxine. They say they've had enough.' I remembered waiting wide-eyed in the gloom. I remembered the wet smell of the place and dancing from foot to foot, expectantly. Maxine would come up with something, I remembered thinking. She did.

'I'm not your imaginary friend,' she said. Even without seeing her I could tell she was in one of her moods by the tone of her voice. Gradually I picked her out of the crowded darkness of the shed. She was sitting cross-legged on a battered old card table. She glared at me. I remember a moment of pure panic. Then I recovered. 'You mean until things cool down,' I said, hopefully. She did not speak for a moment. Just sat there, shoulders squared, staring down at me. 'I've *never* been your imaginary friend,' she said at last. I remembered feeling my legs go weak. I sat down on an inverted water pail. 'You don't mean that,' I mumbled. 'I do so,' she said. Then she smiled, horribly. 'I'm not Winchy's imaginary friend,' she said. 'Winchy's *my* imaginary friend.'

'And you've never forgiven me,' said Maxine. I was snapped back to the moment, the motel from *Psycho*. I was standing at the door of Room One looking out at the night. My lungs were heaving, like a fish in the bottom of a boat. I got hold of myself. I turned. She was still there, grinning at me from the bed.

'No, she didn't die,' I said. 'You're not a murderer this time. But it's happened before and it'll happen again. You've got to figure out what it is that comes over you. You've got to remember what happened.'

Her head dropped. Her hair fell about her face, casting shadows there. I grabbed my jacket from the back of my chair.

'Where you going?' she asked. Her voice was puzzled, a child's voice.

'Back to the club,' I said. 'So are you.'

She sighed. Then she swung her legs out of bed. She gathered up her clothes and was about to enter the bathroom when she changed her mind. She turned and faced me across the room. She dropped my robe to the floor, revealing herself completely. Then she dressed. Slowly. Maxine, thirty years later, in the motel from *Psycho*, becoming less naked by the moment.

It was an hour's drive back to Yorkton. I could hardly see her in the seat beside me, but I could feel her there. I could hear her putting up her hair. Hair she had been growing for a lifetime. It had always been her best feature. Sometimes it had been a secret garden: overgrown and tangled, coarse on the naked calf, wet and heavy with the perfume of wild flowers. Sometimes it had been a playground: sandy, with crazy swings and a slide, too hot to touch, facing into the sun. I wasn't used to having passengers. The company didn't like it for insurance reasons. Still, lots of the guys did it: hitchhikers, and girlfriends. I thought about it a lot.

'I've thought about you a lot, lately,' I said. My tongue clicked miserably.

'Are you disappointed?' she asked.

I didn't answer. I let her think what she wanted. I let the miles roll by while she reconstructed the miracle. She used no clips, no pins. At some point I found her hand resting on my hand on the wheel.

'You must get very lonely,' she said.

It was after four when we entered Yorkton. The club was on the outskirts of town, stuck in the crotch of a crossroad. There was no one around and few cars on the road. There was only one light burning in the huge parking lot. It burned yellow. I pulled my car into the littered shadows by the dumpster near the kitchen doors. I turned off the lights, the motor.

'I can't go through with this,' she said. 'Not again.' She was sitting perfectly erect, her hair piled high, her eyes straight ahead. I spoke quietly, as if to a child.

'She did something to you, Maxine. She pushed you over the edge. You've got to figure out what happened.'

Reluctantly she opened the door. I came around to her. She looked at me with anger and distrust. 'This is not what I had hoped for,' she said. I helped her out of the car. She looked clear through me as if I weren't there. 'This is some kind of a showdown, isn't it?' she said. At first I didn't trust myself to reply.

'Just show me how it happened,' I said. With my hand in the small of her back, I propelled her towards the back door.

'You came out here,' I said, at the doorway.

'I can't remember,' she said.

'I saw you,' I said. I was sweating now, but I was ready for her. She turned to face me, her eyes uneasy. 'You were there?' she asked. I nodded.

'I saw you watching her. I saw you leave. I followed you.'

'Then you saw what happened,' she snapped.

'Maybe,' I snapped back. 'But us imaginary people don't always understand what we see. It's not always clear to us what's happening.' I'd never talked to her like that.

She glared at me, just for an instant, then she stared across the expanse of the parking lot. I could see the recollection growing in her eyes. We were going back again, back. . . .

It was ten o'clock.

'The band was just starting its second set. They were getting louder, keeping pace with the crowd. The songs went on longer and were out of tune. Nobody else seemed to notice.

'I found myself staring at her. The others at the bar made fun of me. I didn't care. She did. She got up to leave. I followed. Out here.'

Maxine began to pick her way through the parked cars. Out across the lot the roads were heavy with Friday night traffic.

'She glanced back about here,' said Maxine. She glanced back at me as she spoke. 'Go on,' I said. She must have remembered the look on her victim's face. Suddenly I knew she was frightened. 'She began to run,' said Maxine. And Maxine began to run, re-living her victim's flight. She was clumsy in her high heels; I caught up with her easily. I grabbed her. 'I grabbed her,' said Maxine, breathlessly. I pulled her around to face me. 'I just wanted to see her face up close,' said Maxine. 'You're hurting me,' she moaned. A Greyhound bus geared down on the highway. I could hear the car radios of teens at the chicken place across the way. 'And when you saw her up close?' I said, shaking her.

'She was going to scream,' said Maxine. 'I covered her mouth with my hand.'

'Like this?' I said and I pressed my hand into her face. I pulled her up close, with my other hand behind her, holding her skinny wrists up high and tight. Maxine nodded at me; her eyes pleaded with me not to hurt her. I had never seen her like this, out of control.

'She looked just like you,' I whispered in her ear. 'Like I always imagined you'd look.' She jerked her head up and down in painful agreement while she blubbered against the weight of my hand in her face. I yanked her wrists up higher between her scapulas, until her eyes rolled back in her head with the pain. Then suddenly I felt her teeth bite deeply into the fleshy part of my thumb.

I yelped and pulled my hand away.

'Please!' she cried. 'You've got the wrong woman.'

My hand was bleeding. I lashed out at her. She staggered out of my reach. I grabbed again. This time I caught her by the hair. She pulled herself free. Her hair came away in my hand.

Immediately, she started to scream like the real mother in

Solomon's tale. She stared at the blonde creature in my fist. I stared at it too. It had seemed so real.

I could hear voices raised, voices shouting. Dimly it registered they were yammering at me. I couldn't move. I dropped the hair. She made no move to pick it up. She was leaning against the car, a few yards away, blubbering. Her makeup was smeared. Her hair was mousy brown, cropped close to the skull. She looked like a stunned mouse wondering where the talons had come from and when they would strike again.

I heard the sirens. Suddenly everything was like a picture on a cheap motel TV. Confusion: the cruisers squealing into the lot, truckers and prairie teenagers and the boozy bewildered bar crowd drifting down to the noise. A strong-armed cop gently cradled Maxine. Only it wasn't Maxine. I faded into the crowd, searching. She was nowhere. I sat in my car a long time trying to figure it out. Then I drove until I couldn't drive any further, until I reached this motel.

I was sitting in the chair by the desk when the high-beamed headlights rushed up the dark walls of my room. I grabbed my jacket off the back of the chair and opened the door in a hurry. I didn't want them to shoot their way in.

As the officers led me towards the cruiser, I could see the palest tint of a prairie dawn in the eastern sky. Behind me I could hear the alarm ringing in Room One. I had planned an early start. I had got fifty miles up the Yellowhead to a cruddy motel. Maxine had got clear. Again. The sound of the alarm filled my head. I couldn't imagine who would turn it off.

ROHINTON MISTRY · b. 1952

The Ghost of Firozsha Baag

I always believed in ghosts. When I was little I saw them in my father's small field of Goa. That was very long ago, before I came to Bombay to work as ayah.

Father also saw them, mostly by the well, drawing water. He would come in and tell us, the *bhoot* is thirsty again. But it never scared us. Most people in our village had seen ghosts. Everyone believed in them.

Not like in Firozsha Baag. First time I saw a ghost here and people found out, how much fun they made of me. Called me crazy, saying it is time for old ayah to go back to Goa, back to her *muluk*, she is seeing things.

Two years ago on Christmas Eve I first saw the *bhoot*. No, it was really Christmas Day. At ten o'clock on Christmas Eve I went to Cooperage Stadium for midnight mass. Every year all of us Catholic ayahs from Firozsha Baag go for mass. But this time I came home alone, the others went somewhere with their boyfriends. Must have been two o'clock in the morning. Lift in B Block was out of order, so I started up slowly. Thinking how easy to climb three floors when I was younger, even with a full bazaar-bag.

After reaching first floor I stopped to rest. My breath was coming fast-fast. Fast-fast, like it does nowadays when I grind curry *masala* on the stone. Jaakaylee, my *bai* calls out, Jaakaylee, is *masala* ready? Thinks a sixty-three-year-old ayah can make *masala* as quick as she used to when she was fifteen. Yes, fifteen. The day after my fourteenth birthday I came by bus from Goa to Bombay. All day and night I rode the bus. I still remember when my father took me to bus station in Panjim. Now it is called Panaji. Joseph Uncle, who was the mechanic in Mazagaon, met me at Bombay Central Station. So crowded it was, people running all around, shouting, screaming, and coolies with big-big trunks on their heads. Never will I forget that first day in Bombay. I just stood in one place, not knowing what to do, till Joseph Uncle saw me. Now it has been forty-nine years in this house as ayah, believe or don't believe. Forty-nine years in Firozsha Baag's B Block and they still don't say my name right. Is it so difficult to say Jacqueline? But they always say Jaakaylee. Or worse, Jaakayl.

All the fault is of old *bai* who died ten years ago. She was in charge till her son brought a wife, the *new bai* of the house. Old *bai* took English words and made them Parsi words. Easy chair was *igeechur*, French beans were *ferach beech*, and Jacqueline became Jaakaylee. Later I found out that all old Parsis did this, it was like they made their own private language.

So then new *bai* called me Jaakaylee also, and children do the same. I don't care about it now. If someone asks my name I say Jaakaylee. And I talk Parsi-Gujarati all the time instead of Konkani, even with other ayahs. Sometimes also little bits of English.

But I was saying. My breath was fast-fast when I reached first floor and stopped for rest. And then I noticed someone, looked like in a white gown. Like a man, but I could not see the face, just body shape. *Kaun hai?* I asked in Hindi. Believe or don't believe, he vanished. Completely! I shook my head and started for second floor. Carefully, holding the railing, because the steps are so old, all slanting and crooked.

Then same thing happened. At the top of second floor he was waiting. And when I said, *kya hai?* believe or don't believe, he vanished again! Now I knew it must be a *bhoot*! I knew he would be on third floor also, and I was right. But I was not scared or anything.

I reached the third floor entrance and found my bedding which I had put outside before leaving. After midnight mass I always sleep outside, by the stairs, because *bai* and *seth* must not be woken up at two A.M., and they never give me a key. No ayah gets key to a flat. It is something I have learned, like I learned forty-nine years ago that life as ayah means living close to floor. All work I do, I do on floors, like grinding *masala*, cutting vegetables, cleaning rice. Food also is eaten sitting on floor, after serving them at dining-table. And my bedding is rolled out at night in kitchen-passage, on floor. No cot for me. Nowadays, my weight is much more than it used to be, and is getting very difficult to get up from floor. But I am managing.

So Christmas morning at two o'clock I opened my bedding and spread out my *saterunjee* by the stairs. Then stopped. The *bhoot* had vanished, and I was not scared or anything. But my father used to say some ghosts play mischief. The ghost of our field never did, he only took water from our well, but if this ghost of the stairs played mischief he might roll me downstairs, who was to say. So I thought about it and rang the doorbell.

After many, many rings *bai* opened, looking very mean. Mostly she looks okay, and when she dresses in nice sari for a wedding or something, and puts on all bangles and necklace, she looks really pretty, I must say. But now she looked so mean. Like she was going to bite somebody. Same kind of look she has every morning when she has just woken up, but this was much worse and meaner because it was so early in the morning. She was very angry, said I was going crazy, there was no ghost or anything, I was just telling lies not to sleep outside.

Then *seth* also woke up. He started laughing, saying he did not want any ghost to roll me downstairs because who would make *chai* in the morning. He was not angry, his mood was good. They went back to their room, and I knew why he was feeling happy when crrr-crr-crrr-crr sound of their bed started coming in the dark.

When he was little I sang Konkani songs for him. *Mogacha Mary* and *Hanv Saiba*. Big man now, he's forgotten them and so have I. Forgetting my name, my language, my songs. But complaining I'm not, don't make mistake. I'm tell you, to have a job I was very lucky because in Goa there was nothing to do. From Panjim to Bombay on the bus I cried, leaving behind my brothers and sisters and parents, and all my village friends. But I knew leaving was best thing. My father had eleven children and very small field. Coming to Bombay was only thing to do. Even schooling I got first year, at night. Then *bai* said I must stop because who would serve dinner when *seth* came home from work, and who would carry away dirty dishes? But that was not the real reason. She thought I stole her eggs. There were six eggs yesterday evening, she would say, only five this morning, what happened to one? She used to think I took it with me to school to give to someone.

I was saying, it was very lucky for me to become ayah in Parsi house, and never will I forget that. Especially because I'm Goan Catholic and very dark skin colour. Parsis prefer Manglorean Catholics, they have light skin colour. For themselves also Parsis like light skin, and when Parsi baby is born that is the first and most important thing. If it is fair they say, O how nice light skin just like parents. But if it is dark skin they say, *arré* what is this *ayah no chhokro*, ayah's child.

All this doing was more in olden days, mostly among very rich *bais* and *seths.* They thought they were like British only, ruling India side by side. But don't make mistake, not just rich Parsis. Even all Marathi people in low class Tar Gully made fun of me when I went to buy grocery from *bunya.* Blackie, blackie, they would call out. Nowadays it does not happen because very dark skin colour is common in Bombay, so many people from south are coming here, Tamils and Keralites, with their funny *illay illay poe poe* language. Now people more used to different colours.

But still not to ghosts. Everybody in B Block found out about the *bhoot* of the stairs. They made so much fun of me all the time, children and grown-up people also.

And believe or don't believe, that *was* a ghost of mischief. Because just before Easter he came back. Not on the stairs this time but right in my bed. I'm telling you, he was sitting on my chest and bouncing up and down, and I couldn't push him off, so weak I was feeling (I'm a proper Catholic, I was fasting), couldn't even scream or anything (not because I was scared—he was choking me). Then someone woke up to go to WC and put on a light in the passage when I sleep. Only then did the rascal *bhoot* jump off and vanish.

This time I did not tell anyone. Already they were making so much fun of me. Children in Firozsha Baag would shout, ayah *bhoot!* ayah *bhoot!* every time they saw me. And a new Hindi film had come out, *Bhoot Bungla,* about a haunted house, so they would say, like the man on the radio, in a loud voice: SEE TODAY, at APSARA CINEMA, R. K. Anand's NEW fillum *Bhoooot Bungla,* starring JAAKAYLEE of BLOCK B! Just like that! O they made a lot of fun of me, but I did not care, I knew what I had seen.

Jaakaylee, bai *calls out, is it ready yet? She wants to check curry* masala. *Too thick, she always says, grind it again, make it smoother. And she is right, I leave it thick purposely. Before, when I did it fine, she used to send me back anyway. O it pains in my shoulders, grinding this* masala, *but they will never buy the automatic machine. Very rich people, my* bai-seth. *He is a chartered accountant. He has a nice motorcar, just like A Block priest, and like the one Dr Mody used to drive, which has not moved from the compound since the day he died.* Bai *says they should buy it from Mrs Mody, she wants it to go shopping. But a* masala *machine they will not buy. Jaakaylee must keep on doing it till her arms fall out from shoulders.*

How much teasing everyone was doing to me about the *bhoot.* It became a great game among boys, pretending to be ghosts. One who started it all was Dr Mody's son, from third floor of C Block. One day they call Pesi *paadmaroo* because he makes dirty wind all the time. Good thing he is in boarding-school now. That family came to Firozsha Baag only few years ago, he was doctor for animals, a really nice man. But what a terrible boy. Must have been so shameful for Dr Mody. Such a kind man, what a shock everybody got when he died. But I'm telling you, that boy did a bad thing one night.

Vera and Dolly, the two fashionable sisters from C Block's first floor, went to a nightshow at Eros Cinema, and Pesi knew. After nightshow was over, tock-tock they came in their high-heel shoes. It was when mini-skirts had just come out, and that is what they were wearing. Very *esskey-messkey*, so short I don't know how their *mai-baap* allowed it. They said their daughters were going to foreign for studies, so maybe this kind of dressing was practice for over there. Anyway, they started up, the stairs were very dark. Then Pesi, wearing a white bedsheet and waiting under the staircase, jumped out shouting *bowe ré*. Vera and Dolly screamed so loudly, I'm telling you, and they started running.

Then Pesi did a really shameful thing. God knows where he got the idea from. Inside his sheet he had a torch, and he took it out and shined up into the girls' mini-skirts. Yes! He ran after them with his big torch shining in their skirts. And when Vera and Dolly reached the top they tripped and fell. That shameless boy just stood there with his light shining between their legs, seeing undies and everything, I'm telling you.

He ran away when all neighbours started opening their doors to see what is the matter, because everyone heard them screaming. All the men had good time with Vera and Dolly, pretending to be like concerned grown-up people, saying, it is all right, dears, don't worry, dears, just some bad boy, not a real ghost. And all the time petting-squeezing them as if to comfort them! Sheeh, these men!

Next day Pesi was telling his friends about it, how he shone the torch up their skirts and how they fell, and everything he saw. That boy, sheeh, terrible.

Afterwards, parents in Firozsha Baag made a very strict rule that no one plays the fool about ghosts because it can cause serious accident if sometime some old person is made scared and falls downstairs and breaks a bone or something or has heart attack. So there was no more ghost games and no more making fun of me. But I'm telling you, the *bhoot* kept coming every Friday night.

264 Robinton Mistry

Curry is boiling nicely, smells very tasty. Bai *tells me don't forget about curry, don't burn the dinner. How many times have I burned the dinner in forty-nine years, I should ask her. Believe or don't believe, not one time.*

Yes, the *bhoot* came but he did not bounce any more upon my chest. Sometimes he just sat next to the bedding, other times he lay down beside me with his head on my chest, and if I tried to push him away he would hold me tighter. Or would try to put his hand up my gown or down from the neck. But I sleep with buttons up to my collar, so it was difficult for the rascal. O what a ghost of mischief he was! Reminded me of Cajetan back in Panjim always trying to do same thing with girls at the cinema or beach. His parents' house was not far from Church of St Cajetan for whom he was named, but this boy was no saint, I'm telling you.

Calunqute and Anjuna beaches in those days were very quiet and beautiful. It was before foreigners all started coming, and no hippie-bippie business with *charas* and *ganja,* and no big-big hotels or nothing. Cajetan said to me once, let us go and see the fishermen. And we went, and started to wade a little, up to ankles, and Cajetan said let us go more. He rolled up his pants over the knees and I pulled up my skirt, and we went in deeper. Then a big wave made everything wet. We ran out and sat on the beach for my skirt to dry.

Us two were only ones there, fishermen were still out in boats. Sitting on the sand he made all funny eyes at me, like Hindi film hero, and put his hand on my thigh. I told him to stop or I would tell my father who would give him solid pasting and throw him in the well where the *bhoot* would take care of him. But he didn't stop. Not till the fishermen came. Sheeh, what a boy that was.

Back to kitchen. To make good curry needs lots of stirring while boiling.

I'm telling you, that Cajetan! Once, it was feast of St Francis Xavier, and the body was to be in a glass case at Church of Bom Jesus. Once every ten years is this very big event for Catholics. They were not going to do it any more because, believe or don't believe, many years back some poor crazy woman took a bite from toe of St Francis Xavier. But then they changed their minds. Poor St Francis, it is not his luck to have a whole body—one day, Pope asked for a bone from the right arm, for people in Rome to see, and never sent it back; that is where it is till today.

But I was saying about Cajetan. All boys and girls from my village were going to Bom Jesus by bus. In church it was so crowded, and a long long line to walk by St Francis Xavier's glass case. Cajetan was standing behind my friend Lily, he had finished his fun with me, now it was Lily's turn. And I'm telling you, he kept bumping her and letting his hand touch her body like it was by accident in the crowd. Sheeh, even in church that boy could not behave.

And the ghost reminded me of Cajetan, whom I have not seen since I came to Bombay—what did I say, forty-nine years ago. Once a week the ghost came, and always on Friday. On Fridays I eat fish, so I started thinking, maybe he likes smell of fish. Then I just ate vegetarian, and yet he came. For almost a whole year the ghost slept with me, every Friday night, and Christmas was not far away.

And still no one knew about it, how he came to my bed, lay down with me, tried to touch me. There was one thing I was feeling so terrible about—even to Father D'Silva at Byculla Church I had not told anything for the whole year. Every time in confession I would keep completely quiet about it. But now Christmas was coming and I was feeling very bad, so first Sunday in December I told Father D'Silva everything and then I was feeling much better. Father D'Silva said I was blameless because it was not my wish to have the *bhoot* sleeping with me. But he gave three Hail Marys, and said eating fish was okay if I wanted.

So on Friday of that week I had fish curry-rice and went to bed. And believe or don't believe, the *bhoot* did not come. After midnight, first I thought maybe he is late, maybe he has somewhere else to go. The clock in *bai*'s room went three times and I was really worried. Was he going to come in early morning while I was making tea? That would be terrible.

But he did not come. Why, I wondered. If he came to the bedding of a fat and ugly ayah all this time, now what was the matter? I could not understand. But then I said to myself, what are you thinking Jaakaylee, where is your head, do you really want the ghost to come sleep with you and touch you so shamefully?

After drinking my tea that morning I knew what had happened. The ghost did not come because of my confession. He was ashamed now. Because Father D'Silva knew about what he had been doing to me in the darkness every Friday night.

Next Friday night also there was no ghost. Now I was completely sure my confession had got rid of him and his shameless habits. But in a few days it would be Christmas Eve and time for midnight mass.

I thought, maybe if he is ashamed to come into my bed, he could wait for me on the stairs like last year.

Time to cook rice now, time for seth *to come home. Best quality Basmati rice we use, always, makes such a lovely fragrance while cooking, so tasty.*

For midnight mass I left my bedding outside, and when I returned it was two A.M. But for worrying there was no reason. No ghost on any floor this time. I opened the bedding by the stairs, thinking about Cajetan, how scared he was when I said I would tell my father about his touching me. Did not ask me to go anywhere after that, no beaches, no cinemas. Now same thing with the ghost. How scared men are of fathers.

And next morning *bai* opened the door, saying, good thing ghost took a holiday this year, if you had woken us again I would have killed you. I laughed a little and said Merry Christmas, *bai*, and she said same to me.

When *seth* woke up he also made a little joke. If they only knew that in one week they would say I had been right. Yes, on New Year's Day they would start believing, when there was really no ghost. Never has been since the day I told Father D'Silva in confession. But I was not going to tell them they were mistaken, after such fun they made of me. Let them feel sorry now for saying Jaakaylee was crazy.

Bai and *seth* were going to New Year's Eve dance, somewhere in Bandra, for first time since children were born. She used to say they were too small to leave with ayah, but that year he kept saying please, now children were bigger. So she agreed. She kept telling me what to do and gave telephone number to call in case of emergency. Such fuss she made, I'm telling you, when they left for Bandra I was so nervous.

I said special prayer that nothing goes wrong, that children would eat dinner properly, not spill anything, go to bed without crying or trouble. If *bai* found out she would say, what did I tell you, children cannot be left with ayah. And then she would give poor *seth* hell for it. He gets a lot anyway.

Everything went right and children went to sleep. I opened my bedding, but I was going to wait till they came home. Spreading out the *saterunjee*, I saw a tear in the white bedsheet used for covering— maybe from all pulling and pushing with the ghost—and was going to repair it next morning. I put off the light and lay down just to rest.

Then cockroach sounds started. I lay quietly in the dark, first to decide where it was. If you put a light on they stop singing and then you don't know where to look. So I listened carefully. It was coming from the gas stove table. I put on the light now and took my *chappal.* There were two of them, sitting next to cylinder. I lifted my *chappal,* very slowly and quietly, then phut! phut! Must say I am expert at cockroach-killing. The poison which *seth* puts out is really not doing much good, my *chappal* is much better.

I picked up the two dead ones and threw them outside, in Baag's backyard. Two cockroaches would make nice little snack for some rat in the yard, I thought. Then I lay down again after switching off light.

Clock in *bai-seth's* room went twelve times. They would all be giving kiss now and saying Happy New Year. When I was little in Panjim, my parents, before all the money went, always gave a party on New Year's Eve. I lay on my bedding, thinking of those days. It is so strange that so much of your life you can remember if you think quietly in the darkness.

Must not forget rice on stove. With rice, especially Basmati, one minute more or one minute less, one spoon extra water or less water, and it will spoil, it will not be light and every grain separate.

So there I was in the darkness remembering my father and mother, Panjim and Cajetan, nice beaches and boats. Suddenly it was very sad, so I got up and put a light on. In *bai-seth's* room their clock said two o'clock. I wished they would come home soon. I checked children's room, they were sleeping.

Back to my passage I went, and started mending the torn sheet. Sewing, thinking about my mother, how hard she used to work, how she would repair clothes for my brothers and sisters. Not only sewing to mend but also to alter. When my big brother's pants would not fit, she would open out the waist and undo trouser cuffs to make longer legs. Then when he grew so big that even with alterations it did not fit, she sewed same pants again, making a smaller waist, shorter legs, so little brother could wear. How much work my mother did, sometimes even helping my father outside in the small field, especially if he was visiting a *taverna* the night before.

But sewing and remembering brought me more sadness. I put away the needle and thread and went outside by the stairs. There is a little balcony there. It was so nice and dark and quiet, I just stood there. Then it became a little chilly. I wondered if the ghost was coming again. My father used to say that whenever a ghost is around it feels chilly, it is a sign. He said he always did in the field when the *bhoot* came to the well.

There was no ghost or anything so I must be chilly, I thought, because it is so early morning. I went in and brought my white bedsheet. Shivering a little, I put it over my head, covering up my ears. There was a full moon, and it looked so good. In Panjim sometimes we used to go to the beach at night when there was a full moon, and father would tell us about when he was little, and the old days when Portuguese ruled Goa, and about grandfather who had been to Portugal in a big ship.

Then I saw *bai-seth*'s car come in the compound. I leaned over the balcony, thinking to wave if they looked up, let them know I had not gone to sleep. Then I thought, no, it is better if I go in quietly before they see me, or *bai* might get angry and say, what are you doing outside in middle of night, leaving children alone inside. But she looked up suddenly. I thought, O my Jesus, she has already seen me.

And then she screamed. I'm telling you, she screamed so loudly I almost fell down faint. It was not angry screaming, it was frightened screaming, *bhoot! bhoot!* and I understood. I quickly went inside and lay down on my bedding.

It took some time for them to come up because she sat inside the car and locked all doors. Would not come out until he climbed upstairs, put on every staircase light to make sure the ghost was gone, and then went back for her.

She came in the house at last and straight to my passage, shaking me, saying wake up, Jaakaylee, wake up! I pretended to be sleeping deeply, then turned around and said, Happy New Year, *bai*, everything is okay, children are okay.

She said, yes yes, but the *bhoot* is on the stairs! I saw him, the one you saw last year at Christmas, he is back, I saw him with my own eyes!

I wanted so much to laugh, but I just said, don't be afraid, *bai*, he will not do any harm, he is not a ghost of mischief, he must have just lost his way.

Then she said, Jaakaylee, you were telling the truth and I was angry with you. I will tell everyone in B Block you were right, there really is a *bhoot*.

I said *bai*, let it be now, everyone has forgotten about it, and no one will believe anyway. But she said, when *I* tell them, they will believe.

And after that many people in Firozsha Baag started to believe in the ghost. One was *dustoorji* in A Block. He came one day and taught *bai* a prayer, *saykasté saykasté sataan*, to say it every time she was on the stairs. He told her, because you have seen a *bhoot* on the balcony by the stairs, it is better to have a special Parsi prayer ceremony there so he does not come again and cause any trouble. He said, many years ago, near Marine Lines where Hindus have their funerals and burn bodies, a *bhoot* walked at midnight in the middle of the road, scaring motorists and causing many accidents. Hindu priests said prayers to make him stop. But no use. *Bhoot* kept walking at midnight, motorists kept having accidents. So Hindu priests called me to do a *jashan*, they knew Parsi priest has most powerful prayers of all. And after I did a *jashan* right in the middle of the road, everything was all right.

Bai listened to all this talk of *dustoorji* from A Block, then said she would check with *seth* and let him know if they wanted a balcony *jashan*. Now *seth* says yes to everything, so he told her, sure sure, let *dustoorji* do it. It will be fun to see the exkoriseesum, he said, some big English word like that.

Dustoorji was pleased, and he checked his Parsi calendar for a good day. On that morning I had to wash whole balcony floor specially, then *dustoorji* came, spread a white sheet, and put all prayer items on it, a silver thing in which he made fire with sandalwood and *loban*, a big silver dish, a *lotta* full of water, flowers, and some fruit.

When it was time to start saying prayers *dustoorji* told me to go inside. Later, *bai* told me that was because Parsi prayers are so powerful, only a Parsi can listen to them. Everyone else can be badly damaged inside their soul if they listen.

So *jashan* was done and *dustoorji* went home with all his prayer things. But when people in Firozsha Baag who did not believe in the ghost heard about prayer ceremony, they began talking and mocking.

Some said Jaakaylee's *bai* has gone crazy, first the ayah was seeing things, and now she has made her *bai* go mad. *Bai* will not talk to those people in the Baag. She is really angry, says she does not want friends who think she is crazy. She hops *jashan* was not very powerful, so the ghost can come again. She wants everyone to see him and know the truth like her.

Busy eating, bai-seth are. Curry is hot, they are blowing whoosh-whoosh on their tongues but still eating, they love it hot. Secret of good curry is not only what spices to put, but also what goes in first, what goes in second, and third, and so on. And never cook curry with lid on pot, always leave it open, stir it often, stir it to urge the flavour to come out.

So *bai* is hoping the ghost will come again. She keeps asking me about ghosts, what they do, why they come. She thinks because I saw the ghost first in Firozsha Baag, it must be my speciality or something. Especially since I am from village—she says village people know more about such things than city people. So I tell her about the *bhoot* we used to see in the small field, and what my father said when he saw the *bhoot* near the well. *Bai* enjoys it, even asks me to sit with her at table, bring my separate mug, and pours a cup for me, listening to my ghost-talk. She does not treat me like servant all the time.

One night she came to my passage when I was saying my rosary and sat down with me on the bedding. I could not believe it, I stopped my rosary. She said, Jaakaylee, what is it Catholics say when they touch their head and stomach and both sides of chest? So I told her, Father, Son, and Holy Ghost. Right right! she said, I remember it now, when I went to St Anne's High School there were many Catholic girls and they used to say it always before and after class prayer, yes, Holy Ghost. Jaakaylee, you don't think this is that Holy Ghost you pray to, do you? And I said, no *bai*, that Holy Ghost has a different meaning, it is not like the *bhoot* you and I saw.

Yesterday she said, Jaakaylee, will you help me with something? All morning she was looking restless, so I said, yes *bai*. She left the table and came back with her big scissors and the flat cone *soopra* I use for winnowing rice and wheat. She said, my granny showed me a little magic once, she told me to keep it for important things only. The *bhoot* is, so I am going to use it. If you help me. It needs two Parsis, but I'll do it with you.

I just sat quietly, a little worried, wondering what she was up to now. First, she covered her head with a white *mathoobanoo*, and gave me one for mine, she said to put it over my head like a scarf. Then, the two points of scissors she poked through one side of *soopra*, really tight, so it could hang from the scissors. On two chairs we sat face to face. She made me balance one ring of scissors on my finger, and she balanced the other ring on hers. And we sat like that, with *soopra* hanging from scissors between us, our heads covered with white cloth. Believe or don't believe, it looked funny and scary at the same time. When *soopra* became still and stopped swinging around she said, now close your eyes and don't think of anything, just keep your hand steady. So I closed my eyes, wondering if *seth* knew what was going on.

Then she started to speak, in a voice I had never heard before. It seemed to come from very far away, very soft, all scary. My hair was standing, I felt chilly, as if a *bhoot* was about to come. This is what she said: if the ghost is going to appear again, then *soopra* must turn.

Nothing happened. But I'm telling you, I was so afraid I just kept my eyes shut tight, like she told me to do. I wanted to see nothing which I was not supposed to see. All this was something completely new for me. Even in my village, where everyone knew so much about ghosts, magic with *soopra* and scissors was unknown.

Then *bai* spoke once more, in that same scary voice: if the ghost is going to appear again, upstairs or downstairs, on balcony or inside the house, this year or next year, in daylight or in darkness, for good purpose or for bad purpose, then *soopra* must surely turn.

Believe or don't believe, this time it started to turn, I could feel the ring of the scissors moving on my finger. I screamed and pulled away my hand, there was a loud crash, and *bai* also screamed.

Slowly, I opened my eyes. Everything was on the floor, scissors were broken, and I said to *bai*, I'm very sorry I was so frightened, *bai*, and for breaking your big scissors, you can take it from my pay.

She said, you scared me with your scream, Jaakaylee, but it is all right now, nothing to be scared about, I'm here with you. All the worry was gone from her face. She took off her *mathoobanoo* and patted my shoulder, picked up the broken scissors and *soopra*, and took it back to kitchen.

Bai was looking very pleased. She came back and said to me, don't worry about broken scissors, come, bring your mug, I'm making tea for both of us, forget about *soopra* and ghost for now. So I removed my *mathoobanoo* and went with her.

Jaakaylee, O Jaakaylee, she is calling from dining-room. They must want more curry. Good thing I took some out for my dinner, they will finish the whole pot. Whenever I make Goan curry, nothing is left over. At the end seth always takes a piece of bread and rubs it round and round in the pot, wiping every little bit. They always joke, Jaakaylee, no need today for washing pot, all cleaned out. Yes, it is one thing I really enjoy, cooking my Goan curry, stirring and stirring, taking the aroma as it boils and cooks, stirring it again and again, watching it bubbling and steaming, stirring and stirring till it is ready to eat.

NOTES ON AUTHORS

AUBERT DE GASPÉ, PHILIPPE-JOSEPH (1786-1871): A French-Canadian aristocrat who became sheriff of Quebec City in 1816, he was imprisoned for debt from 1838 to 1841. In his seventies he began publishing sections of a historical novel, *Les Anciens Canadiens*, which was completed in 1863 and became an enormous success. He also helped his son, Philippe-Ignace-François, write the first French-Canadian novel, *L'influence d'un livre* (1837).

ATWOOD, MARGARET (b. 1939): Poet, fiction writer, and essayist. Her novels include *The Edible Woman* (1969), *Surfacing* (1972), *Lady Oracle* (1976), *Life Before Man* (1979), *Bodily Harm* (1981), *The Handmaid's Tale* (1987), and *Cat's Eye* (1988). Her short stories were collected in *Dancing Girls* (1977) and *Bluebeard's Egg* (1983).

BEAUGRAND, HONORÉ (1848-1906): At seventeen he fought in the Mexican War of 1865; after years of travel in France and the United States, he settled in Montreal where he served as mayor in 1885 and 1886. He founded the newspaper *La Patrie*, but retired from journalism in 1897 and dedicated himself to research into Québécois folklore. He published one novel, *Jeanne-la-Fileuse* (1878) and a collection of Canadian legends, *La Chasse-galérie* (1900). He also wrote travel essays and a history of Montreal.

BLAKE, WILLIAM HUME (1861-1924): He was admitted to the bar in 1885. *A Fisherman's Creed* (1923) discusses religious faith; his two books of essays— *Brown Waters and Other Sketches* (1915) and *In A Fishing Country* (1922)— deal with fishing, camping, and *habitant* legends. Blake translated Louis Hémon's classic *Maria Chapdelaine* into English.

BURNETT, VIRGIL (b. 1928): His books include *Skiamachia: A Fantasy* (1981), *Towers At The Edge Of A World* (1983), *A Comedy of Eros* (1984), and *Farewell Tour* (1986). He has also illustrated *Sir Gawain and the Green Knight* (The Folio Society).

DAVIES, ROBERTSON (b. 1913): His novels include the Salterton novels— *Tempest-tost* (1951), *Leaven of Malice* (1954), and *A Mixture of Frailties* (1958); the Deptford novels—*Fifth Business* (1970), *The Manticore* (1972), and *World of Wonders* (1951); and the latest trilogy, the Cornish novels—*The Rebel Angels* (1981), *What's Bred In The Bone* (1985), and *The Lyre of Orpheus* (1988). Davies has also written criticism, plays, and a collection of ghost stories, *High Spirits* (1982).

DE LA ROCHE, MAZO (1879-1961): The book that made her famous was *Jalna* (1927), the chronicle of the Whiteoaks family, which spawned fifteen more novels in the saga. Her other books include several collections of short stories—*Beside a Norman Tower* (1934), *The Very House* (1937), *Portrait of a Dog* (1930), and *The Sacred Bullock* (1939) among others—and various novels and plays.

DENT, JOHN CHARLES (1841-88): Born in England, he was a free-lance journalist who wrote most of the sketches in the four-volume *Canadian Portrait Gallery* (1880-81). His publications include *The Last Forty Years: Canada since the Union of 1841* (1881), *The Story of the Upper Canadian Rebellion* (1885), and the collection *The Gerrard Street Mystery and Other Stories* (1886).

FINDLEY, TIMOTHY (b. 1930): He began his career as an actor and published his first novel at the age of 37, *The Last of the Crazy People* (1967). This was followed by *The Butterfly Plague* (1969), *The Wars* (1977), *Famous Last Words* (1981), *Not Wanted On The Voyage* (1984), and *The Telling of Lies* (1986). His short stories were collected in *Dinner Along the Amazon* (1984) and *Stones* (1988).

GALLANT, MAVIS (b. 1922): Born in Montreal, she has lived in Paris since 1950. She is the author of two novels, *Green Water, Green Sky* (1959) and *A Fairly Good Time* (1970), and several collections of short stories: *The Other Paris* (1956), *My Heart Is Broken* (1964), *The Pegnitz Junction* (1973), *The End of the World* (1973), *From the Fifteenth District* (1979), *Home Truths* (1981), and *In Transit* (1988).

KINSELLA, W.P. (b. 1935): His short-story collections include *Dance Me Outside* (1977), *Scars* (1978), *Shoeless Joe Jackson Comes To Iowa* (1980), *Born Indian* (1981), and *The Moccasin Telegraph* (1983). His novel *Shoeless Joe* (1982) was made into the 1989 film *Field of Dreams*.

KLEIN, ABRAHAM MOSES (1909-1972): Born in the Ukraine, he moved to Montreal in 1910. His poetry included *Hath Not a Jew . . .* (1940), *The Hitleriad* (1944), and *The Rocking Chair and Other Poems* (1948). He wrote one novel, *The Second Scroll* (1951). His stories were collected posthumously, in 1983, under the title *A.M. Klein: Short Stories*.

LEACOCK, STEPHEN (1869-1924): Born in England, he settled in Ontario in 1876. His first collection of humorous pieces, *Literary Lapses* (1910), was followed by more than thirty volumes including *Nonsense Novels* (1911), *Sunshine Sketches of a Little Town* (1912), *Arcadian Adventures of the Idle Rich* (1914), *Frenzied Fiction* (1918), and *Winsome Winnie* (1920). An excellent selection of Leacock's work was edited by Robertson Davies under the title *The Feast of Stephen* (1974).

MACLEOD, ALISTAIR (b. 1936): He teaches English and creative writing at the University of Windsor, Ontario. He has written two collections of short stories: *The Lost Salt Gift of Blood* (1976) and *As Birds Bring Forth the Sun* (1986). He is the fiction editor of the *University of Windsor Review.*

MAILLET, ANTONINE (b. 1929): The most celebrated of Acadian writers, she chronicled the return of the Acadian settlers to Canada in *Pélagie-la-Charrette* (1979) (Prix Goncourt), *Cent Ans dans les bois* (1981) and others. Her stories appeared under the titles *On a mangé la dune* (1962) and *Par derrière chez mon père* (1972). She has also written several very successful plays, including the monologue *La Sagouine* (1971).

McCORMACK, ERIC (b. 1938): Born in Scotland, he immigrated to Canada in 1966. He has published one collection of short stories, *Inspecting the Vaults* (1987) and one novel, *The Paradise Motel* (1989). He teaches English at the University of Waterloo, Ontario.

MISTRY, ROHINTON (b. 1952): Born in Bombay, he came to Canada in 1975 and started writing in 1983. His first book of short stories, *Tales from Firozsha Baag*, was published in 1987.

MOORE, BRIAN (b. 1921): Born and educated in Ireland, he moved to Canada in 1948. He settled in the United States in 1959, but still retains his Canadian citizenship. His novels include *Judith Hearne* (1955), *The Feast of Lupercal* (1957), *The Luck of Ginger Coffey* (1960), *An Answer From Limbo* (1962), *The Great Victorian Collection* (1975), *Cold Heaven* (1983), and many others.

MOWAT, FARLEY (b. 1921): His involvement with the people of northern Canada and his ecological concerns are reflected in much of his work. His first book, *People of the Deer* (1952), was followed by *The Desperate People* (1959), *The Grey Seas Under* (1959), *Ordeal by Ice* (1960), *A Whale For the Killing* (1972), *Tundra* (1973), *And No Birds Sang* (1979), and many others. His stories about the Inuit were collected in *Snow Walker* (1975).

PARKER, SIR GILBERT (1862-1947): Born in Ontario, he left in 1885 for Australia and four years later for England. He became a member of parliament and later, during the First World War, directed the British government's propaganda effort in the United States. His collected *Works* (1912-23) comprise 23 volumes, many of which are historical romances and adventure novels. His best-known novel is *The Seats of the Mighty* (1896).

RULE, JANE (b. 1931): Born in the United States, she moved to Canada in 1956. Her novels include *Desert of the Heart* (1964), *This Is Not For You* (1970), *Against the Season* (1971), *The Young In One Another's Arms* (1977), *Contract With The World* (1980), *Memory Board* (1987), and *After the Fire* (1989). She has also written many essays and collections of short stories.

SCOTT, DUNCAN CAMPBELL (1862-1947): His work as Deputy Superintendent of Indian Affairs brought him in close contact with the plight of the Canadian native peoples and, with the exception of his first book, *The Magic House and Other Poems* (1893), his work reflects his concern with the native way of life. His collections of poetry include *Labor and the Angel* (1898), *The Green Cloister* (1935) and others. He also published two collections of short stories: *In the Village of Viger* (1896) and *The Witching of Elspie* (1923).

THOMAS, AUDREY (b. 1935): Born in the United States, she later lived in England and emigrated to Canada in 1959. She spent two years in Ghana (1964-6), a landscape that appears in much of her fiction. Her novels include *Mrs Blood* (1970), *Songs My Mother Taught Me* (1973), *Blown Figures* (1974), and *Intertidal Life* (1984). Her short stories have been collected in *Ten Green Bottles* (1967), *Ladies and Escorts* (1977), *Real Mothers* (1981) and *Goodbye Harold, Good Luck* (1986).

VIRGO, SEAN (b. 1940): Born in Malta, he came to Canada in 1966. He has published several books of poetry, including *Pieces For The Old Earth Man* (1973), *Island* (1975), *Kiskatinaw Songs* (1979), and *Deathwatch on Skidegate Narrows* (1979). His short stories appear in *White Lies and Other Fictions* (1981), *Through the Eyes of a Cat* (1983), and *Wormwood* (1989). He has published one novel, *Selakhi* (1987).

WILSON, ETHEL (1888-1980): Born in South Africa, she came to Canada in 1898. Her first novel, *Hetty Dorval* (1947), was followed by *The Innocent Traveller* (1949), *Swamp Angel* (1954), and *Love and Salt Water* (1956). *The Equations of Love* (1954) includes two novellas, and her short stories were collected in *Mrs Golightly* (1961).

WYNNE-JONES, TIM (b. 1948): Born in England, he immigrated to Canada in 1952. His novel *Odd's End* won the Seal First Novel Award. He has since published two more novels, *The Knot* (1982) and *Fastyngange* (1988). He is also the author of several children's books.